Commentary
on the
Book of Mormon

Volume VI

Commentary

on the

Book of Mormon

VOLUME VI

THE BOOK OF ETHER

The record of the Jaredites, taken from the
twenty-four plates found by the people
of Limhi in the days of King Mosiah.

From the notes of:

GEORGE REYNOLDS

and

JANNE M. SJODAHL

Amplified and Arranged by

PHILIP C. REYNOLDS

PUBLISHED BY
DESERET BOOK COMPANY
SALT LAKE CITY, UTAH
1977

Lithographed by

DESERET PRESS

in the United States of America

George Reynolds

In a note near the close of his great contribution to L.D.S. Church literature, *New Witnesses for God*, President B. H. Roberts penned this remarkable tribute to the labors of Elder George Reynolds:

"It is a pleasure to note the work of this my brother, and fellow President in the First Council of the Seventies, in this field of Book of Mormon labor. I feel myself much indebted to him because of his great achievements in this field of research.

"First, for his excellent *Book of Mormon Chronological Table*, published now for many years in connection with the late Elder F. D. Richards' *Compendium*.

"Second, for his *Myth of the Manuscript Found*.

"Third, for his *Story of the Book of Mormon*.

"Fourth, for his *Dictionary of the Book of Mormon*.

"Fifth, for a series of articles appearing in the *Contributor*, Vol. 5, on the *History of the Book of Mormon*.

"Sixth, for a second series of articles in the *Contributor*, Vol. 17, under the title, *Evidences of the Book of Mormon; Some External Proofs of its Divinity*.

"Seventh, and last, and greatest achievement of all, I thank him for his *Complete Concordance of the Book of Mormon*. The amount of patient, painstaking labor required for the production of this magnificent work will never be known to the general reader. Only the close student of the Nephite Scriptures will ever appreciate it. What Cruden and Young have done for Bible students, Elder Reynolds has more abundantly done for Book of Mormon students. The Elders of the Church through all generations to come will, I am sure, feel deeply grateful to Elder Reynolds for his great work which will stand as a monument to his painstaking habits of thorough application to a task; but what is better still, the work will stand as a monument of his love for the Book of Mormon."

Janne M. Sjodahl

An editorial published in the *Deseret News*, June 25, 1939, will serve to acquaint those who know little of the life and labors of the co-author of this *Commentary*.

"Physically frail but mentally energetic; of serious manner, studious volition and sedentary habit; Janne Mattson Sjodahl lived simply and labored faithfully beyond the eighty-fifth anniversary of his birth. A native of Sweden, he was educated in Stockholm and London, becoming identified in early manhood with the Scandinavian Baptist Union having headquarters in Trondhjem, Norway.

"At the age of 33 he came to the United States and was converted to Mormonism after his arrival in Utah over a half century ago. His ability as a writer, his faculty for research, his skill as a translator brought him instant recognition and a life-time of labor.

"As a writer and as an editor he had been connected with the *Deseret News*, the *Improvement Era*, the *Millennial Star* and various foreign language publications once circulated by his Church. He served on various missions to Palestine, Switzerland, England, and Sweden. In the latter country he presented a special edition of the Book of Mormon to the king who received the Utah delegation at the Royal Palace.

"Mr. Sjodahl was the author of many ecclesiastical works and a prolific writer of pamphlets and special articles relating to the organization of which he was a distinguished member. He devoted his whole time, energy, ability, and thought to religious issues and inquiries. Absorbed in meditation almost to a point of asceticism, subjecting his vigor and vitality to constant exertion, he lived many years longer than his acquaintances believed possible for a tireless soul that occupied a frame so fragile."

With the late Elder Hyrum M. Smith, of the Council of Twelve Apostles, Elder Sjodahl was the author of, and the compiler of the *Doctrine and Covenants Commentary*.

A FOREWORD

King Limhi of the Nephites in the Land of Nephi, tells Ammon of the Plates of Gold. The Book of Ether is first brought to our attention in a report of an interview between the King of the Nephites in the country of the Lamanites, the Land of Nephi, Limhi and Ammon, a messenger from Zarahemla. (Mosiah 8:9) The King related a remarkable bit of history. He had, at one time, sent an embassy with an important mission to Zarahemla. The delegates of that legation, being without a competent guide, lost their way in the wilderness and missed their hoped-for destination. Instead of finishing their journey in Zarahemla, they came to a country where there were many ancient ruins, and other evidences of cultural enlightenment. Among the most manifest of these shattered remains of bygone ages was the condition into which the buildings of these venerable people had fallen; all around them were the bones of men and beasts, evincing a terrible devastation. In corroboration of their strange report, they brought back with them twenty-four plates of gold with unknown engravings covering them, besides many other remarkable antiques. King Limhi now desired to know whether Ammon could interpret such writings.

The visitor from Zarahemla replied that he could not, but he hastened to add that the King over the people of his homeland had such a gift, because he had in his possession certain miraculous interpreters. (Mosiah 8:14)

In due time King Limhi and his people broke away from the servitude that enslaved them unto the Lamanites, and found refuge in Zarahemla. King Mosiah, the son of Benjamin, received them with joy and took care of their valuable records. (Mosiah 22:14) Afterwards the royal Prophet translated the twenty-four plates and found thereon an account of a people who had inhabited the land to the north, but had been destroyed through internecine strife. (Mosiah 28:13)

Not an accidental discovery. The twenty-four plates were called the Book of Ether after its author. (Ether 1:2) Their discovery was not an accident. For, when Ether had finished his record thereon, "he hid them in a manner that the people of Limhi did find them." (Ether 15:33) Here is an ideal place to remember that, as the poets have said, "The accidents of man are the inspirations of God, and the incidents of this life are the leadings and the guidings of Him who made it."

The visions of the Brother of Jared. Before the Jaredites, named after Jared, one of the leaders of the people of whom the Book of Ether is a record, left Moriancumer, their camp in the Old Country from which they came, the Brother of Jared was given indescribable visions on Mount Shelem. The Lord instructed him not to make them public during his lifetime, but to place them on record before his death, in the language commonly spoken before the building of the Towel of Babel, but no longer known by later generations. This record was to be sealed up. He also received two stones, prepared so as to "magnify," or make clear, "the things which ye shall write." These stones, known to us as the Urim and Thummim, were also to be sealed up. (Ether 3:21-24, 27, 28)

We know, from the information given by Moroni, the abridger of King Mosiah's translation of the plates of gold, that Mosiah also had the writings of the Brother of Jared, and that he kept them in case the time for their publication should come. We also know that these writings, together with "the interpretation thereof" — the translation by King Mosiah — had come into his (Moroni's) possession, as did the Interpreters. (Ether 4:1-5)

There is, then, no doubt that Mosiah, the son of Benjamin, was the custodian, in his day, of the Jaredite Record and the Two Stones, the Interpreters, which the Lord gave to the Brother of Jared. (Mosiah 28:11-16)

The Jaredite Record was part of the twenty-four plates of gold which the Prophet Ether had hid up unto the Lord, and which came, providentially, into the hands of Mosiah through the expedition of King Limhi. In all probability he received the interpreters from his father, King Benjamin, who may have got them from Mosiah I, his father.

Amaleki, the son of Abinadom, gives, in the Book of Omni, what is, perhaps, the correct clue to the question that has been asked, "How did the Stones of Interpretation, originally given to the Brother of Jared, come into the hands of the kings in Zarahemla? Amaleki says, that a large stone, possibly a monumental pillar or stele, was brought to King Mosiah I, who interpreted the engravings thereon by the *gift and power of God.* We may infer that this means that that Mosiah had the Interpreters. By this power it was found that the stone contained an account of Coriantumr, the last King of the Jaredites, and the slain of his people. (Omni 20:22) Undoubtedly, Coriantumr had brought this information to the Mulekites in Zarahemla. May he not have carried with him the Interpreters also? It must be remembered that this lone survivor after the Battle of Ramah had usurped the highest ecclesiastical as well as the political offices, and that he, therefore, may have had the sacred instrument in his possession, although it was worthless to him. Ether prophesied that he would not fall in the war then raging, but that he would live, to be buried by another people. The inference is not farfetched that he was spared for the very purpose of bringing to the Nephites the story of the dealings of God with the Jaredites.

Mosiah disposes of the Sacred Objects. King Mosiah, the son of Benjamin, was the custodian of the twenty-four plates, his own translation of the contents thereof, the Interpreters, the Plates of Brass, and other records. (Mosiah 1:16) Towards the end of his career, he delivered all of them to Alma, the son of Alma, he being a High Priest and the Chief Judge of the whole country. The Interpreters were included in the sacred collection. (Mosiah 29:42) When transferring the responsibilities of custodial possession to Alma, Mosiah commanded him to keep and preserve the valuable relics, and to cause them to be handed down from one generation to another. (Mosiah 29:11-20)

The Records preserved. At the proper time Alma gave his son, Helaman, charge of the sacred treasures entrusted to him by Mosiah. (Alma 37:1-4) By such transfers they were preserved from generation to generation. About the year 320 of our era, Ammaron, having received them from his brother, Amos, prompted by the spirit, did "hide them unto the Lord, that they might come again unto the remnant of the House of Jacob." (IV Nephi 48-49; compare Words of Mormon 10-11; Alma 37:4)

Mormon instructed concerning the Records. The great Nephite commander and leader, Mormon, relates that when he was about ten years old, Ammaron charged him to go to the Hill Shim, in the Land of Antum, when he should reach the age of about 24, as the Sacred Things had been deposited there. He instructed Mormon to take the Plates of Nephi and complete the records from his own observations. The other plates and articles were to be left in the Hill. (Mormon 1:1-4; 2:17-18)

Cumorah, the final place of safety. Mormon carried out Ammaron's instructions. But later he went to the Hill and "did take up all the records which Ammaron had hid up unto the Lord." (Mormon 4:28) He, finally, hid them all in the Hill Cumorah, having first furnished his son, Moroni, with the entire story of the Plates of Nephi in a much abridged form. (Mormon 6:6)

Moroni finished the tragic chapter telling of the final great battle at Cumorah, and then "hid up the records in the earth," (Mormon 8:4) presumably in the Hill Cumorah. But he also predicted that they would be found and come to light at some future day, (Mormon 8:14-16) a prophecy fulfilled through the instrumentality of the Prophet Joseph Smith.

Moroni gives one final reference to the miraculous interpreters, when he says: "But the Lord knoweth . . . that none other people knoweth our language; therefore He hath prepared means for the interpretation thereof." (Mormon 9:34) This *means* was the very crystals prepared for, and presented to the Brother of Jared on Mount Shelem. (Doctrine and Covenants 17:1)

Only two miraculous Interpreters. History knows of only two sacred instruments of this kind, also known as Urim and Thummim (meaning *lights and perfections*). One was given to Abraham in the City of Ur of the Chaldees (Pearl of Great Price, Abraham 3:1) This was, probably, handed over by Moses to Aaron, the High Priest, who carried them in his "Breastplate of Judgment," an important part of his ecclesiastical equipment. (Exodus 28:30) It was, finally, lost sight of.

The other was given to the Brother of Jared. It was this very same one that the Prophet Joseph had for some time.

The contemporary nations on the eastern continent — Egypt, Chaldea, and Babylonia — were insignificant when compared with the vast extent of territory held and filled by the Jaredites; they were the sole rulers of the whole western hemisphere, and possibly the originals, whence arose the stories of the greatness and grandeur of the fabled Atlantis; for we have no account in the sacred records that God shut them off from the knowledge of the rest of mankind when he planted them in America, as he afterwards did the Nephites; and later research has shown that geographical knowledge of the ancients was much greater in the earlier ages than at the time of the Savior.

The Discovery of the Jaredite Records

Let us turn to the year B.C. 123. At that time the Nephites in the Land of Lehi-Nephi were suffering sore afflictions at the hands of the Lamanites, to whom they were in bondage. In this extremity, Limhi, their King, bewildered and almost ready to despair, sent a company of forty-three able-bodied men, with instructions to discover, if possible, their brethren in the Land of Zarahemla, that peradventure they would bring them succor and ultimately, deliverance. The expedition was unsuccessful insofar as its immediate objective was concerned. The company missed the Land of Zarahemla, pushed northward into Central America, and how far beyond we cannot tell. At last they found the remains of an ancient people who apparently had been destroyed in battle. Among other things, they discovered twenty-four gold plates that were covered with hieroglyphics which they could not decipher. This treasure with some other relics of the vanished race, they took back to King Limhi.

When, shortly after, this section of the Nephite people escaped from their Lamanitish taskmasters and returned to Zarahemla, the twenty-four gold plates were presented to King Mosiah, the younger, and he, being a seer, translated them by the aid of the Urim and Thummim.

These plates were found to contain the history of the world from the Creation to the time of the building of the Tower of Babel, and of the race whose remains had been found by the people of Limhi scattered on the land northward.

This was, however, not the first intimation that the Nephites had of the previous existence of this people. In the days of the elder Mosiah, a large engraved stone was brought to him which he interpreted. It had been found by the people of Zarahemla, and on it was an account of this same race which is known to us as the *Jaredites,* but it more particularly referred to its last ruler, Coriantumr, for he had just previous to his death, resided in their midst for nine months.

The history we have of this remarkable people, as it is recorded in the Book of Mormon, is Moroni's abridgment of their annals as translated by King Mosiah, the younger, from the twenty-four gold plates. It commences with the dispersion of the human family at Babel. The original plates had on them an account of the Creation of the Earth, and then on down to the building of the Tower of Babel. But Moroni did not include this part of their story in his abridgment because of its length, and besides it was already had among the Jews. Interspersed with the narrative are many interpolations of Moroni's, in the shape of reflections, prophecies, and explanations of different passages which he felt that without them, we might misunderstand their Scriptures. As these additions or notes are inserted in the body of Moroni's work and not as footnotes, the reader of his abridgment has to use care in its perusal, or perchance, his ideas of the Jaredites may become confused, and he finds himself troubled to account for statements which are perfectly plain when it is understood that they were written by Moroni nearly four hundred years after the advent of the Savior.

The ancestors of the Jaredites were engaged in the attempt to build the Tower of Babel. It is probable they were of the family of Shem, as they were worshipers of the true God, and upon them he conferred the Holy Priesthood which he, himself, held. How far they had wandered from the Tower, if at all, when the Lord commenced the revelation of His will to them, is not apparent from the sacred text. They were commanded by Him to go "*down* into the valley which is northward," and as the expressions *up and down,* where they are used in the Book of Mormon in connection with geographical locality, are always used with great exactitude, we may venture two surmises: that Jared and his family had already wandered into some not far distant hilly region, or that the valley into which they were commanded to descend sloped towards the north, the flow of its waters, if any, being in that direction.

The Valley into which the Lord led the Jaredites was called *Nimrod* after that mighty hunter of the early post-diluvian age. Here, they tarried for a short time while they prepared for the long journey that was before them. Their flocks and herds they had with them were only part of the impedimenta that slowed their progress to the Promised Land. They went to work snaring wild fowls, they carried with them hives of honeybees (known to them as *Deseret*). They prepared a vessel in which they transported the fish of the waters. Everything that possibly could be of use to them in their travels, they appear to have collected. They were going to a land which we may suppose was or had been swept clean by the waters of the Deluge. It had been bereft of all its animal life, and seeds of grains and fruits for the use of man, had not yet germinated in cultivated abundance for the benefit and blessing of humankind. The little colony had to replenish the continent with the animal and vegetable life so necessary to the comfort and sustenance of their own life, as well as the beasts of the field they took along with them. They were compelled to look ahead and provide all such provisions and worldly goods as if they were going to a new earth which to all intents and purposes they were.

When in the Valley of Nimrod the Lord came down from His dwelling *On High,* and talked with the Brother of Jared. But Jared's brother *saw Him not* for the Lord remained concealed in a cloud. The Lord directed that the little company should go forth into the wilderness, "into that quarter where there never had man been." As they journeyed the *Heavenly Presence* went before them in the cloud and instructed them and gave directions as to which way they should travel. In the course of their journey they had many waters — seas, rivers, and lakes — to cross, on which occasions they built barges as directed by the Lord. It must have been an arduous labor, requiring much time and great patience, to transport their flocks and herds, with all their cumbrous freight across these many waters.

We shall not attempt to trace the wanderings of the company on their way to the Promised Land. The account given in the Book of Ether is entirely too meager for that purpose.

Some suppose that they went as far north as the Caspian Sea, which they crossed; then turning eastward, slowly journeyed along the Central Asian Plateau. That led them to the Pacific Seaboard, most probably on the Coast of China. These suppositions may be correct; the writers do not know enough to either affirm or deny them, but one thing is certain, the journey must have been a long and tedious one. The region through which they passed was one in which no man dwelt, they could purchase no supplies, and if they did not live entirely on wild fruit, fish, and small game, it is probable that they tarried now and then, at favorable points, long enough to plant and harvest a crop. As they advanced to a greater distance from the center of population in western Asia, it is possible that they traveled beyond the limits to which the larger animals had, by that time scattered; and if so, they were entirely without the aid of the food obtained by the chase. On the other hand, it is probable that the fish in the rivers and lakes formed a valuable source of food supply; yet it must also be remembered that they carried fish in a vessel with them.

Through their faith and prayers the founders of the Jaredite Nation obtained many precious promises of the Lord. Among these was the assurance that their language should not be confounded, and that the Lord, Himself, would go before them, and lead them into a land that was choice above every other land upon the face of the Earth. And again, that the nation they should found, there would be none greater among all the nations of the world. The history of their descendants proves how fully this last promise was realized. The contemporary nations upon the eastern Continent — Egypt, Chaldea, and Babylonia — were insignificant when compared with the vast extent of territory held and filled by the Jaredites; they were the sole rulers of the whole western Hemisphere, and possibly the originals whence arose the stories of the greatness and grandeur of the fabled Atlantis. We have no account that God shut them out from the knowledge of the rest of mankind when He planted them in America as He afterwards did the Nephites, and late research has shown that the geographical knowledge of the ancients was much greater in the earlier ages than at the time of the Savior and a few hundred years previous to His advent.

Led personally by the Lord, instructed from His own mouth, protected by His presence, the colony, of which Jared's brother appears to have been the prophet and leader, at last reached the borders of the great sea which divides the Continents. To the place where they tarried they gave the name, Moriancumer. Here they remained for a period of four years, at the end of which time the Lord again visited the Brother of Jared in a cloud and chastened him and his brethren because of their neglect to call upon His Name. Repentance followed this reproof, and on their repentance their sins were forgiven them.

The Brother of Jared was then commanded by the Lord to build eight barges after the pattern of those he had previously constructed. This command he obeyed with the assistance of the company. The vessels were small, light in construction, and water tight. As they were dark in the interior, by reason of there being no windows, the Lord, at the entreaty of Jared's brother, touched sixteen white stones which the latter had molten out of a high mountain called Shelem. After the Lord had touched them they shone forth and gave light to the vessels in which they were placed. When the Lord put forth His finger to touch the stones, the veil was taken from the eyes of the Brother of Jared and he saw the finger of the Lord; and he beheld that it was as the finger of a man, like unto flesh and blood. Then the Brother of Jared fell down before the Lord, for he was struck with fear, but because of his faith the Lord not only permitted him to see His finger, but showed Himself to him.

Furthermore, the Lord said to the Brother of Jared, "Behold, I am He Who was prepared from the foundation of the world to redeem My people. Behold, I am Jesus Christ. I am the Father and the Son. In Me shall all mankind have light, and that eternally, even they who shall believe on My Name; and they shall become My sons and daughters. And never have I showed Myself unto man whom I have created, for never has man believed in Me as thou hast. Seest thou that ye are created after Mine own image? Yea, even all men were created in the beginning, after Mine own image. Behold, this body, which ye now behold, is the body of My Spirit; and even as I appear unto thee to be in the Spirit, will I appear unto My people in the flesh."

All things being prepared, Jared and his people, with their animals, fishes, bees, seeds, and multitudinous other things, went on board. A favorable wind wafted them from shore and they gradually drifted to the American coast. At the end of the voyage which lasted three hundred and forty-four days, the colony landed on this continent. It is generally understood that the place where they landed was south of the Gulf of California and north of the Isthmus of Panama.

When the members of the little colony set their feet upon the shores of America, they humbled themselves before the Lord, and shed tears of joy because of the multitude of His tender mercies over them. Then they went forth and began to till the earth, and soon grew strong in the land which God had given them; they being a righteous people, were taught directly from On High.

Before long the question of government arose, and the people desired a king. This thing was grievous to their divinely inspired leaders, for they saw that it would lead to captivity; but perceiving the determination of the people, they consented. It was difficult to find any suitable man who would consent to occupy the royal position. At last, when all the other sons of Jared were eliminated because of their refusal to reign as a king, the youngest of Jared's sons whose name was Orihah, consented, and he was anointed King.

It appears altogether probable that this choice was taken as a precedent, for among this people there seems to have prevailed a custom entirely opposite that of other nations — that of having one of the younger, generally the youngest instead of the eldest, succeed his father on the throne. The Jaredites were a very long-lived race, full of vitality, often having sons and daughters born to them until the very end of their days. The number of generations mentioned during the period embraced in their history is much fewer than the general average for the same number of centuries, notably so, where the eldest son succeeds to the rank and title of his sire.

The kings of the Jaredites, in the order of their succession, were Orihah, Kib, Corihor, Kib restored, then follows Shule. In the days of Shule the kingdom was divided. Noah, the son of Corihor, established a separate monarchy over a portion of the land. After his death he was succeeded by his son, Cohor, who was slain in battle by Shule, when the whole kingdom was restored to the last named.

Shule was succeeded by his son, Omer, who was deposed and imprisoned by his son, Jared, but two other sons afterwards defeated Jared and restored the kingdom to the rightful ruler, their father. In this civil war between Omer and his son, Jared, when the latter had been defeated by his brothers, they spared his life on condition that he recognize the right of his father to the throne.

Jared became very sorrowful at his defeat, as he had set his heart on being king. While in this state of mind, his daughter, who was exceedingly fair, came to him, and learning the cause of his discontent, made a most extraordinary and villainous proposition to him, which showed she was as conscienceless as her father. It was that he should invite a friend, named Akish, to visit him; when he came she would dance before him and use her charms to captivate his heart. If her plan succeeded and Akish desired her to wife, Jared was to grant his request on condition that Akish brought him the head of his father, Omer. To enable him to accomplish this diabolical scheme, the daughter of Jared reminded her father of the signs and covenants of the ancients, whereby they entered into compact one with another for mutual aid and comfort, including protection in carrying out any great wickedness they might desire to commit.

Her plan was accepted and proved in every way to be successful. After the manner she suggested, Akish gathered his kinsfolk, and persuaded them to swear, with terrible oaths, that they would be faithful to him in all that he might require of them. By these wicked combinations the Kingdom of Omer was overthrown. But he, being warned of the Lord, escaped to a distant land, which was called Ablom. Then Jared was anointed King, and gave his daughter to Akish to wife.

But Akish was not satisfied. He plotted with his associates and they slew Jared as he sat upon his throne, and Akish reigned in his stead. But after committing these crimes, he became suspicious of his partners in sin, and grew jealous of one of his own sons whom he shut up in prison and starved him to death. Before long, other sons of Akish seduced the people from their allegiance to their father, a civil war of the utmost magnitude ensued which ceased not until all the people were slain except thirty, and those who had fled to Omer in the Land of Ablom. After this, Omer returned and reigned over the few souls that remained.

Omer was succeeded by his son, Emer; Emer by his son, Coriantum; Coriantum by his son, Com. Com was slain by his son, Heth, who took possession of the Kingdom after he had murdered his father.

In the days of Heth, there was a great famine which destroyed the greater portion of the people, among them the King himself. He was succeeded by Shez, Shez by his son, Riplakish, who was dethroned by Morianton, whose son, Kim, afterwards followed him in the kingly power. Kim was brought into captivity, through rebellion, and it was not until the next reign, that of his son, Levi, that the usurpers were driven from the throne. Then follow the reigns of Corom, Kish, Lib, and Hearthom. The last named was deposed after reigning twenty-four years, and held in captivity all the remainder of his days. So also were his son, Heth, his grandson, Aaron, his great grandson, Amnigaddah, and the latter's son Coriantum.

We are not informed what were the names of the kings of the usurping dynasty who reigned while the royal family served in captivity; but in the days of Coriantum's son, Com, the reigning prince was named, Amgid. Com went to war against him, overthrew him, and gained possession of the throne of his ancestors. Shiblon, the son of Com, succeeded his father, but was slain, his son, Heth, being made captive and was thus held all his days.

In the next generation, Ahah, Heth's son, regained the throne and reigned over the whole people for a short time. Few and iniquitous were his days. Ethem, called a descendant and also the son of Ahah, was the next king. His son, Moron, succeeded him. In Moron's days there were renewed rebellions which ended, as had so frequently been the case before, in the captivity of the king. Moron was a captive all the rest of his life, and his son, Coriantor, passed his whole earthly existence in captivity.

Ether, the Prophet, was the son of Coriantor. The King in his days was named Coriantumr, the last king of his race, for the wars that desolated the land in his reign culminated in the destruction of the Jaredites. This very short sketch of the reigns of their kings shows how thoroughly were the fears of Jared and his brother realized — that the anointing of a king to rule them would lead to captivity.

Like their successors, the Nephites, the troubles of the Jaredites grew out of their iniquities. Many mighty prophets ministered to them, but only occasionally were they listened to. Like the Nephites, in another phase of their existence, they owed many of their misfortunes to cherishing the secret bands of Gadianton-like assassins, who, bound by infernal covenants, perpetuated the most unnatural and bloodthirsty crimes. In the days of Omer, the daughter of Jared (who in more than one respect reminds us of the daughter of Herodias) was instrumental in first introducing these soul-destroying confederacies with Satan among the Jaredites; and in after ages they dwindled or flourished according to the amount of their faith and integrity of the people.

Materially, the Jaredites were wonderfully blessed. It could scarcely have been otherwise. They had all the treasures of this choice land at their disposal. In the days of Emer, the sacred historian describes them as having become exceedingly rich, having in their possession all manner of fruit, grain, silks, fine linen, gold, silver, and precious things; and also all manner of cattle, sheep, swine, goats, and also many other kinds of animals which were useful for the food of man; and they also had horses, and asses, and there were elephants and cureloms and cumons; all of which were useful to men, and more especially the elephants, cureloms and cumons. What the last two above named were, we do not know.

Owing to their gross and abounding wickedness, the Lord on several occasions visited the Jaredites with partial destruction. These judgments came in the shape of fratricidal war, pestilence, drought, and famine. In the days of Heth there was a great dearth of water in the land, through which the inhabitants were destroyed exceedingly fast, while poisonous serpents came forth "and did poison many people." These serpents drove, it is said, the flocks and herds south, and then congregated at the narrow neck uniting the two great divisions of the land, thus hedging up the way so that the people could not pass, adding another factor to their misery, for their crops were not only destroyed because of the lack of rainfall, but the resource to animal food was taken from them. Thus they became a broken people, but when through their misery they had sufficiently humbled themselves before the Lord, He sent the long desired rain, and there began to be fruit in the north countries and in all the countries round about. Other desolations at various times came upon them because of their disobedience to the behests of Heaven.

The war which ended in the entire destruction of the Jaredite government as an enemy, was one of the most bloodthirsty, cruel, and vindictive that ever cursed this fair planet. Men's most savage passions were worked up to such an extent that every better feeling of humanity was crushed out. The women and children armed themselves for the fray with the same fiendish activity, and, fought with the same intense hate, as the men. It was not the conflict of armies alone; it was the crushing together of a divided house that had long tottered because of internal weakness, but now fell in upon itself.

The war was not the work of a day; it was the outgrowth of centuries of dishonor, crime and wilful disobedience to God's laws. And as this continent was once cleansed of its unrighteous inhabitants by the overwhelming waters of a universal Deluge, and only eight souls left, so this second time, as a flood, through the promises of the Lord to Noah, was no longer possible, instead thereof the wicked slew the wicked until only two men remained, the King and the historian; the one to wander wounded, wretched, and alone, until found by Mulek's colony; the other to record the last dreadful throes of his people for the profit of succeeding races, and then to be received into the loving care of his Father and his God. Both the Nephites and ourselves are indebted to him for our acquaintance with the earlier history of the American Continent, which otherwise would have been entirely shut out from our knowledge.

Some four or more years before the final battle near and around the Hill Ramah, otherwise, Cumorah, two millions of warriors had been slain, besides their wives and children. How many millions actually fell before the last struggle ended, and Coriantumr stood alone, the sole representative of his race, it is impossible to tell from the record handed down to us, but we think we are justified in believing that for bloodshed and desolation no such war ever took place before, or has occurred since in the history of this world; if the annals of any nation have the record of its equal, it is not known to us.

The duel between the leaders of the two contending hosts, Coriantumr and Shiz, when their fellows were all slain, was a unique and horrible one, for when all had fallen except these two, Shiz, one of them, fainted for loss of blood. Then Coriantumr, after having taken a short rest, raised his sword and smote off the head of his foe. Shiz raised himself on his hands, fell, struggling for breath and died. Then utterly exhausted, Coriantumr dropped to the ground and became as though he had no life.

Coriantumr, when he regained consciousness, wandered forth, aimlessly and alone, the last of his race. A whole continent lay round about him, but there was nothing in any place to invite him to tarry or to depart. Companions, he had none; every creature in the image of God, save himself, had moistened the soil with his life's blood. All had been swept into unsanctified graves or poisoned the air with the smell of their unburied bodies. The savage beasts alone remained to terrify him with their hideous calls as they held high carnival over the unnumbered slain. Weak from loss of blood, he staggered on, placing as great a distance as his failing powers would permit between himself and the horrors of the last battleground.

He passed onward through each deserted valley, each tenantless town; in neither was there any human voice to greet him; the homes of his own people and those of his enemies were alike — a silent desolation; all the land was a wilderness.

How long Coriantumr wandered to and fro, wretched, comfortless and forelorn, we do not know; but at last he reached the southern portion of the northern continent, thousands of miles from Ramah, and there, to the great astonishment of both, he found the people of Mulek, who had been led by the hand of the Lord from Jerusalem. With them he spent his few remaining days, and when nine moons had grown and waned he passed away to join the hosts of his people in the unknown world of spirits.

All this was in fulfillment of the prophecies of Ether, who, years before, had been sent by the Lord to Coriantumr with the fateful message that if he and all his household would repent, the Lord would give him his kingdom, and spare the people; otherwise they should be destroyed save it were himself, and he should live only to see the fulfilling of the prophecies which had been spoken concerning another people receiving the land for their inheritance; and Coriantumr should receive a burial by them; and every soul should be destroyed save it were Coriantumr.

But Coriantumr did not repent, neither did his household; and all the words of the Lord, through Ether, came to pass. Not the least of them remained unfulfilled.

MORONI
The Abridger of the Jaredite Records

THE BOOK OF ETHER

The son of Mormon, and the last representative of the Nephite race. He was an officer under his father and commanded a corps of ten thousand men at the battle of Cumorah. He wrote the concluding portions of the Book of Mormon, from the commencement of the 8th chapter of the book bearing his father's name to the end of the volume. This includes the book bearing his own name and his abridgment of the history of the Jaredites known to us as the Book of Ether. He takes up the history of the continent from the time of the slaughter at Cumorah and tells us (A.D. 400) that "the Lamanites are at war one with another and the face of the land is one continued round of murder and bloodshed; and no man knoweth the end of the war." And again, yet later, he writes, "Their wars are exceeding fierce among themselves, and because of their hatred they put to death every Nephite that will not deny the Christ, and I, Moroni, will not deny the Christ, wherefore I wander whithersoever I can, for the safety of mine own life." Such was the sad condition of the Lamanite race in the early part of the fifth century after Christ. There (A.D. 421) the inspired record closes; thenceforth we have nothing but uncertain tradition until the veil was withdrawn by the discovery of America.

In the course of nature Moroni died and in the Lord's due time he was resurrected. *The sacred record and other holy things, buried in Cumorah, still remained in his care. On him the duty fell to watch that no unsanctified hands disturbed their rest. When the time set in the councils of heaven for their translation came he delivered them to the instrument chosen by the Holy Ones, Joseph Smith, the prophet, who, when he had accomplished his work, returned them to Moroni, who still keeps ward and watch over these treasures.

But was there any fear that the records would be disturbed by unholy hands? We believe there was. It must not be forgotten that

---

*Joseph Smith's answer to the question, How and where did you obtain the Book of Mormon?—Moroni, who deposited the plates (from whence the Book of Mormon was translated) in a hill in Manchester, Ontario County, New York, being *dead and raised again* therefrom, appeared unto me, and told me where they were, and gave me directions how to obtain them. I obtained them, and the Urim and Thummim with them, by the means of which I translated the plates and thus came the Book of Mormon.

the Lamanites of the days of Moroni were not the benighted savages of earlier centuries. They were not the pure blood of Laman and his associates. They were dissenters from the Nephites, apostates from the true church; and they were as well acquainted with the fact that the records existed as the prophet himself. In the days of Mormon he removed the plates from the hill Shim, for the very reason that he feared the Lamanites would get hold of and destroy them. There were the same reasons for fear should they discover their resting place in Cumorah.

The tradition of the existence of these records remained for long ages with the Lamanites; undoubtedly growing fainter and fainter and more confused as the centuries rolled by, but still not entirely extinguished. Indeed the remembrance is not utterly obliterated in the minds of some of Lehi's children to this very day.

So strong was this recollection in earlier days, that we are told of a time when a council of wise men, with royal consent, made an attempt to rewrite them. How successful they were we have no means of telling; but this we know, that when the Spaniards conquered Mexico the land was full of sacred books. These so much resembled the Bible of the Christians that the Catholic priests came to the conclusion that it was a trick of the devil to imitate the holy scriptures, and in this way lead the souls of the Indians to perdition. In their bigoted zeal they burned every copy of these books or charts that they could find, and inflicted abominably cruel punishments upon those who were found concealing them. In this way almost every copy of these valuable works was destroyed.

Though the original records were hidden by the power of God, it is quite possible that many copies of the scriptures remained in the hands of the Lamanites when the Nephites were destroyed. In the Book of Mormon frequent reference is made to the abundance of these copies. No doubt in the last desolating wars between the Nephites and Lamanites but little care was taken of these scriptures. Both peoples had sunken deeply in iniquity; they cared nothing for the word of God, and probably, as we may infer from Mormon's apprehensions, the Lamanites destroyed all the copies of the holy books that they found. Still, it is not improbable that some few of these works remained untouched; and when the Lamanites had gotten over their first overwhelming bitterness and aversion to everything Nephite, and again began to grow in civilization, they would search for these records, if for nothing else than as valued curiosities; though we think they sometimes prized them much more highly.

The plates having been guarded by the power of God, were

translated by the same power. No book was ever translated more accurately; none, by human wisdom, as faultlessly as the Book of Mormon.*

Joseph Smith, the youth whom God honored by making him the instrument in His hands of restoring these precious records to the knowledge of mankind, was born in the town of Sharon, Windsor County, Vermont, on the 23rd of December, 1805. When about ten years of age his parents, with their family, moved to Palmyra, in the State of New York, in the vicinity of which place he lived for about eleven years; the latter portion of the time in a village called Manchester. Joseph helped his father on the farm, hired out at day-work, and passed his years very much after the manner common to young men in the rural districts. His advantages for obtaining anything beyond the rudiments of education were exceedingly small: he could read without much difficulty, write an imperfect hand, and had but a limited understanding of arithmetic.

The circumstances attending Joseph's first vision in the early spring of 1820, when he saw the Father and the Son, have been so often published, and must necessarily be so familiar to our readers, that with this bare reference to the fact we will pass them by. It is sufficient for the purpose of our present research to know that this marvelously important event did happen. Then and there the corner-stone was laid of the vast fabric to God's glory of which Joseph was the master builder, when mortal beings alone are considered.

---

*In council with the Twelve Apostles, Joseph Smith said, I told the brethren that the Book of Mormon was the most correct of any book on earth, and the keystone of our religion, and a man would get nearer to God by abiding by its precepts, than by any other book.

A Word of Wisdom to the Student
of the Book of Mormon

Scholars among the early arrivals in America after Columbus were at a loss to account for the similarity they observed between some Indian traditions and ideals and those of the patriarchal (or even Mosaic) age of the Old Testament.

Others, who have spent years studying the records of the first European invaders and what little remains of aboriginal literature, have been similarly impressed.

Among such scholarly writers we believe Lord Kingsborough has a prominent and representative place. According to Mr. Bancroft's review of his conclusions (*Native Races*, Vol. V, pp. 84-91), the noble Lord found, for instance, that the Mexicans anciently acknowledged the unity of God in Tezcatlipoca, and that they, at the time, revered angels, thrones, principalities, dominions, powers, as did the people of Old Testament times. The Toltecs, probably, were acquainted with the story of the *Fall* as related in Genesis; the story of the deception by the *Serpent*, (the Nahash), who in the Pearl of Great Price (Moses 4:6-7), is said to have been the agent and mouthpiece of Satan. Lord Kingsborough found striking resemblance between the Creation, Flood, and Dispersion traditions of the Hebrews and the American aborigines. He also believed it probable that some of the Indians had a seventh-day Sabbath. The Mexicans, as the Hebrews, he pointed out, poured sacrificial blood upon the earth; they sprinkled it and they marked persons with it. In Palestine, no one was permitted to enter the holiest compartment of the temple. That was the law in Peru. That man was created in the image of God, was a Mexican, as well as Hebrew conception.

According to Lord Kingsborough, it is impossible, on reading what Mexican mythology records of the *War in Heaven* and the *Fall of Tzontemoc and the other rebellious spirits;* of the *Creation of Light* by the word of Tonacateculiti, and on the *Division of Waters,* of the *Sin of Ytztlacoliuhgui,* and his blindness and nakedness; of the *Temptation of Suchiguecal* and her disobedience in gathering roses from a tree, and the consequent misery and disgrace of herself and all her posterity — not to recognize Scriptural analogies.

It is certainly not scientific to deny the logical force of such conclusions by men who speak after years of research — men of undisputed credibility in all common affairs of life. Scientific considerations demand a more reasonable view. The Book of Mormon, in relating the story of the migration of the Jaredites and showing their descent from Shem; and also the latter immigration of Lehi and his family, and Mulek and his guardians, about 600 B.C., enables us to account for the strictly Hebrew and Semitic features of Indian institutions and achievements, as shown by remains from remote millenniums as well as from more recent dates.

ALEXANDRIAN MANUSCRIPT

The Alexandrian Manuscript, known as *A* in theological literature, also by the name *Alexandrinus Codex*, corroborates in an astounding way the form of the name JARED as it appears in the Book of Ether.

That manuscript consists of four volumes containing a Greek translation of the entire Old Testament and most of the New. It has, besides, an epistle of the famous Athanasius to Marcellinus, and an assortment of early writings. According to one tradition, the copy was made in Alexandria about the middle of the 4th Century by an English lady by the name of Theclah. It was presented to King Charles I by the Patriarch of Constantinople in the year 1628, and it has been in the British Museum since 1753.

The value of the manuscript is very great for the textual criticism of the Bible, and its reading of *Jared* (as in the Book of Ether) for *Jerah*, a form of spelling in some earlier translations of the Book of Moses (Genesis), is of importance to students of ancient American history and not only to readers of the Book of Ether.

THE JAREDITES

According to the Book of Mormon, a colony, now known as Jaredites (Moroni 9:23), some time shortly after the attempt to build the famous Tower of Babel, came to America from the region occupied by the tower builders.

Very little is known about these colonists and their descendants, but we may suppose that their migration was part of a general movement in all directions which took place at that time, from the Land of Shinar, afterwards called Chaldea.

A GENERAL MIGRATION FROM BABYLON

That such a general migratory movement actually took place can hardly be doubted. Josephus, who drew information from both Hebrew and Greek sources, says:

"After this they were dispersed abroad, on account of their languages, and went out by colonies everywhere, and each colony took possession of that land which they lit upon, and unto which God led them; so that the whole continent was filled with them, both the inland and the maritime countries. There were some, also, who passed over the sea in ships and inhabited the islands."[1]

In a much more recent work we read:[2]

"All history demonstrates that from that central focus (Babylon) nations were propelled over the globe with an extraordinary degree of energy and geographical enterprise."

A Chinese tradition is mentioned by Dr. Fisher of Yale, thus:

"The nucleus of the Chinese Nation is thought to have been a band of immigrants, who are supposed by some to have started from the region southeast of the Caspian Sea, and to have crossed the headwaters of the Oxus. They followed the course of the Hoang Ho, or Yellow River, having entered the country of their adoption from the northwest, and they planted themselves in the present province of Shan-se." (*Improvement Era,* Feb., 1927, p. 314)

It is not impossible that others of the Jaredite Race followed the pioneers of the Book of Ether, and remained at the seashore, laying the foundation of the Chinese Empire. The annual pilgrimage of

---

[1]*Antiquities of the Jews,* Book 1, Chapter 5.
[2]Schoolcraft, *Hist. and Statist. Information,* Vol. 1, p. 14; Philadelphia, 1852.

Chinese to the top of their sacred mount just at the point of the peninsula of Shantung confirms this supposition.

DATE OF THE JAREDITE MIGRATION

According to the chronology of Bishop Usher, which appears in English versions of the Bible, the building of the Tower was undertaken about B.C. 2,200. Dr. Joseph Angus, in his *Bible Handbook*, suggests 2,247. According to Babylonian traditions, the City of Babel was founded about the year B.C. 2,230. But as early as B.C. 2,000, there were clay tablets in the Babylonian Library, now preserved in the British Museum, which contained the story of the Tower-building. It must have been ancient history already at that time. Everything considered, the great dispersion can hardly have taken place much later than B.C. 2,500.

LOCATION OF THE TOWER

Near a place called *Hillah* on the east bank of the Euphrates, there is a splendid ruin known as *Birs Nimrud*, standing like a watch-tower on a vast plain. It is in the shape of a pyramid and is 150 feet high. On its top there is a solid mass of vitrified bricks. From inscriptions Sir Henry Rawlinson found its name to be *The Temple of the Seven Planets*.[3] This ruin has been supposed to be what is left of the Tower of Babel.

THE JAREDITES AT MORIANCUMER

According to the Book of Ether (Ether 1:42; 2:1) the Jaredites began their journey by going northward into the Valley of Nimrod. In the course of their travels from this valley, they crossed many waters — lakes and rivers — and eventually they came to that *great sea which divideth the lands*, and there they pitched their tents and called the place Moriancumer, probably after the Brother of Jared who was the leader and head of the little colony. Here they remained four years.

JAREDITE CIVILIZATION

The Jaredites were far from being savages, or even barbarians, as these terms are used by modern writers. They were agriculturists familiar with *seeds of every kind*, and they had *flocks of every kind*. They were hunters and trappers, and bee-keepers[4] and they understood how to utilize the food supply in the rivers and lakes, for as part of their equipment for the journey into the wilderness *where there never had man been*, they made a vessel *in which they did*

---

[3] *Assyrian Discoveries*, p. 59.

[4] Their name for honey-bee was *deseret*, a word which seems to have survived to our day in the Arabian *aseleth*, which means honey.

carry with them the fish of the waters. All this indicates a civilization further advanced than we generally give the people of the so-called Stone Age credit for. A people cultivating the soil, taking care of flocks, keeping bees, hunting and fishing and constructing boats, (Ether 2:6) must have known a great variety of industries.

But, as a further evidence of the high intellectual and spiritual level attained by the Jaredites, their records tell us that they had revelations of the most exalting truths concerning God and man, which presupposes a high degree of intellectual and spiritual advancement.

BUILDING BARGES

At Moriancumer the Jaredites constructed eight barges, or vessels, in which they crossed the ocean.

Let us note one remarkable circumstance connected with the *building of these ships.* When they were completed, the question of illumination presented itself. The barges had no windows, and the travelers were not permitted to make a fire. The Brother of Jared, consequently, prompted by the most sublime, childlike faith, presented the difficulty before the Lord. But, the Divine Architect, instead of giving His faithful servant direct instructions on the matter, referred the question back to him: "What will ye that I shall do?" The ingenuity of the Brother of Jared thus being put to the test, this great leader of men, went up on a mountain, and there he did *molten* out of a rock, sixteen small stones, clear and transparent. These stones he presented before the Lord and asked that He make them luminous. God did so. He touched them with His finger, and they became light-bearers.[5]

SETTLEMENTS IN THE LAND OF PROMISE

The first country settled in the Land of Promise was called Moron.[6] Where that country was, we do not know, except it was near the Land which by the Nephites was called *Desolation.* From

---

[5]It should be noted here that some scholars are of the opinion that the *window* which God commanded Noah to make for the Ark, was just such a luminous stone. The word in the original is *tsohar,* which is said to mean something *bright,* or *clear,* and Jonathan Ben Uzziel understands it to mean a precious luminous stone, which Noah, by Divine command, took from a certain river and carried it into the Ark. If this is correct, the Brother of Jared merely asked the Lord to do for him that which He had done for that ancient patriarch, Noah.

[6]This name is in all probability akin to the name Merom (Joshua 11:5), now known as *Marum.* It may also be akin to Maran (I Corinthians 16:22), where it means *Our Lord.* In passing it may be observed that *Maranatha* should be written *Marana tha,* and be rendered, *Come, O our Lord.* For it is, no doubt, the same expression which we find in Revelation 22:20, *Come Lord.*

this center the Jaredites spread out in all directions, and became so numerous that there was no greater nation *upon all the face of the earth,* according to the word of the Lord.

Orson Pratt was of the opinion that the "Jaredite colony . . . landed on the western coast of Mexico, and extended their settlements over all the North American portion of the Continent, where they dwelt until about six centuries before Christ, when, because of wickedness they were all destroyed." (*Mill. Star,* Vol. 38, p. 693)

Very early in their history the people made Orihah, the youngest son of Jared, their *King.* He walked humbly before the Lord, exercised his judicial functions in righteousness, and lived a happy domestic life, being the father of thirty-one children.

Omer, the fourth successor of Jared, had a rebellious son whom he named Jared. This son and his followers left the Country of Moron and established themselves in the Land of Heth.

Omer, being warned in a dream to leave his country because of the secret combinations, *"traveled many days and came over and passed by the Hill of Shim, and came over by the place where the Nephites were destroyed, and from thence eastward, and came to a place which was called Ablom,"* possibly after Abel. Here, Omer was joined, later, by Nimrah and his followers.

During a season of drought and famine, in the days of Heth, the eighth from Jared, many of the Jaredites fled "towards the land southward, which was called by the Nephites, Zarahemla," and many perished, being attacked by poisonous serpents: nevertheless, "there were some who fled into the land southward." These were separated from the rest of the people, for the Lord caused the serpents ". . . that they should hedge the way that the people could not pass."

Although the history of the Jaredites in the Book of Ether is merely a faint outline, it makes it clear that, while Moron was the center of interest to the historian, the people had spread from there in various directions.

The first king of Moron was Orihah, the son of Jared.[7]

Shule was one of the great rulers of the Jaredites. His reign, however, was exceedingly stormy, with wars and rebellions, and he

---

[7]The following list of Jaredite rulers is given in the Book of Ether:

Orihah	Coriantum	Morianton	Lib	Coriantum	Ethem
Kib	Com	Kim	Hearthom	Com	Moron
Shule	Heth	Levi	Heth	Shiblon	Coriantor
Omer	Shez	Corom	Aaron	Seth	
Emer	Riplakish	Kish	Amnigaddah	Ahah	

The last ruler, the contemporary of Ether, the Prophet, was Coriantumr. (Ether 12:1)

fought with varying success, until he had overcome his enemies and given his people peace. He was a righteous judge and a wise lawgiver, as well as a mighty warrior.

The success of Shule as a warrior is attributed to his superior arms. The historian says: "Wherefore, he came to the Hill Ephraim, and he did molten out of the hill, and made swords out of steel for those whom he had drawn with him."

STEEL

The Jaredites, in all probability, did not know iron in the particular form which we call *steel*, but from the earliest days of history the people had a metal which in the Old Testament Hebrew is called *nechushah* and *nechushet*, and which our Bible translators have rendered "steel" in four places, and "brass" twice. In Genesis 4:22, we read that Tubal-cain, a descendant of Cain, was an expert in "brass" (nechushah), and Job says of this metal that it is *molten* out of the stone, using an expression almost identical with that of Ether. In II Samuel 32:35; Job 20:24; Psalm 18:34; and Jeremiah 15:12, the same word has been rendered "steel." It means, in fact, neither. According to Gesenius it means "copper," "mostly as hardened and tempered in the manner of steel and used for arms and other cutting instruments." That was the kind of "steel" that Tubal-cain converted into implements, and may also have been the kind that Shule used in making swords.[8]

CORIANTUMR

The last king of Moron was Coriantumr. In his day the country was the scene of incessant warfare. It was invaded by Shared, by Gilead, a brother of Shared, by Lib, and by Shiz, his brother, in succession, and so fierce were the conflicts during these invasions that two million men, and many women and children perished. (Ether 15:2) Coriantumr, appalled at the loss of life, made overtures for peace, but in vain. The opposing armies then took up strong positions near the Hill Ramah. For four years, Coriantumr and Shiz prepared themselves for a final battle. Each gathered his followers, "that they might receive all the strength which it was possible that they could receive." Even women and children were conscripted. The outcome of that battle was that both armies were annihilated. Shiz was slain. Coriantumr escaped and eventually reached the Country of Zarahemla. (Omni 21)

---

[8]This takes us back to the beginning of the bronze age. How far back the use of iron can be traced in this country is another question. J. W. Foster says that in shell heaps at Grand Lake on the Teche have been found in mounds "unique specimens of axes of hematite iron ore," and also they were found in mounds covered with soil in which large oaks were growing and had been growing for centuries. (*Prehistoric Races of the United States,* p. 159)

ALL JAREDITES NOT SLAIN?

The general understanding, we believe, is that the entire Jaredite Race was exterminated in this sanguinary battle, with the exception of Coriantumr. It is, of course, possible that the narrative is to be so understood, but the probability is that the Prophet Ether only refers to the annihilation of the two armies and the end of the monarchial form of government.

At the time of the Battle of Ramah there must have been probably millions of Jaredites in this hemisphere; that is evident from the fact that two million souls had perished in the four years before that battle. But it would be absurd to suppose that every Jaredite, men, women, and children, old and young, sick and cripples, as well as strong and well-informed individuals, were enlisted in the armies and encamped around the Hill. It, furthermore, would be contrary to human experience to suppose that there were no desertions from the armies during the long and deadly encounters. It is much more probable that some escaped and when missing, were counted as dead. Again, is it improbable that some of the wounded recovered and survived, without any record having been made of their recovery? We know, from Ether 9:32, that some Jaredites escaped into the "Land Southward," during the famine in the days of Heth, and they must also have become numerous and possibly were not directly interested in the war between Coriantumr and Shiz.

It is very customary to speak of an entire nation when we mean only the more important part of it. We say, for instance, that the Kingdom of Judah was carried away into captivity, when, as a matter of fact, only a small portion, though an important one, was transported to Babylon. Thus, in the first captivity, B.C. 598, the Babylonians carried away 3,023 souls, leaving the common people in their homes. Ten years later 832 captives, and in B.C. 584, 745 more were expatriated — 4,600 in all;[9] or, if these figures give only the number of men, say 15,000, including women and children. In the same way, we speak of the return of the captives, when, as a matter of fact, only half of them, 31,629, according to one estimate, and 42,360, according to another, left the land of captivity.[10]

Furthermore, it seems to us that some Indian traditions regarding the migration of their forefathers, some of their religious ideas, especially the place of the heavenly bodies and the serpents in their symbolism, and many linguistic peculiarities point to a Jaredite origin, which cannot be explained on the supposition that the entire race was wiped out.

[9]Flinders Petri, *Egypt and Israel,* p. 81.
[10]Ezra 2:6-65; Nehemiah 7:6-67.

Destruction does not always mean extermination. We speak of the destruction of Jerusalem and the Jews (I Nephi 10:3), but they still exist. Compare II Nephi 25:9, where the Jews are said to have been destroyed "from generation to generation."

If we set Bishop Usher's chronology aside as too short[11] and assume that the building of the Tower and the dispersion took place about B.C. 2,500, and if the Battle of Ramah took place not long after the arrival of the Mulekites in America, the history of the Jaredites in the Book of Ether covers a period of about 1900 years. During all that time the people built cities, cultivated the ground, engaged in arts, industries, and trade; they lived, loved, and died, until, because of moral degeneration, their governments were broken up and their countries made desolate, through famine, pestilence, and war.

JAREDITES HAD TIME TO INCREASE

Nineteen centuries may not be a long period in the history of the Earth, but what a multitude of events are crowded into 1900 years of human records! Or even much less time than that. Here is an illustration:

In 1865, one of the big trees in Calaveras County, California, was cut down. Edgar de la Rue calculated that it began to grow about 620 A.D.; then he went over history since that time to see what had happened during the lifetime of that venerable tree. His article found its way into print, in the form of a dispatch, dated Red Bluff, Cal., February 4, 1922.

The tree was born about the time Mohammedanism began to take root, and, we may add, when papacy was established by the imperial decree of Emperor Phocas, in 607 A.D.[12] It was 110 years old when the Battle of Tours was fought. Figuratively speaking, the tree saw the introduction of Christianity in Scandinavia in 830; the beginning of the Reign of Alfred the Great in England; the Cru-

---

[11]Short correctly observes that the authors of the Bible do not profess to give a complete chronology, or even to furnish data for an infallible system. Their accounts are condensed. In their genealogies they leave out several generations, which can be seen if we compare the genealogy of our Lord as given in the Gospels with those of the Old Testament. Their purpose was not to give a complete list of descendants, but to prove descent through a certain line, and their condensed lists serve that purpose only. (Short's *North Americans of Antiquity*, p. 199)

[12]Boniface III was a deacon of the Roman Church, who in 603 A.D., was sent to Constantinople by Gregory the Great as a legate (apocrissarius). There he supported Phocas, a usurper of the throne of the vilest character, and in return when Boniface had been elected pope in 607, Phocas issued, at his request, a decree against Cyriacus, Bishop of Constantinople, in which it was ordained that "the see of blessed Peter, the apostle, should be the head of all the churches," and that the title of "universal bishop" belonged exclusively to the Bishop of Rome. And this was, evidently the keystone in the arch of apostasy.

sades; the signing of the Magna Charta in 1220; and the conquest of Wales in 1280. The tree was growing and developing when Columbus discovered America in 1492, and when Balboa, in 1520, first viewed the Pacific Ocean. The tree was 1,030 years old when Oliver Cromwell was made Protector, and had reached the age of 1,156 years when America's Declaration of Independence was signed in 1776. It was, finally, 1,244 years old at the close of the Civil War, in 1865, when it was cut down. If to this age of a tree we add six or seven centuries for the history of the Jaredites, we can form some idea of the immensity and infinite diversity of the contents of that history, of which only a fraction, and that in mere outline, has been handed down to us. Consider also, that it is about 1,900 years since the Christian Religion, itself, was revealed.

THE JAREDITE LANDS

PLACE OF LANDING NOT KNOWN

The Jaredites, led by Divine Power, landed on the shores of the Promised Land, after a perilous voyage across the deep, that had lasted 344 days. Such is the information contained in the Book of Ether. But where they disembarked, the historian does not say. (Ether 6:11-12)

MULTIPLYING AND SPREADING

The next fact concerning the newcomers is, that "they went forth upon the face of the land, — the Promised Land, the North American Continent — "and began to till the land." We read further, that "they began to spread upon the face of the land, and to multiply and to till the earth; and they did wax strong in the land."

These two statements read together can only mean that the various families of the Jaredites, soon after their arrival, separated and occupied each its own territory for cultivation, under the administration of the great leaders, as appears later. From the outset, they were avoiding the mistake of the tower builders. They were not centralizing the population, but distributing it. Settlers went forth from the place of landing as soon as naturally convenient, and established themselves in new localities. This process was repeated in the following generations, and the whole continent became gradually well populated.

The record, having stated that the country had a numerous population, breaks the historical chain of events, and joins the disconnected links years afterwards, when the Brother of Jared let it be known that he felt old age and dissolution approaching. Many years, with their rapidly progressing developments, are thus passed by in silence. How many we know not. But the two sons of Joktan, Jared and his brother, must have reached a very high age before they realized that their work was nearly finished. They were, perhaps, nearing the end of their second century. We venture this supposition on the strength of Genesis 11:11-26, where the age of each of the ancestors of Abraham is given.

Peleg, the brother of Joktan, lived 239 years. Regu, the son of Peleg, was also 239 years of age when he died. Serug, Regu's son, was 230 at the time of his death. Nahor, the son of Serug and the grandfather of Abraham, reached the age of 148 years. It is a reasonable conclusion that the two sons of Joktan, Jared and his brother, reached at least the average age of the mentioned descendants of Peleg, the brother of Joktan, or about 214 years. During that time, important geographic changes must have occurred in the Jaredite settlements, as well as progress in other directions, for the purposes of replenishing the Earth (Genesis 9:1), not gathering.

Another conclusion is, also, in our judgment, unavoidable. We must not expect to find the administration of the two great leaders of the people, a century or a century and a half after the landing, to be located at the coast. As settlers went forth in various directions and founded colonies, the centers of population changed, and, at a time when the means of communication were not what they are today, the convenience of the government must have demanded that its seat be moved to the more populous and influential of communities. Jared and his brother must, therefore, at the end of their long career, have had their capital, probably far from the coast. If, as some have said, the landing place was somewhere "south of the Gulf of California and north of the Isthmus of Panama," such moves, either north or south, would have been feasible.

The foregoing comments are offered on Ether 6:19-20, where we read that the Brother of Jared proposed to take a census preparatory to submitting the question of the future form of government to a general vote. The necessity of a registration of the voters indicates that the Jaredites were numerous at that time.

THE LAND OF NEHOR

This is the first American Land, or country, which is mentioned by name in the Book of Ether. Jared had passed away, also his Brother. Orihah, Jared's son, was no more. Kib, the son of Orihah, was the reigning head of the government.

One of Orihah's sons was named Corihor. He forsook his father's house and homeland and established himself in the Land of Nehor. Here, after some years of preparation, he placed himself at the head of a rebellion. Kib, the King, was captured by the insurgents and became a prisoner of war, and Corihor usurped his place in the government.

The name of the country, supposing it to be a Semitic word, may give a clue, at least to the direction in which to look for it. *Nehar* is the Hebrew for river. As a verb it is used metaphorically (Jeremiah 31:12; 51:44; Micah 1:4) for the *flowing together* of nations into one place. *Nehor*, the Jaredite form of the word, almost certainly has the same meaning as the Hebrew *nahar*, a river, or a place, a land, by a river; a country into which people are *flowing*.

Nehor is said to be Egyptian for the Nile. To the Hebrews and other Semites, *nahar* was the Euphrates. The country between the Missouri and the Mississippi may well have reminded the Jaredites of Mesopotamia. The Mississippi may well have been the Nahar, or Nehor, of the Old Country to them.

Here it may be mentioned that the American press, a few years ago, announced that recognized archeologists had come to the conclusion that a city-building people had inhabited Illinois, Ohio, Indiana, and Wisconsin, as far back as B.C. 3000. This would take us back further than the beginning of the Jaredite era, according to the chronology of Ussher, and it is not necessary to go back that far. But the point is this, that the mighty Mississippi River is flowing through the very area that is mentioned by the archeologists as the habitation of a city-building people. This raises the question whether the Nehor of the Book of Ether is not the Mississippi, and the Land of Nehor the Mississippi Valley and an adjacent indefinite area, where today innumerable mounds prove a numerous population in the remote antiquity.

THE LAND OF MORON

The king dwelt here. (Ether 7:5-6; 17) It was the capital, the center of Jaredite culture. To the generation of Orihah and Kib, following immediately after that of Jared and his brother, Moron was the *Land of their first inheritance,* (vv. 16-17) because it was a land which the two great leaders, before they passed away, undoubtedly, bequeathed to their posterity. In time it became the center of Jaredite history as well as culture. (Ether 14:11)

The literal meaning of the word *Moron,* supposing *marana,* meaning *our Lord* (I Corinthians 16:22) to be its Aramæan kindred, would also be *our Lord.* Applied to a country it would mean *The Land of Our Lord.* It had, undoubtedly, been dedicated to His service. Compare Ether 2:12, where it is expressly stated that nations living in this Promised Land are under obligation to serve *the Lord of this land, Who is Jesus Christ,* in return for the blessings of liberty.

Moroni, who abridged Mosiah's translation of the Twenty-four gold plates which contained the full account of the Jaredite history, gives the information that Moron was near the *Land which is called Desolation* by the Nephites. (*See,* Alma 22:30-32; 46:17; 50:34; 63:5) If, as is probable, Moron was in a south-western direction from Nehor, the land by the river, and north of Desolation, it would include in its area what is now known as Missouri, and, consequently, Jackson County, where Independence City is located. It would also embrace Adam-ondi-Ahman, about fifty miles north of Jackson County, an area made sacred during the time of Adam, and which is again to attain to extraordinary prominence in the Kingdom of God, *when the Ancient of Days shall sit, as spoken of by Daniel, the Prophet.* (Doctrine and Covenants 116) Orson Pratt says *Adam-ondi-Ahman* means, *The Valley of God.* (*Journal of Discourses,* Volume 16, p. 48), almost the same as Moron. (Also, read Doctrine and Covenants 107:53-57)

Independence has become an almost sacred place in the history of the Church of Jesus Christ of Latter-day Saints. It will again, in due time, be the stage on which the glory of the Almighty will be manifest to all the world. Revelation says of Missouri: "This is the Land of Promise, and the place for the city of Zion. Behold, the place which is now called Independence is the center place." (Doctrine and Covenants 57:2-3) "There the center place, or Zion, will be built up."[1] A magnificent temple will be erected there. There the New Jerusalem will be built, beginning at the Temple Lot (Doctrine and Covenants 84:2-5; also *see,* III Nephi 20:22; 21:23-25; Ether 13:3-6).

Missouri, and especially Independence, Jackson County, is, accordingly, destined to become the attraction of the world, when the Holy City rises there in splendor, with, figuratively speaking, streets of gold and gates of precious stones; when the first temple-palace ever built by man is reared in which the King of kings, with His glorified attendants, will receive His Holy Priesthood in audience, to confer with them and give instructions concerning the affairs of His Kingdom.

Does anyone, half doubtful, ask why such signal honor should be bestowed upon a region such as of which we are speaking?

The answer is: Adam-ondi-Ahman was, undoubtedly dedicated to the Lord by our great progenitor, himself, during the Adamic dispensation, before the Flood. Moron, in all probability the same land as that in which Adam-ondi-Ahman was situated, was similarly dedicated by the Brother of Jared, during the dispensation of Noah, after the deluge. Such a dedication is a covenant between God and man, similar to the Covenant of God with Abraham concerning Palestine. But, as far as God is concerned, a covenant stands forever. It is everlasting, even if it be temporarily set aside by the

---

[1]"Remarks have been made as to our staying here in the Rockies. I will tell you how long we shall stay here. If we live our religion, we shall stay here in these mountains forever *** and a portion of the Priesthood will go and redeem and build up the center stake of Zion." (President Brigham Young, *Journal of Discourses,* Volume 11, p. 16)

other part. That we believe, is the reason for the selection by the Lord of Missouri to be a Land of Promise, the place for the New Jerusalem, the place for the City of Zion.

EPHRAIM

This is the name of a hill, or, perhaps, a hilly region, near the City of Nehor, the Capital of the Land of Nehor. The meaning of the word is *fruitful,* indicating a prosperous part of the country. It must have been known especially for its wealth of minerals, for when Shule decided to begin military operations against his brother, Corihor, on behalf of their father, Kib, he went to the Hill Ephraim, and there he made *swords of steel* for his army. Thus equipped he attacked and deposed his wicked brother, liberated their father, and placed him again at the head of the government. (Ether 7:9)

There seems to be no doubt that the ancient dwellers of the region through which the Mississippi flows were miners. Bancroft (*Native Races,* Volume 4, p. 783) says that ancient miners have left numerous traces of their work in the region of Lake Superior. At one place a piece of copper—almost pure—weighing over five tons has been found fifteen feet below the surface. It bore marks of fire.

THE LAND OF THEIR FIRST INHERITANCE

This seems to be Moron. (Ether 7:17) Corihor had a son named Noah. He organized a rebellion against Shule, the King, and Corihor, his father. Having become the ruler over the Land of their First Inheritance, he made Shule a prisoner of war and carried him captive into *Moron.* That identifies Moron as the *Land of their First Inheritance.*

THE LAND OF HETH

(Ether 8:2) Where this Land, or, district, was, we do not know. Heth, according to Genesis 15, was the second son of Canaan, a descendant of Ham, and the ancestor of the Hittites, who at one time were a powerful people, strong enough to wage war against Egypt and Assyria. They inhabited Canaan at the time of the Exodus. The name means *terror.* Perhaps there were descendants of Ham among the friends who followed Jared and his brother from the Tower. That would account for the name of this Land.

ABLOM

(Ether 9:3) The name means *green meadows.* The country was situated possibly on the Atlantic Seacoast. That was the opinion of

Orson Pratt as stated in a footnote in earlier editions of the Book of Mormon.

The Hill Shim, which Omer and his family passed on their flight to Ablom was located in a Country called Antum. (Mormon 1:3) This name, as some other Book of Mormon words, is evidently the Kechua, *anta*, which Garcilasso de la Vega translates, *copper*. It is, no doubt, related to *antion*, a piece of gold (Alma 11:19), and *onti*, a piece of silver (Alma 11:6). It is suggestive of a mining region.

Nimrah, after his brother had been murdered by their father, fled to Ablom, to the colony of Omer.

THE LAND SOUTHWARD

This, as the Prophet Moroni explains (Ether 9:31), was known as Zarahemla by the Nephites. It was the Land Southward to the Jaredites, while Moron, Nehor, and *the countries round about*, were the *north countries*. (v. 35)

THE NARROW NECK OF LAND

The Isthmus of Panama. *See,* Ether 10:20.

THE VALLEY OF GILGAL

In the fourth year of the war that ended in the disaster at Ramah, Coriantumr, the last King of the Jaredites, met his bitter enemy, Shared, in this valley. The murderous combat lasted for three days. Shared was defeated and fled precipitately to the Plains of Heshlon (Ether 13:27-28). *See,* Ether 6:14. The name *Gilgal* means *circle*. It may have been given to the valley on account of its circular form, or because of certain mounds erected there for dwellings, or for sepulchral purposes or for fortifications. The mounds were of different forms. Some were in the shape of animals. One mound in Ohio is thought to represent a snake swallowing an egg. Other mounds are circular. Circleville, Ohio, has its name from mounds of that form.

WILDERNESS OF AKISH

(Ether 14:3-7) There is a Semitic word, *akash*, to be froward, false, etc., as in Psalm 101:4, "A froward heart shall depart from me." Akish, the name, may be a derivative from the same root as this word. Its meaning would describe accurately the character of Akish, the son of Kimnor, in Ether 8:10.

Two years after the death of Shared, his brother, Gilead, attacked Coriantumr. The Battle of the Wilderness of Akish ensued. Gilead succeeded in usurping the throne of Coriantumr in Moron, and the latter entrenched himself and his followers in the Wilderness of Akish. They remained there for two years. During that time Gilead was murdered by his chief ecclesiastical official, who, in his turn was slain by an ambitious individual named Lib. Coriantumr now attacked Lib, but he was defeated and fled to a place called Agosh. Here another battle occurred. Lib fell, but his brother Shiz assumed the leadership.

The people, at this time, began to split into two parties. Many thousands had been slain upon the battlefields during the years of war. Of the survivors, some joined Coriantumr, others Shiz. The next battle was fought "upon the seashore," possibly on the shore of some great inland lake. (Ether 14:11-26)

LAND OF CORIHOR

(Ether 14:27-31) Coriantumr continued his retreat, closely pursued by Shiz. So terrible were the losses inflicted on the armies of Shiz by the rear guard of Coriantumr's troops that the inhabitants in the settlements through which the armies passed, fled in terror and panic, to the Land of Corihor. After a battle of three days at the seashore, Shiz went into camp in the Valley of Corihor, and Coriantumr pitched his tents in the Valley of Shurr. A battle was fought at the Hill Comnor. Coriantumr was severely wounded and was carried from the battlefield as though dead.

THE HILL RAMAH

(Ether 15:11) The Jaredite name for Cumorah. When Coriantumr recovered sufficiently from his wounds, and then realized that two million men, and in addition their wives and children, making perhaps a total of between three and four million souls, had been slain during the years of warfare, he offered his antagonist the Kingdom if he would end further bloodshed. Shiz rejected the offer. He demanded the life of Coriantumr. So the war was continued.

Coriantumr took his stand near the waters of Ripliancum, probably an inland lake. Shiz attacked and was defeated. He fled with his soldiers to a place called Ogath. Coriantumr, who was again wounded, did not pursue, but went—probably northward—to the country and Hill Ramah. The two deadly enemies each had its own gathering place—one at Ramah, the other at Ogath.

The next four years preparations were made in both these camps for a final conflict. All things being made ready, the massacre at Ramah took place, as is described in Ether 15:15-34.

CONCLUSION

In order to get a correct picture of the conflict at Ramah, its antecedents and consequences, certain facts should be remembered.

The disaster was brought about when the leaders of the people had apostatized from the Lord, rejected His Government, and persecuted His Holy Prophets.

The Jaredites, in this country, had an experience similar to that of the Israelites and Jews in their Promised Land, ages afterwards, who, after the destruction of their City and Sanctuary, were slain or driven and scattered all over the globe, where they became *lost* both to themselves and to the world.

It should also be remembered that the reign of Lib, the son of Kish, a considerable exodus of Jaredites took place from the North Countries to the South. (Ether 10:19-28) This movement was primarily for the purpose of procuring food, clothing, and we dare say, materials for implements, weapons and ornaments, for the agriculturists in the north who had seen their stock perish, and their farms burn up during the years of drought. Many of these *hunters,* as they are termed, did not return. They remained in the south. They built at least one *great city* by the narrow neck of land on the place where *the sea divides the land.* (Ether 10:20) How many more cities they founded we do not know, but they must have multiplied at least at the same rate as their kindred in the north. (Ether 9:16; 10:4; 12:22) If the Jaredites in the north were counted by the millions (Ether 15:2), there may have been other millions in the south. Coriantumr, the last and only individual who survived the war between him and Shiz, and who wandered many miles south of the scene of that last battle at Ramah, may have been hopeful of finding these very same people.

We should be reminded, further, of the fact that the conflict at Ramah was the final settlement of the chief issue between two political parties, or their leaders, Coriantumr and Shiz, respectively. Both were in the field for power and royal honors. Shiz, in addition, was consumed by an unquenchable thirst for revenge. He wanted the life of his antagonist. Their campaign during the four years preceding Ramah (Ether 15:14) was a tireless effort to bring as many people as possible together in their two gathering places, but especially men for service on the battlefield, together with their resources.

THE BOOK OF ETHER

CHAPTER 1

1. *The Book of Ether.*

2. *Not a full account.*

The record of the Jaredites, taken from the twenty-four plates found by the people of Limhi in the days of king Mosiah.

The prophet Ether's genealogy—The great tower—Jared and his brother—Their language not confounded—Preparing for migration as directed by the Lord.

1. And now I, Moroni, proceed to give an account of those ancient inhabitants who were destroyed by the hand of the Lord upon the face of this north country.

2. And I take mine account from the twenty and four plates which were found by the people of Limhi, which is called the Book of Ether.

3. And as I suppose that the first part of this record, which speaks concerning the creation of the world, and also of Adam, and an account from that time even to the great tower, and whatso-

---

VERSES 1-2. *The Book of Ether.* In the Book of Ether, Moroni, the son of the Prophet Mormon, presents an account of the ancient inhabitants of America who were destroyed by the hand of the Lord in the "north country."

The land referred to is evidently that in which Moroni sojourned at the time he made his version of this Book, which land is also known as Desolation. It was probably in North America, where the Battle of Cumorah had been fought.

The account of Moroni's is, substantially, a summary of the translation of King Mosiah of the twenty-four gold plates found by the explorers of Limhi (Mosiah 21: 25-29). They became known as "The Book of Ether," from the name of the author (Ether 1:6).

VERSES 3-5. *The story of the beginnings not told.* Moroni explains that the stories of the Creation and of Adam, and the history of the world to the time of the building of the great tower occupied the first part of the twenty-four plates, but that this section was omitted from his version because it was "had among the Jews," referring to the records of Moses. This is a notable testimony to the genuineness and the authenticity of the first eleven chapters of the Book of Genesis in the Bible, and, by inference, of the whole five Books of Moses. Here, as elsewhere, the Book of Mormon is, in the language of many scholars, "A New Witness for God."

ever things transpired among the children of men until that time, is had among the Jews—

4. Therefore I do not write those things which transpired from the days of Adam until that time; but they are had upon the plates; and whoso findeth them, the same will have power that he may get the full account.

5. But behold, I give not the full account, but a part of the account I give, from the tower down until they were destroyed.

VERSE 5. *Not a full account*. In the first paragraph Moroni informs us that the subject of his historical sketch is the ancient inhabitants who were destroyed "upon the face" of this "north country." He is relating the tragic fate of that part of the Jaredites. In the fifth verse he adds that he does not copy the full account as committed to writing by Ether, but only a part of it.

The Jaredites, at the time of Ether, were widely scattered on the American Continents. All students of the Book of Ether agree on that. The divine promise to Jared, before he left for America, was, "There will I bless thee and thy seed, and raise up unto Me of thy seed, and of the seed of thy brother, and they who shall go with thee, a great nation. And there shall be none greater than the nation which I will raise up unto Me of thy seed, upon all the face of the earth." This promise was fulfilled during the centuries that intervened between the arrival of Jared in America and the Battle of Ramah.

Orson Pratt says:

"In process of time they became a very numerous and powerful people, occupying principally North America; building large cities in all quarters of the land; being a civilized and enlightened nation." (*Remarkable Visions*, Edinburgh, 1840)

President George Reynolds says:

"The contemporary nations on the Eastern Continent—Egypt, Chaldea and Babylonia—were insignificant when compared with the vast extent of territory held and filled by the Jaredites; they were the sole rulers of the whole Western Hemisphere, and possibly the originals whence arose the stories of the fabled Atlantis; for we have no account that God shut them out from the knowledge of the rest of mankind when He planted them in America, as He afterwards did the Nephites; and late researches have shown that the geographical knowledge of the ancients was much greater in the earlier ages than at the time of the Savior and a few hundred years previous to His advent." (*The Story of the Book of Mormon*, p. 325, Edition of 1957)

When studying the Book of Ether it is important to remember that neither the original author, or authors, nor the later copyist, intended to produce a handbook on American archaeology or ancient ethnography; Ether gives, very briefly, some of the main historical features of the people governed by Jared and his descendants through Orihah. Of the descendants of the Brother of Jared we are informed that one of them, "a mighty man," overthrew Moron, the grandfather of Ether, and kept him prisoner and his son, Coriantor, the father of the prophet, in captivity all their days. (Ether 11:17-23) But what of the other immigrants who left the site of the Tower with Jared and his brother and accompanied them to what is now called America? In Ether 6:16 we read that, "The friends of Jared and his brother were in number about twenty and two souls, and they also begat sons and daughters before they came to the Promised Land; and therefore they began to be many." At the time of the Battle of Ramah there must have been Jaredites of the many various lineages in favorable locations all over the Western Hemisphere, as amply evidenced by shell heaps, mounds, and mysterious ruins in widely separated places.

3. *Genealogy of Ether.*

6. And on this wise do I give the account. He that wrote this record was Ether, and he was a descendant of Coriantor.

7. Coriantor was the son of Moron.

8. And Moron was the son of Ethem.

9. And Ethem was the son of Ahah.

10. And Ahah was the son of Seth.

Verses 6-32. *There are thirty generations, beginning with Jared.*

SEMITIC NAMES

On closer examination of the names of Ether's progenitors, we find a large percent of them to be related to Semitic stems. For instance, *Jared* means in Hebrew, one who descends, or, according to others, one who rules. Compare Ether 2:1, where it is stated that the journey began with Jared and his companion "descending" into the Valley of Nimrod. *Shule* (possibly from "shaal," to ask for, to desire) meaning a man of prayer. His biography (Ether 7:7-27) justifies this appellation. *Omer* and *Emer* (possibly from "amar") means a speaker, or perhaps (like Omri) one to whom God speaks. *Com* and *Kim* (from kum or koom) meaning to arise, to stand up, and is applied to a hill, a height. *Levi* (from the stem "lavah" to join or to associate with; compare Genesis 29:34), meaning a joining. *Aaron,* meaning a mountain of strength; *Kish,* straw, forage; *Lib,* whiteness; *Seth,* put; *Ethem,* their strength; *Ether,* abundance.

It is evident from this genealogical record that Jared was a descendant of Shem, that son of Noah of whom it is said that he was the "father of all the children of Eber"; that is, of all the peoples later known as Hebrews (Genesis 10-21).

THE JAREDITES IN GENESIS

The story of the Jaredites, as preserved by Ether, lends added interest to the brief notes concerning the lineage of Eber in Genesis.

This patriarch had two sons. One he called Peleg (division), "for in his days was the earth divided." (Genesis 10:25) The other was called by him, Joktan (meaning either "small," or "dispute," "contention." Both names were a reminder of some historic event by which the human families in the early stage of their existence had been separated and dispersed.

The names of the ancestors of Eber from Shem, and his descendants through Peleg to Abraham, are found in Genesis 11:1-26, proving the Semitic and Hebrew lineage of the Israelites or Jews. This is one of the highest importance for the identification of our Lord as the Messiah of the Old Testament prophecies.

A shorter list of names of the families of Eber, from Shem to the sons of Joktan, is given in Genesis 10:21-32, representing a Hebrew line different from that of Abraham. This brief genealogical record closes with the significant words: "These are the sons of Shem, after their families, after their tongues, in their lands, after their nations * * * and by those were the nations divided in the earth after the flood"; so that, although the record of names is small, the history covered by it concerns many people, countries, and cultures. This may be sufficient ground for the assumption that the Jaredites, too, have a place among the links of this genealogical chain; that, in fact, Jared was a descendant of Joktan, as Abraham was of Peleg.

11. And Seth was the son of Shiblon.

12. And Shiblon was the son of Com.

13. And Com was the son of Coriantum.

14. And Coriantum was the son of Amnigaddah.

JOKTAN AND JUCATAN

There are geographical names in America, which can best be accounted for on this supposition. Yucatan is one of them, for that is, we have no doubt, the same as Joktan, and it may have been brought to America by descendants, perhaps a son, of that great-great-grandson of Shem.[1] The Arabians who claim that Joktan was one of the principal founders of their nation call him, "Kahtan."

OPHIR

One of the sons of Joktan was so named. Very early some place, famous for its gold, also became known as Ophir. The name signifies, it is said, "red," or, as a name of a certain place, a "fruitful place," the same as "Bountiful," a prominent name in the story of the Book of Mormon. In the Book of Job, one of the earliest literary productions of the Old Testament, the "gold of Ophir," is mentioned twice. Eliphas, a friend of the sorely tried patriarch, tells him that if he would repent and put aside iniquity, God would give him *"gold as dust and gold of Ophir as stones of the brook."*[2]

WHERE WAS THE LAND OF OPHIR?

That question has been very much debated. The preponderance of opinion has placed it in southern Arabia, where other sons of Joktan settled and became the ancestors of mighty Arabian tribes. But Armenia has also been suggested as the Land of Ophir. Some have thought that one of the Moluccas, or Spice Islands, in the Malay Archipelago, was Ophir, while others have regarded the region about the delta of the Indus River in India as the marvelous land of gold. Bancroft and others note that Columbus believed the Island of Haiti (Hispaniola) to be the

---

[1]Descendants of Joktan colonized the southern part of Arabia, from Mesha to Sephar, "a mount of the east (Genesis 10:30), and Josephus had it from learned rabbis that there was a Joktan in India. Dr. Miles Poindexter (in *Ayar Incas*, Vol. 2, p. 208) suggests that the name Yuthan, in Turkestan, is an abbreviated form of "Yu-kho-than" (Joktan). Perhaps a similar suggestion might apply to "Cathay," the China of the day of Marco Polo. "Cathay" was originally "Khitan." Dr. Poindexter found the name "Kautan" in Peru. It was the name of an ancient village. He believes that it is another form of the name, "Yucatan."

[2]The argument of Eliphas may be rendered thus:
"If thou return to the Almighty, thou shalt be restored;
But thou must put away iniquity far from thy tent;
Throw away thy gold as dust, and thy Ophir among the stones of the brook;
Then the Almighty shall be thy golden Treasure,
He shall be thy finest silver." (Job 22:23-25)

Job mentions gold of Ophir when he speaks of the value of wisdom, thus:
"It cannot be had for gold,
Silver cannot be weighed for the price thereof.
It cannot be valued with gold from Ophir,
Nor with precious onyx or for sapphire." (Job 28:15-16)

In one of the Psalms the poet sings the praise of the king:
"Thy garments smell
of myrrh, of aloes and cassia;
From palaces of ivory,
Stringbands made thee glad.
King's daughters were thy maids of honor,
Upon thy right hand stood the queen
In gold of Ophir. (Psalm 45:8-9)

15. And Amnigaddah was the son of Aaron.

16. And Aaron was a descendant of Heth, who was the son of Hearthom.

17. And Hearthom was the son of Lib.

18. And Lib was the son of Kish.

19. And Kish was the son of Corom.

20. And Corom was the son of Levi.

21. And Levi was the son of Kim.

22. And Kim was the son of Morianton.

23. And Morianton was a descendant of Riplakish.

24. And Riplakish was the son of Shez.

Ophir of King Solomon. (*Native Races*, Vol. 5, pp. 64-65) He must, consequently, have thought that a vast commercial traffic connected the Old World with the Western Hemisphere more than a thousand years before our era. Bancroft also quotes notable authority for the hypothesis that Ophir was Peru in South America. Finally, it should be noted that both Jeremiah (10:8-10) and Daniel (10:5) refer to Ophir under the name of "Uphaz."

Perhaps, as suggested by Dr. John Fiske and others, "Ophir" was a common designation for valuable articles of merchandise, which daring merchant-sailors brought from almost mythical localities outside the boundaries of the more generally known world. Perhaps Hebrew writers, anciently spoke of gold of Ophir as we speak of "foreign" products and contrast them with domestic goods.[3]

JERAH

This is another interesting and, for this inquiry, important name in the genealogical list of the descendants of Noah, through Shem. It is, in Genesis, the name of a son of Joktan, the brother of Peleg in whose days the earth was divided. It is the same name as that by which the great hero of the Book of Ether, Jared, is known. There is little doubt that the Jerah of Genesis is the Jared of Ether.

This may call for a word of explanation. *Varients of the same name.* The spelling in Genesis is Jerah (English) and Jarach (Hebrew), the *ch* representing an audible *h-sound.* According to *Smith's Bible Dictionary,* the Alexandrian Codex, one of the oldest and most useful guides on questions relating to the genuineness of the Scripture texts, spells the name, Jarad, which is, letter for letter, when the consonants alone are read, the same as in the Book of Ether. It is always to be remembered that in the earliest Hebrew manuscripts there were no vowel points, only consonants. The Septuagint of the Complutensian Polyglott edition has, Jerach. In I Chronicles 1:2, the Aldine of the Septuagint reads, Jader instead of Jared, while the Compluten-

---

[3]Hebrew historians relate that King Solomon, having completed the Temple in Jerusalem (about B.C. 1005), built a merchant fleet at Ezion-geber, near Eloth on the coast of the Red Sea, in the Land of Edom. The ships, it is said, went as far as Ophir and returned from there with 420 talents of gold for the King in Jerusalem (I Kings 9:26-28; 2 Chronicles 8: 16-18). Several reasons force the conclusion that this goldland was situated a considerable distance from Ezion-geber. The traffic was maintained by two mighty navies, one belonging to King Solomon and the other to King Hiram of Tyre (I Kings 10:11), and the round trip required no less than three years (I Kings 10:22). The voyages of these vessels were not mere coasting expeditions. Solomon required for their success the expert services of Phoenician navigators, "shipmen that had knowledge of the sea" (I Kings 9:27). They may have been skilled and experienced enough to cross either the Atlantic or the Pacific, stopping at various islands. Their cargoes representing almost fabulous values. If a talent was worth $55,000, four hundred-twenty talents was an immense fortune even for a king. Such cargoes were not for small craft, but must have been carried by large and seaworthy ships.

25. And Shez was the son of Heth.

26. And Heth was the son of Com.

27. And Com was the son of Coriantum.

28. And Coriantum was the son of Emer.

29. And Emer was the son of Omer.

30. And Omer was the son of Shule.

31. And Shule was the son of Kib.

32. And Kib was the son of Orihah, who was the son of Jared;

4. Jared, and the Brother of Jared.

33. Which Jared came forth with his brother and their families, with some others and their families, from the great tower, at

---

sian edition has, Jare, the final letter apparently missing. The two forms, Jader and Jare, are most likely probably slips of the copyists, easily accounted for. Letters will sometimes, in copying, become transposed inadvertently, and sometimes omitted. Compare "Jarad," "Jerach," "Jader," "Jare," with "Jared." The Arabian is, "Yerakh." But they are all the same name.[4]

THE DIVISION OF THE EARTH

According to Genesis (10:25 and 31-32), during the days of Peleg and his brother Joktan, the earth was divided between various families, tongues, and nations. Several of the sons of Joktan settled in southern Arabia, but Jerah does not seem to have been among these. In *Smith Dictionary of the Bible,* the information is given that "he has not been satisfactorily identified with the name of any Arabian place or tribe, though a fortress (and probably an old town, like the numerous fortified places in the Yemen of the old Himyarite Kingdom) named Yerakh is mentioned as belonging to the district of Nijjad." This is perfectly intelligible, if, as the Book of Ether relates, Jared and one of his brothers were, by Divine inspiration, appointed to lead a company of colonizers to America. And why should not this hemisphere have been peopled, as well as the eastern continents, when "the nations were divided in the earth after the flood?" (Genesis 10:32)

VERSE 32. *Oriah, the son of Jared.* The genealogical record of Ether begins with the names outlined in verses 6-32. The names connecting Jared, or Jerah, with Shem, the son of Noah, and through him with Adam as in Genesis, are all omitted. Moroni has already explained that he begins his story with the dispersion at the Tower, because history of previous events "is had among the Jews." (Ether 1:35)

VERSE 33. *Jared came forth with his brother.* Joktan had thirteen sons: *Almodad, Sheleph, Hazarmaveth, Jerah* (or *Jared*), *Hadoram, Uzal, Diklah, Obal, Abimael,*

---

[4]Lineage of Abram Genesis 11:10-26		Lineage of Jared Genesis 10:21-32	Lineage of Ether Ether 1:6-32
Shem		Shem	
Arphaxad		Arphaxad	
Salah		Salah	
Eber		Eber	
Peleg	————his brother————	Joktan	
Reu		Jerah, or	
Serug			
Nahor			Jared
Terah			Orihah
Abram			Kib
			Shule
			Omer, Etc.
			Down to Ether

the time the Lord confounded the language of the people, and swore in his wrath that they should be scattered upon all the face of the earth; and according to the word of the Lord the people were scattered.

34. And the brother of Jared being a large and mighty man, and a man highly favored of the Lord, Jared, his brother, said unto him: Cry unto the Lord, that he will not confound us that we may not understand our words.

Sheba, Ophir, Havilah, and *Jobab* (Genesis 10:26-29). Each of these names stands for some characteristic, some act, or experience, of the owner of it. *Almodad* means "Measure of God." *Hazarmaveth,* a place name, "Dwelling of death," the same as "desolation." *Abimael* means "my father from God." *Jobab* is said to mean "howling or mourning." The first part of the name, Jobab, seems to connect it with the patriarch in the Land of Uz, "whose name was Job." (Job 1:1)

VERSE 34. *The Brother of Jared.* It is stated in this verse that the Brother of Jared was a "large and mighty man, and a man highly favored of the Lord." His name is not given. We think it is a striking testimony to his humility and self-negation that he, notwithstanding his spiritual endowments and physical characteristics, which made him a great leader of men, was content with being known as Ahijared (the Brother of Jared) or some such subordinate title.

In the absence of direct revelation on the question of his name we can only form opinions. It is reasonably certain that it was one of the other twelve sons of Joktan, who went with Jared and became prominent in early American history. But which one of them? There were twelve. And they were all brothers of Jared.

Everything considered, we are inclined to think that Ophir, the eleventh son of Joktan, is the Brother of Jared of the Book of Ether; chiefly for the reason that he became the best known, the most famous, of the twelve others, next after Jared. Very early his fondness for gold, or his ability to acquire it, prompted his contemporaries to attach his name to any place in the far away, dimly known regions of the earth where the precious metal abounded. The gold was the "gold of Ophir." And in one place (Job 22:24), "ophir," is in the mouth of Eliphas of Theman, means *gold.* His message to the patriarch has been quoted in a previous paragraph of this chapter, but it is worth repeating. This is what he said literally:

> "Yes, throw in dust gold,
> And on rocks of brooks, ophir."

If ophir is understood to mean gold, Peru in olden times certainly was a "land of ophir." The story of Inca Atahualpa and Pizarro is well known. The Spaniard promised the Inca to give him life and liberty, if he would fill a certain room with gold as high as a man could reach. Atahualpa did so. The value of the precious metal thus collected at a short notice is, by Prescott, estimated at fifteen and one-half million dollars, and it would be worth much more at this time. At the time of King Solomon there may have been more than one land of ophir, or gold, but the commercially famous Eldorado of that age was so far distant from Ezion-geber that three years were required for the round trip. That was far enough away from the port of embarkation to make the suggestion that Ophir was in Peru seem more than a dream. May not Ophir have been the brother who accompanied Jared to America at the time of the dispersion? (*See* note under "Moriancumer," Ether 2:13)

35. And it came to pass that the brother of Jared did cry unto the Lord, and the Lord had compassion upon Jared; therefore he did not confound the language of Jared; and Jared and his brother were not confounded.

36. Then Jared said unto his brother: Cry again unto the Lord, and it may be that he will turn away his anger from them who are our friends, that he confound not their language.

37. And it came to pass that the brother of Jared did cry unto the Lord, and the Lord had com-

---

THE DISPERSION

The familiar story of the Dispersion is told in Genesis 11:1-9. While the human family as yet had but one language, some of them, journeying eastward, came to the Plain of Shinar, where, later, the famous City of Babylon was built. In this inviting locality they decided to build a world city, with a tower, or sanctuary, to become known throughout the entire inhabited world. By this means, they argued, their unity as one people with one speech and one religion would be preserved. Perhaps they also thought that the privileged class might find a refuge in the tower in case of another flood. At all events, the plan was displeasing to the Lord. It disregarded the commandment to Noah: "Be fruitful, and multiply, and replenish the earth." And, in all probability, it was an evidence of doubt and contempt as regards the sacred covenant of God with all living beings on earth, of which the rainbow was made the glorious symbol. (Genesis 9:12-13) And so the Lord frustrated their plans by confounding their language.

THE ACCOUNT AMPLY CONFIRMED

The Hebrew account of the Dispersion is amply confirmed. Fragments of a document with cuneiform text, discovered by Professor George Smith, the English Assyriologist, tell of men who had turned against God and essayed to build a mound at Babylon. But the winds blew down their tower and *Anu* confounded great and small on the mound and "made strange their counsel."

Plato refers to a tradition according to which men and animals, at one time, had one language. But men became too ambitious in their quest for immortality, wherefore Jupiter confounded their speech, and they were dispersed.

In the Sibylline Oracles which at one time were supposed to be inspired by a prophetess in Babylonia, an alleged relative of the Egyptian Isis, the Dispersion is referred to thus: "The gods sent storms of wind and overthrew the tower, and gave everyone his peculiar language, and for this reason it was that the city was called Babylon." (Josephus, *Antiquities* 1:4)[5]

THE CALL OF JARED, HIS BROTHER, AND THEIR FRIENDS

This section contains information concerning the origin of ancient Americans. It connects them by means of an historic chain, through the lineage of Shem, with

---

[5]The explanation here and in Genesis 11:9: "Therefore is the name of it called Babel, because the Lord did there confound the language of all the earth," is to be understood as a play on words: They began to build a *Babil* (a gate of God); the result was a *Belil* (an abominable mixture, such as that which afterwards was prohibited in the Mosaic Law, Leviticus 19:18, and to which Isaiah delicately alludes, 1:3).

passion upon their friends and their families also, that they were not confounded.

38. And it came to pass that Jared spake again unto his brother, saying: Go and inquire of the Lord whether he will drive us out of the land, and if he will drive us out of the land, cry unto him whither we shall go. And who knoweth but the Lord will carry us forth into a land which is choice above all the earth? And if it so be, let us be faithful unto the Lord, that we may receive it for our inheritance.

the post-diluvian ancestor of the human race, Noah. It shows that in the providential division of the earth, the Western Hemisphere was included. It shows how the descendants of the patriarch actually did "replenish the earth," and not only the Eastern Continents.

THE STORY OF JARED

Jared, impressed by the apparent divine favors enjoyed by his younger brother,—let us call him Ophir—asked him to pray that the Lord would not confound their language.

This seems to indicate that the calamity which ended the building of the tower did not overtake them in a moment, all at one time, but that it came gradually, and that those who were willing to turn to God had time for repentance and prayer.

The Brother of Jared prayed, and God granted his petition.

Again, at the direction of Jared, his brother prayed for some of their friends. This prayer was also heard. (Verse 37) Their language was not confounded.

Jared now instructed his brother to ask God for information as to where He wanted them to go, in case they were to be expelled from the flourishing Valley of Shinar. He rather intimated that, in his opinion, the Lord would be owing them a choice piece of property in exchange for their present home. The Brother of Jared did pray as instructed, and the Lord heard and answered the prayer. But, in answering, He actually placed the Brother at the head of the expedition. He told him to gather the flocks, to lay in a supply of grain, and to bring the people together, including Jared and his family, and, the Lord said, "Thou shalt go at the head of them down into the valley northward. And there will I meet thee, and I will go before thee into a land which is choice above all the lands of the earth." The Lord was evidently not entirely pleased with the Brother of Jared. But, He, nevertheless, promised to make the Jaredites the greatest nation on the face of the earth, because of the prayers of the Brother of Jared: "Because this long time ye have cried unto Me."

ETHER

The last great prophet of the Jaredites to whom we are indebted for the history of that race, for it is an abridgment of Ether's writings, made by Moroni, that we have in the Book of Mormon, under the title of the Book of Ether. Ether was of the royal race, his father Coriantor, one of those unfortunate monarchs who lived

39. And it came to pass that the brother of Jared did cry unto the Lord according to that which had been spoken by the mouth of Jared.

40. And it came to pass that the Lord did hear the brother of Jared, and had compassion upon him, and said unto him:

41. Go to and gather together thy flocks, both male and female, of every kind; and also of the seed of the earth of every kind; and thy families; and also Jared thy

---

in captivity all his days. In the reign of Coriantumr, the last king of the Jaredites, Ether came forth and proclaimed the near destruction of the entire people, a prophecy which many of his predecessors had also uttered; but he also promised that the king should survive all his subjects and live to see another race occupy the land. Great and marvelous were the prophecies of Ether. He saw the days of Christ and the great work of the last dispensation, even to the coming of the new Jerusalem. Indeed, he appears to have had revealed to him a complete history of the dealings of the Lord with the inhabitants of this earth from his own day to the end of time. But the people heeded not his words and ultimately grew weary of this threatenings and drove him from their midst. He hid himself in a cavity of a rock, coming forth in the night time to view the course of events and occasionally appearing and repeating his warnings. While thus hidden, he wrote the history of contemporaneous events, and, year by year, watched the fulfillment of the word of the Lord, as the people gradually destroyed each other in unrelenting warfare. He lived to record the utter destruction of his people at Ramah (Cumorah) with the sole exception of Coriantumr, who survived as a witness to the unfailing word of God. We are not told whether Ether died or was translated. We incline, from his own words (Ether 15:33), to the latter opinion. When he had finished his record he hid the twenty-four golden plates on which it was engraven in the place in which they were afterwards found by the people of King Limhi (B.C. 123).

CORIANTOR

The father of the Prophet Ether; he was the son of Moron, one of those unfortunate kings of the Jaredites who was deposed through treason and rebellion and held a prisoner the remainder of his life. Coriantor was born in captivity and remained so all his days. This period of Jaredite history is a particularly sad one; it is an epoch of sin and war. Many prophets appeared, who proclaimed that the Lord would execute judgment against the Jaredites to their utter destruction and that he would bring forth another people to possess the land as he had their fathers; but the people rejected all the words of these servants of God "because of their secret societies and wicked abominations"; nevertheless, in that and the succeeding generation these prophecies were all fulfilled—the Jaredites were destroyed and the land was given to a branch of the house of Israel.

MORON

One of the last and most wicked kings of the Jaredites; his father, Ethem, also ruled in unrighteousness. During his reign the Gadianton-like bands, which at that time flourished among the Jaredites, led a rebellion against the king and succeeded in wresting from him half the kingdom but after many years Moron succeeded in reconquering his lost provinces. Soon after, a descendant of the brother of Jared, who is described as "a mighty man" headed another revolution against Moron and was so successful that he took possession of the whole of the kingdom and held Moron

brother and his family; and also thy friends and their families, and the friends of Jared and their families.

42. And when thou hast done this thou shalt go at the head of them down into the valley which is northward. And there will I meet thee, and I will go before thee into a land which is choice above all the lands of the earth.

43. And there will I bless thee and thy seed, and raise up unto me of thy seed, and of the seed of thy brother, and they who shall go with thee, a great nation. And

---

in captivity all the rest of his days. In captivity Moron begat Coriantor who was the father of the prophet Ether. Moron, in all probability, lived in the seventh century B. C.

ETHEM

A wicked king of the later Jaredites, living, most probably, in the eighth century before Christ. He was the son and successor of Ahah. In Ethem's days many prophets came and prophesied that unless the Jaredites repented the Lord would utterly destroy them from the earth. But the people hardened their hearts and repented not; the prophets mourned over their depravity and withdrew from among them. Ethem was as his people and did wickedly all his days; when he died he was succeeded by his son Moron, who was like unto his father.

AHAH

A wicked king of the Jaredites, who reigned in the latter days of that nation. His father's name was Seth. Seth, owing to internal commotions, was brought into captivity and thus remained all his life. But Ahah obtained the kingdom and reigned over the people until his death. He did all manner of iniquity by which he caused the shedding of much blood but providentially his reign was a short one. He was succeeded on the throne by his son Ethem.

SETH

A Jaredite prince, the son of King Shiblom, who, in the war in which his father was slain, was brought into captivity and so held all the rest of his life. His son, Ahah, regained the kingdom. Of Seth's character we have no details.

SHIBLOM OR SHIBLON

The son of Com; one of the later monarchs of the Jaredites. In his day, because of the iniquity of the people, many prophets appeared and foretold the woes that would mark the extinction of the race. Wars and grievous calamities also marked the reign of Shiblom. First, his brother inaugurated a bloody civil war which extended throughout all the land. The wicked combinations, akin to the Gadianton robbers of the Nephites, did their part to render anarchy more complete. Famines and pestilence followed rapine until "there was a great destruction, such an one as never had been known upon the face of the earth." In the extreme of their misery and degradation the people began to repent and then the Lord had mercy upon them. Finally Shiblom was slain and Seth, his son, was brought into captivity. Of Shiblom's character we have no record but his rebellious brother issued

there shall be none greater than the nation which I will raise up unto me of thy seed, upon all the face of the earth. And thus I will do unto thee because this long time ye have cried unto me.

---

the infamous mandate that all the prophets who prophesied of the destruction of the people should be put to death. (Ether 11:4-9)

COM

A righteous king of the Jaredites, who reigned in the latter days of that nation. Like the preceding, his father's name was Coriantum, though they appear to have lived nearly a thousand years apart. Com's father was one of the dynasty of monarchs who were deposed and held in captivity by the successful house. In that captivity Com was born but when he attained manhood he rebelled and gained possession of half the kingdom. When he had thus reigned 42 years he made war with Amgid, the ruler of the other half and after a desolating conflict of many years he gained power over the whole realm. While he was king, robber bands, like unto the Gadiantons, began to appear who administered secret and damnable oaths, after the manner of the ancients and sought again to destroy the kingdom. Com fought these robbers with vigor but without success, for they had the sympathy of the masses of the people, who were rapidly ripening for destruction. Many prophets came in these days who foretold the impending destruction of the race if the people did not repent and turn unto the Lord. But the voice of mercy and warning was rejected and the sin-sunken Jaredites sought the lives of the heaven-inspired messengers. The prophets fled to Com for preservation and he appears to have valiantly protected them. While with him they prophesied many things for his comfort and edification and he was blessed of the Lord all the remainder of his days. He lived to a good old age and begat Shiblom, who, at his death, reigned in his stead.

CORIANTUM

One of the royal dynasty of the Jaredites who was held in captivity during his entire life; his father's name was Amnigaddah. In the days of his ancestor, Hearthom, the reigning family was deposed and for several generations they were held as prisoners. Com, the son of Coriantum, rebelled and after a lengthy war, regained possession of the kingdom.

AMNIGADDAH

A Jaredite king, the son of Aaron and the father of Coriantum. His father, himself and his son were kept prisoners all their lives by the dynasty that had usurped the throne. In his grandson Com's days the kingdom was recovered.

AARON

One of the royal race of the Jaredites. He was the son of Heth, a descendant of Jared. In the days of his grandfather, Hearthom, who was the reigning monarch, the kingdom was taken away from him and he was kept a prisoner all his days. His son Heth, his grandson Aaron, and Aaron's son Amnigaddah were also kept in captivity all their lives by the triumphant party. In the days of Aaron's great-grandson, Com, the kingdom was reconquered for the dynasty of which Aaron was a member. At a rough guess we should image that Aaron lived about a thousand years before Christ.

HETH

A Jaredite prince, who was, by the usurping dynasty, held in captivity all his days. He was the son of King Hearthom who was deposed and kept a prisoner all his life. Heth's son, Aaron, was also held captive from the day of his birth to his death.

HEARTHOM

A king of the Jaredites; he was the son of Lib, whom he succeeded. When he had reigned twenty-four years the kingdom was wrested from him and he was held in captivity by the successful party all the remainder of his life. Only one of his sons is mentioned whose name was Heth. Of Hearthom's private character the record is silent.

LIB

A righteous king of the Jaredites in whose reign the nation prospered and multiplied greatly. He was the son and successor of Kish. In the reign of a former monarch named Heth the Lord had deeply afflicted the people because of their sins and among other things he had caused numbers of poisonous serpents to occupy the regions in the neighborhood of the Isthmus of Panama and thus prevented the people from gaining access to the southern continent. In Lib's days these venomous reptiles were destroyed and the land southward was found to be full of beasts of the forest. That country was preserved as one enormous hunting ground of the race. Lib himself becoming a great hunter. He also built a large city at the narrowest portion of the Isthmus, apparently for the purpose of guarding the regions south from settlement, so that it might be the source of their meat supply for the country northward was covered with inhabitants. In this region the people greatly developed in the arts of civilization. They prosecuted mining with much vigor, improved in the manufacture of textile fabrics, agriculture made marked advance through the invention and application of improved machinery in the cultivation of the earth and the harvesting of their crops. They also made all manner of weapons of war, though, as this was a time of profound peace this can only be regarded as a precautionary measure. In fact, to use the words of the sacred historian: "never could be a people more blessed than were they, and more prospered by the hand of the Lord. And they were in a land that was choice above all lands, for the Lord had spoken it."

Lib lived many years, was blessed with a numerous posterity and when he died he was succeeded by his son Hearthom.

KISH

A king of the Jaredites. He was the son of Corom and succeeded his father on the throne. Nothing is said in the Book of Ether about his character, the events of his reign or the length of his life. All we are told of him is that he reigned in the place of his father and that when he died, he was succeeded by his son Lib.

COROM

One of the few righteous kings of the Jaredites. It is said of him that he did good all his days. He was the son and successor of Levi and when he died at a very advanced age, leaving a numerous posterity, his son Kish reigned in his stead.

LEVI

A Jaredite prince, the son of Kim. His father was driven from the throne and held in captivity for the remainder of his days. Levi was born in captivity and so remained until 42 years after the death of his father when he rose in rebellion against his uncle who occupied the throne, deposed him and reigned in his stead. During his reign he did that which was right in the sight of the Lord and his people were greatly prospered. He lived to a good old age, was blessed with a large family and when he died his son Corom succeeded him as king.

KIM

A king of the Jaredites. He was the son of Morianton, born to him when he (Morianton) was very aged.

The days of Morianton were among the most prosperous that the Jaredites saw; they grew exceedingly rich during his reign. But when he became very aged he abdicated in favor of Kim, who reigned in his father's place for eight years before the latter died. Kim, however, did not reign in righteousness and by his wickedness he displeased the Lord, so that he permitted the brother of Kim to rebel against him, dethrone him and hold him in captivity all the remainder of his life. During his captivity he begat sons and daughters, the only one whose name is mentioned is Levi, who was born to him in his old age.

MORIANTON

A king of the Jaredites. It appears that Riplakish, a monarch of that race, became so obnoxious to his people on account of his tyranny and abominations that they rose in rebellion, slew him and drove his descendants out of the land. After many years one of these descendants, named Morianton, gathered an army of outcasts and invaded the Jaredite country. The war that followed was an exceedingly severe one and lasted a number of years. One by one the cities of the Jaredites fell into the hands of Morianton until he had made himself master of the entire country. When established in power he conciliated the people by lightening their burdens so that they anointed him king. During his mild though energetic reign the people were greatly prospered, many new cities were built and the nation grew exceedingly rich. He lived to a very great age and when too old to hold the reins of government he abdicated in favor of his son Kim, Morianton surviving this action eight years. His character is thus summarized in the Book of Ether, "he did do justice unto the people, but not unto himself, because of his many whoredoms; wherefore he was cut off from the presence of the Lord."

RIPLAKISH

An unrighteous king of the Jaredites. He greatly afflicted his people by imposing upon them grievously heavy taxes and when they could not, or would not pay these exactions he cast them into prison, where he compelled them to labor continually to sustain him in his whoredoms and abominations and in the erection of costly and magnificent edifices that conduced to his luxury; if any prisoner refused to labor he was put to death. In this way he greatly adorned his kingdom but he also filled it with prisons. For forty-two years the people groaned under his oppressions when they rose in their anger, slew Riplakish and drove his descendants out of the land. What form of government immediately followed is uncertain; we have no information on this point but we are told that after many years one of his descendants, named Morianton, established himself as king.

SHEZ

A king of the Jaredites, the son of Heth. By reason of the great wickedness of the Jaredites in the days of Heth, the Lord permitted a severe famine to come upon them by which the far greater portion of the people were destroyed. Of the royal family, all perished except Shez, who, when the crops again began to grow commenced to build up this desolate race. He was a virtuous man and taught his people righteousness and the sun of prosperity shone upon them. His peace, however, was marred by the treason of his son Shez who rebelled against him. This son, however, was slain by a robber and peace was restored. In the later years of his lengthy reign Shez built many cities and the rapidly increasing people spread out in various directions. This monarch lived to an exceeding old age, was blessed with numerous children and when he died was succeeded on the throne by his son Riplakish, who was apparently the youngest of his family. (Ether 10:1-4)

HETH

A cruel and vicious king of the Jaredites. He was the son of Com. His grandfather, Coriantum, was a righteous ruler and the people prospered greatly during his reign; but in the days of Com the increase of wealth and prosperity was accompanied by an increase of wickedness and the old secret plans and associations were revived. Heth became a leader in these things and rose in rebellion against his father, slew him with his own sword and became king in his stead. The Lord then sent many prophets who called upon the people to repent, declaring that if they did not a terrible famine should come upon the land. The people, led and inspired by Heth, rejected the words of the prophets and cruelly persecuted them; some they cast out, some they threw into pits and left them to perish. Before long the rains from heaven ceased and there was a great dearth over all the land and poisonous serpents made their appearance and killed many people. These serpents also attacked the flocks of the Jaredites and drove them in vast bodies towards the southern continent. Many perished by the way but some reached the land known to the Nephites as Zarahemla. Restrained by the power of God, the serpents stopped at the Isthmus of Panama where they formed a cordon, preventing the Jaredites from further following their scattered flocks. The carcasses of the beasts which fell by the way were ravenously eaten by the famished people until they had devoured them all. We can scarcely imagine the horrors that must have attended this famine when the people consumed the poisoned flesh of the creatures thus killed. Disease in its most terrible form must have followed famine. Before long then this loathsome food was all consumed and the people rapidly perished. Then those who remained began to repent of their sins and call on the Lord; and when they had humbled themselves sufficiently, the Lord sent the long-needed rain and the remnants of the race began to revive. Soon there began to be fruit in the north country and the regions around about and Shiz, the only survivor of the royal house, reigned over the few that were left; for Heth and all his household, except Shiz, had perished in the famine.

COM

A king of the Jaredites, the son of Coriantum. Com was born when his father was very aged, evidently considerably over one hundred years old, for Coriantum's first wife died at the age of 102 years, after which he married a young maid who became the mother of several children, among whom was Com. In Com's reign the Jaredites increased greatly in numbers; they also spread widely over the face of the land; but they also grew in iniquity and the secret associations (*see* Akish) that a few generations before had caused the almost entire destruction of the race, were revived. One of the leaders in these crimes was a son of Com, named Heth, who was born when Com had reigned 49 years. This young man conspired against his father, slew him with his own sword and reigned in his stead.

CORIANTUM

A good king of the Jaredites. He was the son of Emer, who, four years before his death anointed Coriantum to reign in his stead. He was a righteous, just and vigorous ruler and in his days the Jaredites were greatly prospered and many large cities were built. But he had no children until he was exceedingly old; his wife died when she was 102 years of age, after which he married a young maid who bore him a large family. He lived until he was 142 years old, when he died and was succeeded on the throne by his son Com.

EMER

One of the early kings of the Jaredites. Two years before his death, Omer, his father, anointed him to reign in his stead. Emer was one of the best kings of his race. He executed judgment in righteousness all his days. In his reign the people greatly increased in numbers and in wealth, becoming the owners of large herds of useful animals and rich agricultural and mineral products, in gems and fine manufactured goods. The curse, also, which had come upon the land during the days of Akish because of the iniquity of the people, began to be removed as they were now living more righteously. Emer's was a lengthy reign, sixty-two years are mentioned; but it is not evident whether this period covers the whole of his reign or not. When he died, full of years and honor, he was succeeded by one of his numerous sons, named Coriantum, whom he had anointed king four years before his death. It is recorded of Emer that he saw the Son of Righteousness and did rejoice and glorify in his day.

OMER

A righteous but unfortunate king of the early Jaredites. He was the son of Shule and the father of a prince named Jared. Jared rebelled against his father and by his flatteries led away the people of half the kingdom. He then gave battle to his father and took him prisoner, holding him in servitude half his days. While thus in bondage Omer begat several children, among whom were two sons named Esrom and Coriantumr. When these young men grew to manhood they espoused the cause of their father, raised an army, attacked the forces of Jared by night and utterly routed them. Jared retained his life by renouncing his rights to the throne and Omer was reinstated in the kingly authority. Jared, greatly chagrined at the loss of the royal power, entered into secret combination with Akish, a friend of Omer, to assassinate the king and restore Jared to the throne. Their attempt was partially successful. Omer was driven from the throne but being warned by the Lord in a dream, he fled with the faithful portion of his family to the far off north Atlantic seaboard, passing in his journey the hill Shim, where the Nephite records were in after ages hid, and the hill Ramah. From the direction of his journey we are justified in believing that the land Ablom, where he established himself, was on the New England coast. From time to time others joined Omer while the Jaredite people were rent by internecine wars which ended in their almost entire destruction. Then Omer returned with his followers and reigned over the remnant of a once numerous people. He lived to be exceedingly old and two years before his death he anointed his son Emer to reign in his stead. His days were many and full of sorrow.

SHULE

Shule was one of the Jaredite Kings in the early ages of that people. He was the son of Kib, born to him in his old age while he was held in captivity by another son, named Corihor, who had rebelled against him and deposed him as the legal ruler. When Shule grew to manhood, he became mighty in judgment and in bodily strength, and being angry with his brother, Corihor, for rebelling against their father, raised an army, armed it with swords made by himself, gave battle to his brother at a city named Nehor, defeated the latter's forces and restored their father to the throne. Kib, being very aged, placed the sovereign power in the hands of Shule, who reigned in righteousness and extended the borders of his growing people in all directions. Corihor, repentant of his former treason, received many favors from Shule, and was placed in positions of high power in the nation, the trusts whereof he faithfully performed. But as he had rebelled against his father in his early days, so in like manner one of his sons, named Noah, rebelled against him, and in this rebellion drew away all his brothers. At first Noah was successful. He obtained possession of the Land of the Jaredite's First Inheritance, called by them, Moron, and reigned King of that region of Central America.

Again, he attacked Shule, and this time took him prisoner, carrying him captive to Moron with the intention of putting him to death. But before he had carried out his bloodthirsty designs, his cousins, the sons of Shule, broke into his house and killed the usurper. They then went to the prison where their father was held, released him from his confinement and replaced him on the throne of that part of the country not held by the son of Noah. There were now two kingdoms, both of which were growing, while that one under Shule "did prosper exceedingly and waxed great." After a time Corihor, the son of Noah, commenced war with Shule in which Corihor was deservedly unsuccessful and in the conflict that followed he was slain. His son Nimrod, knowing the unrighteousness of his father's cause, restored Noah's Kingdom to Shule, so that the latter again, as in the beginning, reigned over the whole of the Jaredite Race. For this act of magnanimity, Shule bestowed great favors upon Nimrod, who did in the whole kingdom "according to his desires."

Though the people were highly prospered at this time, they gave way to idolatry, and grew hard in their hearts. This, no doubt, was intensified by the bad example of the royal family, and the miseries and cruelties of the wars which their wars induced. During Shule's days the Lord sent many prophets to the Jaredites who warned the people of His impending judgments. For a time these prophets were rejected and reviled. But Shule made a law that the prophets should have free access wherever they wished to go, and further decreed a punishment for all those who persecuted and reviled them. The preaching of these holy men eventually brought the Jaredites to repentance and because of their penitence the Lord spared them and turned away His judgments and the people prospered again. In his old age Shule begat Omer who succeeded him on the throne. Shule's days were full of trouble and sorrow, but he reigned in righteousness, was faithful to the Lord and executed judgment in justice towards his people. We are of the opinion that Shule was a contemporary of the Patriarch Abraham.

KIB

The second king of the Jaredites. He was the son of Orihah and grandson of Jared. He was born in his father's old age and succeeded him to the throne. Among Kib's sons was one named Corihor, who, when he was thirty-two years old rebelled against his father and drew many people after him. He first established himself in the land of Nehor and when strong enough came against Kib in the Land of Moron, which Moron was near the land called Desolation by the Nephites. Having taken his father prisoner, Corihor held him in captivity for many years. In his old age Kib begat Shule, who, when grown to manhood overthrew Corihor and replaced his father on the throne. His father having then arrived at an exceedingly great age resigned the kingdom to Shule who reigned in his stead.

ORIHAH

The youngest of Jared's four sons and the first king of the Jaredites. When Jared and his brother had grown old they desired to know the wishes of their people before they went down to their graves. The people desired to be ruled by a king. This idea was displeasing to their leaders but they ultimately consented to one being chosen. All the sons of Jared and of his brother refused this dignity until Orihah was reached and he accepted the kingly honor. He reigned in righteousness, executing judgment in justice, walking humbly before heaven and instructing his subjects in the ways of the Lord. He lived to a very great age, was the father of thirty-one children, twenty-three of whom were sons and when he died he was succeeded on the throne by his son Kib. The Jaredites prospered and multiplied greatly under his wise and beneficent reign.

JARED

The founder of the Jaredite race. He was apparently one of those engaged in the building of the Tower of Babel. It is presumable that he was a descendant of Shem, as he and most certainly his brother, held the holy priesthood. We are inclined to believe, from the brief narrative in the Book of Ether, that Jared's brother was the leading spirit of the colony that accompanied these brothers on their toilsome journey to this continent. Of Jared's private character we are told but little but he appears to have been more conservative, more pliable and less energetic than his brother. The race was named after him, we presume, because one of his sons, Orihah, became its first king and Jared's thus became the royal family. Jared had four sons and eight daughters: the names of his sons were Jacom, Gilgah, Manhah and Orihah, Jared lived to a great age. He died and was buried in the Land of Moron. (For particulars of the journey of Jared and his people see Jared, Brother of.)

JARED, BROTHER OF

The prophet and leader of the founders of the Jaredite race. His name is not given in the Book of Mormon, but we learn through modern revelation that it was Mahonri Moriancumer. He was in all probability a descendant of Shem and was present at the building of the Tower of Babel, if not actually engaged in that work; though he and his brother had not fallen into idolatry as had so many of the builders of that notorious edifice. When God scattered these presumptuous builders, Jared and his brother pleaded with the Lord that their language and that of their friends might not be confounded. Their prayer was heard, their mother tongue was preserved. In answer to their further entreaties the Lord promised to lead them into a land choice above all others where he would make of them a great people and he himself would go before them as their guide. In obedience to the heavenly command Jared, his brother and their friends, with their respective families gathered their flocks and seeds of various kinds and started to follow as the Lord should lead.

The valley into which the Lord first led them was called Nimrod after that mighty hunter of the early post-diluvian age. Here the people of Jared tarried for a time while they prepared for the long journey which was before them. Their flocks and herds they had with them; they now went to work and snared fowls; they carried with them hives of honey bees (known to them by the name of deseret) and prepared a vessel in which they transported the fish of the waters. They appeared to have collected everything that could possibly be of use to them. They were going to a land that had been swept clean by the waters of the deluge; it had been bereft of all its animal life; the seeds of grains and fruits no longer germinated in its soil and the colony had to replenish the continent with the animal and vegetable life necessary for their comfort and sustenance, as though it was a new earth. When in the valley of Nimrod the Lord came down and talked with the brother of Jared. But the brother of Jared saw him not for the Lord remained concealed in a cloud. But God directed that the company should go forth into the wilderness, into that quarter where man had never yet been. As they journeyed the Heavenly Presence went before them in a cloud, instructed them and gave directions which way they should travel. In the course of their journey they had many waters—seas, rivers and lakes—to cross, on which occasions they built barges, as directed by the Lord. It must have been an arduous labor, requiring much time and great patience to transport their flocks and herds, with all the rest of their cumbrous freight across these many waters. As they advanced to a great distance from the centre of population in western Asia, it is possible they traveled beyond the limtis to which the larger animals had by that time scattered and if so, they were entirely without the aid of the food obtained by the chase; on the other hand, it is probable that the fish in the lakes and rivers formed a valuable source of food supply; yet it must also be remembered they carried fish in a vessel with them.

Led by the Lord personally, instructed by his own mouth, protected by his presence, the colony, of which Jared's brother appears to have been the prophet and leader, at last reached the borders of the great sea which divides the continents. To the place where they tarried they gave the name of Moriancumer. Here they remained for a period of four years, at the end of which time the Lord again visited the brother of Jared in a cloud and chastened him and his brethren because of their neglect to call upon his name. Repentance followed this reproof and because of their repentance their sins were forgiven them.

The brother of Jared was then commanded by the Lord to build eight barges after the same pattern as those he had previously constructed. This command he obeyed with the assistance of the company. The vessels were small, light in construction and water tight. As they were dark in the interior, by reason of being without windows, the Lord, at the entreaty of the brother of Jared, touched sixteen small white stones, which the latter had molten out of a high mountain called Shelem; and after the Lord touched them they shone forth and gave light to the vessels in which they were placed. When the Lord put forth his finger to touch these stones the veil was taken from before the eyes of the brother of Jared and he saw the finger of the Lord; and it was as the finger of a man, like unto flesh and blood.

And because of the brother of Jared's great faith the Lord showed himself unto him and declared himself to be Jesus Christ who should come into the world to redeem his people.

All things being prepared, Jared and his people, with their animals, fish, bees, seeds and multitudinous other things, went on board; a favorable wind wafted them from shore and they gradually crossed to the American coast. At the end of a somewhat stormy voyage of three hundred and forty-four days the colony reached this continent. It is generally understood that the place where they landed was south of the Gulf of California and north of the land Desolation which was north of the Isthmus of Panama.

No sooner had the people of Jared landed than they humbled themselves before the Lord, many of them shedding tears of joy because of the multitude of his tender mercies in bringing them so safely to this new land of promise. Their next duty was to prepare for the future. They commenced to till the soil and perform the other labors incidental to founding a new home. In these efforts they prospered greatly. They began to grow and increase in numbers and in wealth; and even better than this, they were a righteous people, being taught directly from on high. In process of time Jared and his brother grew old and perceiving that their course on earth was nearly finished the latter proposed that they gather the people, number them, give them necessary teachings and learn their wishes. This was done; but to the grief of the brother of Jared the people desired a king be anointed to rule over them. He saw, by the spirit of prophecy, that this action would lead to many evils and he was inclined to refuse their request but Jared pleaded that the wishes of the people be granted and his brother finally consented. It was the first step in the wrong direction and led to much sin, misery, contention and captivity. The people having the privilege granted them, chose Pagag the eldest son of their prophet. He declined, as did all of his brothers and also all the sons of Jared except Orihah. The last named accepted the royal dignity and was anointed king. Soon after this, the brother of Jared died, full of years and honor. Like Enoch, he had been privileged to enter the presence of the Lord and to have revealed to him the history of the world in all its generations. He was also a seer, having received the priceless gift of a Urim and Thummim. His faith was never exceeded by the sons of men; he laid hold of the promises of the Almighty with unshaken confidence. By that faith he performed miracles; Moroni tells us that by its power he "said unto the mountain Zerin, Remove—and it was removed" (Ether 12:30) but of the circumstances that attended this manifestation of divine power we have not the slightest details. The brother of Jared is also said to have been "mighty in writing," the uncorrupted language which he used being, unquestionably, most favorable for expressing niceties of thought in written characters. He was a "large and mighty man" in personal appearance and undoubtedly as strong in his integrity to God and in his moral courage as he was in physical characteristics. Altogether, we deem him one of the greatest prophets and leaders of God's people that ever graced this Earth. When he died he left behind him twenty-two sons and daughters.

CHAPTER 2

1. In the Valley of Nimrod—2. Comments of Moroni on Liberty—3. Morian-cumer On the Sea which Divideth the Lands—4. The Barges.

1. *In the Valley of Nimrod.*

1. And it came to pass that Jared and his brother, and their families, and also the friends of Jared and his brother and their families, went down into the valley which was northward, (and the name of the valley was Nimrod, being called after the mighty hunter) with their flocks which they had gathered together, male and female, of every kind.

2. And they did also lay snares and catch fowls of the air; and they did also prepare a vessel, in which they did carry with them the fish in the waters.

Verse 1. *Nimrod.* Nimrod was the son of Cush, the eldest son of Ham (Genesis 10:8-10). The general understanding of the biographical notes in that section of Genesis is that Nimrod had great bodily strength, and was eminent as a hunter of wild, dangerous animals; that he became popular among young men who gladly joined him in his hunting expeditions, and whom he organized into a military force by the aid of which he assailed and subjugated the inhabitants of Shinar; that he was a despot who built forts, towns and cities, chief among which was Babel. Other important places were called after his name. There was a Birs Nimrod (Borsippa) near Babylon; a Tel Nimrod (Hill of Nimrod) near Baghdad, and a mound, later known as Calah. In the Book of Ether we learn that there was a Valley of Nimrod, probably the region now known as Irak. In Persian and Greek mythology Nimrod is supposed to be represented by the magnificent constellation Orion.

Verse 2. *Fish of the waters.* These colonists had a vessel in which they carried fish as part of their provisions. This information reminds us of the fact that the early Americans were largely dependent on sea-food for their subsistence as proved by the contents of the shell heaps, or kitchen middens.

SHELL HEAPS

These are found along the coasts of America and inland by the rivers. There are such remnants from a distant past in Newfoundland, Nova Scotia, Massachusetts, Louisiana, Maine, Minnesota, Iowa, Illinois, Indiana, Tennessee, Florida, California, Oregon, Alaska, Mexico, Nicaragua, and Terra del Fuego.

Some of these mounds are very large, covering from sixty to one hundred acres, or even larger. Some are only a few feet high, while others are over forty feet in height. In some localities they are quite numerous. Colonel Island, Georgia, is said to be covered with them. Forty of such have been explored.

The contents of these mounds show the people around whose dwellings they accumulated engaged in fishing as well as hunting. They have yielded the bones of the elk, the beaver, the seal, the mud turtle, the great auk, the wild turkey, as well as the reindeer and the dog. Bones of fishes and reptiles have also been

3. And they did also carry with them deseret, which, by interpretation, is a honey bee; and thus they did carry with them swarms of bees, and all manner of that which was upon the face of the land, seeds of every kind.

4. And it came to pass that when they had come down into the valley of Nimrod the Lord came down and talked with the brother of Jared; and he was in a cloud, and the brother of Jared saw him not.

---

found, but more particularly shells of mussels and oysters. At the bottom of one, a pit in one of these mounds in Little Miami Valley, Florida, a Mr. F. W. Putnam found a large quantity of carbonized corn, covered with husks and matting of reeds indicating agriculture and a sedentary life.

The date of the early shell heaps is unknown, but it is certain that they are the accumulations of many generations. Those in California are considered more recent than those in Florida.

The shell heaps, as the name indicates, are simply the refuse, the garbage, left behind-when the people departed for new homes, or camping grounds. But they also contain so many objects of value to students of ancient cultures. Deposits in Peru have yielded, among other things, little figures of gold and of silver, representing fishes. Also numerous fragments of pottery. The Peabody Museum of Cambridge, Mass., owns twenty gold ornaments from the Chincha Islands, off the coast of Peru. They consist of very thin plates arranged in parallelograms from seven to eight inches long by three to four inches wide, covered with dotted lines and furnished with a hole by means of which they can be hung around the neck, or fastened to the clothes. To all appearances these deposits belong to the same periods as the shell heaps.[1] We need hardly remind the reader of the Twenty-four Gold Plates of Ether, found by the explorers of King Limhi (Mosiah 8:9).

VERSE 3. *Deseret.* Moroni says this word, "by interpretation," means "honey bee." Possibly in the original language, spoken before the confusion of tongues and the dispersion of peoples, this was so. The Hebrew for *honey* is debesh (Exodus 3:8), or nophet (Psalm 19:10), or yahar (1 Samuel 14:25). *Bee* is generally deborah (Deuteronomy 1:44). None of these words seem to be etymologically related to deseret. But there is an Arabian word for honey, *'asal,* which may be near enough akin to the word for *honey bee* as used in the Book of Ether to suggest a common stem.

VERSE 4. *The Lord appears to the Brother of Jared.* In the Valley of Nimrod God revealed Himself to the Brother of Jared, surrounded by a cloud. Not the dark mass in which electric forces are concentrated and which manifest themselves in blinding, destructive lightning flashes and terrifying, rolling, rumbling, thunder claps; but rather the softly falling, friendly evening shades, which enable mortal eye to view the setting sun as the most glorious wonder of nature. (*See* Exodus 33:17-23.) As in the case of Elijah, the Lord manifested Himself to the Brother of Jared in a *still small voice*, that of man speaking to another; not in a devastating cyclone; not in an all order and law-defying earthquake; nor in an all-consuming fire. God had a message to convey to the Brother of Jared. He had a mission for him to perform. He had certain authority to confer upon him. And all this was done without ostentation, but nonetheless effectively. (Compare the story of Elijah on Mt. Horeb 1 Kings 19:9-13).

---

[1]Marquis de Nadallac, *Pre-Historic America,* p. 68.

5. And it came to pass that the Lord commanded them that they should go forth into the wilderness, yea, into that quarter where there never had man been. And it came to pass that the Lord did go before them, and did talk with them as he stood in a cloud, and gave directions whither they should travel.

6. And it came to pass that they did travel in the wilderness, and did build barges, in which they did cross many waters, being directed continually by the hand of the Lord.

7. And the Lord would not suffer that they should stop beyond the sea in the wilderness, but he would that they should come forth even unto the land of promise, which was choice above all other lands, which the Lord God had preserved for a righteous people.

8. And he had sworn in his wrath unto the brother of Jared, that whoso should possess this land of promise, from that time

---

We note that whenever God reveals Himself in person to man, He appears as a man. And this is true of every divine personal revelation of God on record, from the time He walked with Adam in the Garden of Eden where our progenitor was listening to hear His voice (Genesis 3:10), to the day when He appeared to the Prophet Joseph Smith in the Sacred Grove. True, Divine Spirit is everywhere (D. and C. 88:5-13; 41). As the poet will have it: "Every bush alive with God." But, nevertheless, the God of Creation, the God of Abraham, Isaac, and Jacob, the God of Jesus Christ, His Beloved Son, has individuality and personality, as His children have.

VERSES 5-7. *The Lord commanded them.* Through the Brother of Jared, the Lord gave unto the colonists His further commandments. From now on the divine guidance came through him.

INTO THE WILDERNESS

The following particulars concerning the route the little company traveled are given: (1) It went through an uninhabited region (v. 5). (2) There were many waters—rivers and lakes—which they crossed by means of barges. God was their Pilot (v. 6). (3) There was a *sea*, possibly a lake in the wilderness, where the prospects of a settlement seemed inviting, but the Lord would not permit them to stay there. He had, He said, a better home for them, a land of promise, *choice above all other lands.* At the same time the Lord warned the company that it was a land preserved *for a righteous people.* (v. 7)

Several notable rivers originate in the mountainous district known as Ararat (Holy Land). The Euphrates and the Tigris flow into the Persian Gulf; the Araxes and the Cyrus into the Caspian Sea, and the Acampsis into the Black Sea. These and other rivers may have been the *many waters.* If so, the *sea* in the wilderness may have been the Caspian Sea. But as to this, nothing certain is known.[2]

VERSE 8. *He had sworn in His wrath.* This should be read in conjunction with Ether 1:38-39. It appears that Jared instructed his brother to ask the Lord for guidance as to where to go in case they were driven from their homes. In doing so, he hinted broadly that he would expect *a land which is choice above all the earth* as a com-

---

[2]The general impression is that the colonists first went northward; then they turned eastward across the Asiatic wastes. Orson Pratt calls these seas the "inland waters of Asia."

henceforth and forever, should serve him, the true and only God, or they should be swept off when the fulness of his wrath should come upon them.

2. Comments of Moroni, the last historian of the whole Book of Mormon, on Liberty.

9. And now, we can behold the decrees of God concerning this land, that it is a land of promise; and whatsoever nation shall possess it shall serve God, or they shall be swept off when the fulness of his wrath shall come upon them. And the fulness of his wrath cometh upon them when they are ripened in iniquity.

10. For behold, this is a land which is choice above all other lands; wherefore he that doth possess it shall serve God or shall be swept off; for it is the everlasting decree of God. And it is not until the fulness of iniquity among the children of the land, that they are swept off.

11. And this cometh unto you, O ye Gentiles, that ye may know the decrees of God—that ye may repent, and not continue in your iniquities until the fulness come,

---

pensation for their abandoned homes. The Brother of Jared prayed as instructed, not even adorning the petition with meaningless diplomatic phrases. The Lord at once saw through the character of the prayer. He heard it, and answered it. But it was granted in—humanly speaking—righteous anger. The Lord was angry. He told the petitioners that they would be led to a land *choice above all other lands,* but the Lord added that whoso should possess it *"should serve Him, the true and only living God, or they should be swept off when the fulness of His wrath should come upon them."* Having made this covenant with the Brother of Jared, the Lord conferred the authority of leadership upon him instead of Jared: "Thou shalt go at the head of them (Ether 1:42). One of the most instructive stories ever written!

VERSES 9-10. *The decrees of God concerning this land.* In these two paragraphs, Moroni, by way of comment, repeats and emphasizes the solemn obligations which the inhabitants of this land of promise assume when making their homes here, under the covenant of God with the Brother of Jared: "Whatsoever nation shall possess it," Moroni says, "shall serve God, or they shall be swept off when the fulness of His wrath shall come upon them." (v. 9) That is the covenant. It is a mortgage resting on the entire land.

Owing to His special interest in this portion of the Earth, the Lord raised up unto Him, wise men, and caused them to establish a Constitution "for the rights and protection of all flesh, according to just and holy principles." He even "redeemed the land by the shedding of blood," this being inevitable at the time of the revolutionary conflict. (D. and C. 101:77-80) It was God who inspired and established the American Constitution. The Lord further said that it is He Who has made the people free; therefore, they are free indeed.

VERSE 10. *An everlasting Decree.* The Covenant is here again stated. "He that doth possess it shall serve God or shall be swept off." And this is added: "For it is an everlasting decree of God." It is as much in force today, as it was thousands of years ago.

that ye may not bring down the fulness of the wrath of God upon you as the inhabitants of the land have hitherto done.

12. Behold, this is a choice land, and whatsoever nation shall possess it shall be free from bond-age and from captivity, and from all other nations under heaven, if they will but serve the God of the land, who is Jesus Christ, who hath been manifested by the things which we have written.

3. Moriancumer on the sea which divideth the lands.

13. And now I proceed with my record; for behold, it came to pass that the Lord did bring Jared and his brethren forth even to that great sea which divideth the lands. And as they came to the sea they pitched their tents; and they called the name of the place Moriancumer; and they dwelt in tents, and dwelt in tents upon the seashore for the space of four years.

VERSE 11. *This cometh unto you,* refers to the Book of Ether. One of the purposes of this literary composition is to make all the world acquainted with the fact that the Lord has, as it were, a special encumbrance on this portion of the Earth, by virtue of the covenant He made with the Brother of Jared. People who make their homes here have a right to know that by living here they assume the obligations of serving the Lord. If they are dissatisfied with the conditions, they are at liberty to move somewhere else, but not to rise up in rebellion against God. "Blessed is the nation whose God is the Lord: and the people whom He hath chosen for His own inheritance." (Psalm 33:12)

VERSE 12. *Freedom promised.* Moroni here assures us that obedience to *the God of this land, Who is Jesus Christ,* will be rewarded with freedom from bondage and captivity *from all nations under Heaven.*

> "The Earth is the Lord's and the fulness thereof,
> The world and they that dwell therein;
> For He hath founded it upon the seas,
> And established it upon the floods."
>
> (Psalm 24:1-2)

VERSE 13. *That great sea.* Whether this refers to the Pacific or Atlantic Ocean is not known for certain. In the absence of any authoritative information on the question, we prefer to accept the suggestion of Elder Orson Pratt. It is at least plausible that the Jaredite migration was an eastward movement.[3]

---

[3]Students of ancient history are pretty well agreed on locating settlements of the descendants of the sons of Joktan in Yemen, in the southwestern part of the Arabian Peninsula. They have found traces of districts and cities originally named after Hazarmaveth, Uzal, Sheba, Ophir, and Havilah, and it is considered well established that the early inhabitants of these localities had commercial connections with India as well as Ethiopia. This leads us to think that the colonists of Jared and his brother probably turned eastward when they left their first home at Moriancumer on the sea which divideth the lands, and that they may have landed on the west coast of what is now called North America. Even in our day an occasional fisherman from Japan has crossed the Pacific to our west coast, driven by the winds and the Japanese Current.

MORIANCUMER

Moriancumer is the name the colonists gave to the first camp on the shores of the great sea. It was the name of the Brother of Jared. As customary anciently, the central settlement of a community was named after the chief leader. And thus the first resting place of this company was called Moriancumer.

This is a matter of history.

In the *Messenger and Advocate,* April 1835, pp. 108-112, there is a letter on the early days of the Church. Oliver Cowdery was the editor of the magazine, and the Prophet Joseph Smith had recently offered to look over the historical matter in order to see that "our narrative may be correct." (*Messenger and Advocate,* Oct., 1834, p. 11) In this letter we read: "It is said, and I believe the account, that the Lord showed the Brother of Jared all things which were to transpire from that day to the end of the earth, as well as those which had taken place."

At this place we record an authoritative statement regarding the name of the Brother of Jared. In the *Juvenile Instructor,* Volume 27, p. 282, one of the authors hereto, President George Reynolds of the First Council of Seventy, furnishes this information:

"While residing in Kirtland, Elder Reynolds Cahoon had a son born to him. One day, while the Prophet Joseph Smith was passing by his door, he called the Prophet in and asked him to bless and name the baby. Joseph did so and gave the baby the name of Mahonri Moriancumer. When he had finished the blessing he laid the child upon the bed, and turning to the father, Elder Cahoon, he said, 'The name I have given your son is the name of the Brother of Jared; the Lord has just shown (or revealed) it to me.' Elder William F. Cahoon, who was standing nearby, heard the Prophet make this statement to his father; and this was the first time the name of the Brother of Jared was known in the Church in this dispensation."

In a previous note we have expressed the thought that Ophir, the eleventh son of Joktan, may have been the brother that was called to accompany Jared on the long and perilous journey. This was only by way of suggestion. But whosoever he was, his name was no doubt changed at the time when he was called to take the lead of the expedition (Ether 1:42). Such changes of name were not uncommon. *Jacob* was called Israel: "Thy name shall be called no more Jacob, but Israel," (Genesis 32:28). Jethro, the father-in-law of Moses, was also known as Hobab (Numbers 10:29). Daniel was called Belteshazzar (Daniel 4:8). And in New Testament times, we have John, the evangelist, also known as Mark (Acts 12:12); Bartholomew was called Nathanael (John 1:45). Our Lord changed the name of Simon, the son of Jona, to Cephas (John 1:42), and Saul, after his conversion, became known as Paul.

THE MEANING OF THE NAME

Concerning the meaning of the name, Moriancumer, we can offer only a brief suggestion. The first part of the name, *Morian,* may be related to the Aramic, Mara, which means lord or master. Or to *Moreh,* a teacher, the name of the place where Abraham first rested on his arrival in Canaan (Genesis 12:6). In the second part of the word, the main idea is expressed in *cume,* which means to stand up, or to rise (Mark 5:41). The final *r* is in many languages, ancient and modern, expresses the idea of being, or making. Witness such nouns as *maker, doer, hunter, lover,* etc., etc., in English, and their equivalents in cognate languages. If this analysis of the name, Morian - cume - r, is correct, it would mean, *One who stands up for God,* that is, one who speaks for, or represents the Lord. As applied to a locality, it would mean a place, a hill, a camp specially claimed for the Lord. It would express the same idea as the name, *Cumorah,* in which the identical grammatical elements appear.

14. And it came to pass at the end of four years that the Lord came again unto the brother of Jared, and stood in a cloud and talked with him. And for the space of three hours did the Lord talk with the brother of Jared, and chastened him because he remembered not to call upon the name of the Lord.

15. And the brother of Jared repented of the evil which he had done, and did call upon the name of the Lord for his brethren who were with him. And the Lord said unto him: I will forgive thee and thy brethren of their sins; but thou shalt not sin any more, for ye shall remember that my Spirit will not always strive with man; wherefore, if ye will sin until ye are fully ripe ye shall be cut off from the presence of the Lord. And these are my thoughts upon the land which I shall give you for your inheritance; for it shall be a land choice above all other lands.

The meaning of the first name, Mahonri, given to the baby by the Prophet Joseph, is not entirely unknown. We believe we are safe in analyzing it thus: Mahon - r - i. *Mahon*, or *Mahan*, means one who is *the master of a great secret*. When Cain had sold himself to the fallen angel, and had been instructed in the awful art of committing murder, he said, *Truly I am Mahan, the master of this great secret*. (*See* Moses, Pearl of Great Price, 5:29 and 45-49) That is the literal meaning of the term. The name given to the Brother of Jared signifies that he, too, had become the possessor of a great secret; but his secret was a revelation from God, while the secret of Cain came from the opposite source. For this is a mystery of Godliness[4] as well as mysteries of satanic origin. The *r* may be an abbreviation of the *nr* which is one of the original languages, means (we understand) *man*.[5] The *i* may be an abbreviation of Jah. The name, *Mahonri Moriancumer*, would then be, "The Master of the mystery of Jehovah, who stands up for the Lord."

VERSE 14. *The Lord came again.* Four years after the first manifestation of the Lord to Moriancumer, the Brother of Jared, He again revealed Himself in a cloud, as He had done the first time. But on this occasion He rebuked His servant because he had neglected his prayers.

VERSE 15. *The Brother of Jared repented.* After a severe rebuke, Moriancumer asked for forgiveness, and the Lord assured him that He was willing to forgive both him and his brethren, if they would sin no more.

Here the important truth is taught that neglect of prayer is a sin. The consequence of continuance in neglect would be that they would be *cut off from the presence of the Lord.* Prayer is a connecting wire between God and His children in their temporary absence from their eternal home. They need it every day, every hour, in their daily lives. And if they are leaders among men their need of prayer is still more urgent, for no one can be entrusted with leadership safely, who is not, himself or herself, in uninterrupted communication with God. Officials of Church and State, teachers of children, parents, who are supposed to be the representatives of God in the home, all need the Spirit of the Lord, and *My Spirit will not always strive with man.*

---

[4]"And without controversy great is the mystery of godliness: God was manifest in the flesh, justified in the Spirit, seen of angels, preached unto the Gentiles, believed on in the world, received up into glory." (I Timothy 3:16)

[5]*Sanscrit,* nala, nara, man; compare *Greek* anar; *Latin,* Nero. (*Mexican Linguistics,* Denison)

4. *The barges.*

16. And the Lord said: Go to work and build, after the manner of barges which ye have hitherto built. And it came to pass that the brother of Jared did go to work, and also his brethren, and built barges after the manner which they had built, according to the instructions of the Lord. And they were small, and they were light upon the water, even like unto the lightness of a fowl upon the water.

17. And they were built after a manner that they were exceeding tight, even that they would hold water like unto a dish; and the bottom thereof was tight like unto a dish; and the sides thereof were tight like unto a dish; and the ends thereof were peaked; and the top thereof was tight like unto a dish; and the length thereof was the length of a tree; and the door thereof, when it was shut, was tight like unto a dish.

18. And it came to pass that the brother of Jared cried unto the Lord, saying: O Lord, I have performed the work which thou hast commanded me, and I have made the barges according as thou hast directed me.

19. And behold, O Lord, in them there is no light; whither shall we steer? And also we shall perish, for in them we cannot breathe, save it is the air which is in them; therefore we shall perish.

20. And the Lord said unto the brother of Jared: Behold, thou shalt make a hole in the top, and also in the bottom; and when thou shalt suffer for air thou shalt unstop the hole and receive air. And if it so be that the water shall come in upon thee, behold, ye shall stop the hole, that ye may not perish in the flood.

21. And it came to pass that the brother of Jared did so, ac-

---

VERSES 16-25. *Instruction concerning the barges.* The barges were to be small and light on the waters (v. 16); perfectly watertight, peaked both fore and aft, the length of the longest trees available, so as to insure the perfect solidity of the hulk; and they were to have a door that would keep out the water when closed (v. 17); also proper ventilation (vv. 19-21) and necessary light (vv. 22-25).

GENERAL NOTES

The following is from an editorial in the "Juvenile Instructor," April 15, 1892, by President George J. Cannon:

"There are wide-spread traditions which connect Nimrod, the grandson of Ham, with this Tower of Babel. By some it is asserted that he was the leader or king of the people who essayed to build it. Certainly it was not earlier than his day, for when Jared and his people first began their journey they passed northward into a valley named after this same Nimrod.

"But the date that Nimrod dwelt on the earth is quite uncertain. Tradition has it that he was born to his father Cush, in the latter's old age, and some rabbinical and Mahometan traditions make him a contemporary of the Patriarch Abraham. As man in those days lived to be several hundred years old, this is not impossible,

cording as the Lord had commanded.

22. And he cried again unto the Lord saying: O Lord, behold I have done even as thou hast commanded me; and I have prepared the vessels for my people, and behold there is no light in them. Behold, O Lord, wilt thou suffer that we shall cross this great water in darkness?

23. And the Lord said unto the brother of Jared: What will ye that I should do that ye may have light in your vessels? For behold, ye cannot have windows, for they will be dashed in pieces; neither shall ye take fire with you, for ye shall not go by the light of fire.

24. For behold, ye shall be as a whale in the midst of the sea; for the mountain waves shall dash upon you. Nevertheless, I will bring you up again out of the depths of the sea; for the winds have gone forth out of my mouth, and also the rains and the floods have I sent forth.

25. And behold, I prepare you against these things; for ye cannot

---

although it would bring the confusion of languages to a much later date than is given in the generally accepted chronologies.

"Too much trust must not, however, be placed upon chronologies dealing with those times. Two varying ones, now before us, give the building of Babel at 2247 and 2207 B.C., respectively, and the birth of Abraham at 2056 and 1996 B.C. We incline to the opinion that the first named event occurred at a greater distance from the universal flood than is generally asserted.

"Having no fixed date upon which we can depend for the confusion of tongues, we cannot with any exactness compute the length of time that the Jaredites occupied this continent. It also prevents us from forming any trustworthy estimate of who among these people were the contemporaries of the Hebrew patriarchs and prophets of the Israelitish kings. When we reach the later ages of their history we can form some slight idea by tracing backward from Coriantumr and Ether, who evidently lived at the time as Lehi and Nephi, Zedekiah and Mulek. On the other hand, while Abraham and Jared may possibly have lived simultaneously on the earth, the probabilities, almost amounting to a certainty, are that Orihah, the son of Jared, and the first King of the Jaredites, was, either in his early or his later years, a contemporary of the Father of the Faithful."

A CHOICE LAND

"Behold, this is a choice land, and whatsoever nation shall possess it it shall be free from bondage, and from captivity, and from all other nations under heaven, if they will but serve the God of this land, Who is Jesus Christ, who hath been manifested by the things we have written." (Ether 2:12)

DOUBLE RESPONSIBILITY

"From out of this comes both our opportunity and our responsibility, and these two are double. We have from our civil ancestors, from Washington and all the rest, the gift of free government which has come to us out of their God-given wisdom, their trials, hardships and sacrifices, even to the last sacrifice of all—life itself. We have from these same ancestors the wealth of guiding advice, admonition, and experience. All this, every one of our fellow citizens has likewise.

| cross this great deep save I prepare you against the waves of the sea, and the winds which have gone forth, and the floods which shall | come. Therefore what will ye that I should prepare for you that ye may have light when ye are swallowed up in the depths of the sea? |

But we have also the word of God, direct and through His prophets, giving us His promises regarding this land and this government, and the conditions upon which these promises are based. The world does not believe these, but the Lord has given to us the testimony of their truth and reality.

NO CHANGE

God has never changed or modified or withdrawn one whit of His promises or their conditions. This we must always and poignantly remember.

Since our knowledge is doubled, our obligation is twice multiplied. We ought not to escape this obligation if we could; we cannot escape it if we would.

The Lord has repeatedly declared in our day that this continent—hemisphere— is Zion.

To Isaiah of old the Lord revealed:

"And it shall come to pass in the last days, that the mountain of the Lord's house shall be established in the top of the mountains, and shall be exalted above the hills; and all nations shall flow unto it."

"And many people shall go and say, Come ye, and let us go up to the mountain of the Lord, to the house of the God of Jacob; and He will teach us of His ways, and we will walk in His paths; for out of Zion shall go forth the law, and the word of the Lord from Jerusalem.

"And He shall judge among the nations, and shall rebuke many people; and they shall beat their swords into plowshares, and their spears into pruninghooks: nation shall not lift up their sword against nation, neither shall they learn war any more." (Isaiah 2:2-4)

Nephi repeated these words to his people.

WASHINGTON'S PLEDGE

Washington had a vision of all this when in his Farewell Address, he pledged his:

"unceasing vows that Heaven may continue to you the choicest tokens of its beneficence; that your union and brotherly love may be perpetual; that the free Constitution, which is the work of your hands, may be sacredly maintained; that its administration in every department may be stamped with wisdom and virtue; that in fine, the happiness of the people of these States, under the auspices of liberty, may be made complete by so careful a preservation and so prudent a use of this blessing as will acquire to them the glory of recommending it to the applause, the affection, and adoption of every nation which is yet a stranger to it."

This is the destiny of America—that all men shall come to freedom and the blessings of liberty, through our good works, "for the Law shall go forth from Zion and the Word of the Lord from Jerusalem." (President J. Reuben Clark, Jr., *Deseret News, Church Section*, March 4, 1939)

MORIANCUMER, LAND OF

The place on the shore of the great ocean where Jared and his people tarried four years before crossing to America. It was evidently named after the Brother of

Jared (Mahonri Moriancumer). Here the Lord Jesus Christ appeared to him and gave him many glorious revelations and here, by divine command, the company built the eight barges that carried them across the great waters. We have no direct information in regard to the locality of Moriancumer, but those who believe that the Jaredites traveled eastward through Central Asia, are of the opinion that it was near the mouth of one of the great rivers that flow through the Chinese Empire into the Pacific Ocean.

NIMROD, VALLEY OF

The Valley of Nimrod was in Mesopotamia, or in the adjacent regions, and was so called after the mighty hunter who founded the Babylonian Empire. There the Jaredites assembled and organized their journey. In this Valley the Lord talked with the Brother of Jared, and commanded him that the company of which he and his brother were the leaders, should go forth into that region where man had never yet been, but Jared's brother did not at that time see the Lord for He was hidden in a cloud.

CHAPTER 3

1. *Moriancumer prays for light.*

1. And it came to pass that the brother of Jared, (now the number of the vessels which had been prepared was eight) went forth unto the mount, which they called the mount Shelem, because of its exceeding height, and did molten out of a rock sixteen small stones; and they were white and clear, even as transparent glass; and he did carry them in his hands upon the top of the mount, and cried again unto the Lord, saying:

2. O Lord, thou hast said that we must be encompassed about by the floods. Now behold, O Lord, and do not be angry with thy servant because of his weak-

---

VERSE 1. *Shelem.* After the vessel had been prepared, Moriancumer ascended a mount to which the pilgrims had given the name, Shelem. Zebach Shelem is the Hebrew for thank offering, wherefore we safely conclude that this mount had been set apart for sacred purposes (See Leviticus 7:12, 15; 22:27). Hence the name.

TRANSPARENT STONES

Moriancumer now presented sixteen small stones, clear as transparent glass, before the Lord and asked Him to make them luminous (v. 4). Dr. Adam Clark, in his commentary on the Bible, says that, according to Rabbinical tradition, the word translated window in the story of the Ark of Noah, in Genesis, was a shining object; a stone which the Patriarch had found in the River Pison, and which had been made luminous. If this tradition were founded upon facts, Jared and his family would have heard it from their parents.

A practical application to our own spiritual lives of this account of Moriancumer praying for light, is the lesson that when a servant of the Lord has done all he can to overcome the difficulties he is sure to encounter, he may confidently ask the Lord to do for him what he cannot do for himself. That is the privilege of a child in his father's house. And

> When God has touched our efforts
> With the finger of His might,
> Then every worthless pebble
> Is a bright and shining light.

VERSES 2-5. *The prayer.* The prayer of Moriancumer might profitably be made a special study by every reader of the Book of Mormon. It should be used as a pattern for own private devotions.

Moriancumer first reminded the Lord that the difficulty he had met had arisen in the divine command itself. "Thou hast said" (v. 2). Also: "Thou hast given us a commandment that we must call upon Thee." Moriancumer did not feel that he was an intruder before the Almighty. He then humbly asked the Lord not to be angry with him for his weakness, his failure to solve the problem before him; or

ness before thee; for we know that thou art holy and dwellest in the heavens, and that we are unworthy before thee; because of the fall our natures have become evil continually; nevertheless, O Lord, thou hast given us a commandment that we must call upon thee, that from thee we may receive according to our desires.

3. Behold, O Lord, thou hast smitten us because of our iniquity, and hast driven us forth, and for these many years we have been in the wilderness; nevertheless, thou hast been merciful unto us. O Lord, look upon me in pity, and turn away thine anger from this people, and suffer not that they shall go forth across this raging deep in darkness; but behold these things which I have molten out of the rock.

4. And I know, O Lord, that thou hast all power, and can do whatsoever thou wilt for the benefit of man; therefore touch these stones, O Lord, with thy finger, and prepare them that they may shine forth in darkness; and they shall shine forth unto us in the vessels which we have prepared, that we may have light while we shall cross the sea.

5. Behold, O Lord, thou canst do this. We know that thou art able to show forth great power, which looks small unto the understanding of men.

2. *Jesus Christ shows Himself.*

6. And it came to pass that when the brother of Jared had said these words, behold, the Lord stretched forth his hand and touched the stones one by one with his finger. And the veil was taken from off the eyes of the brother of Jared, and he saw the

---

his unworthiness on account of the Fall. Thou, he said, art holy, and dwellest in the Heavens; we because of the Fall have become evil continually. That is, our natures have been permanently affected by the transgression in Eden.

VERSE 3. Next, the Prophet acknowledged the mercy of God unto the people while in the wilderness, who had been driven forth because of their iniquity, referring to the building of the Babylonian Tower.

VERSE 4. Because of the mercy already experienced, Moriancumer felt emboldened to ask to be favored with light to illumine the barges.

VERSE 5. Finally, Moriancumer said that he realized he asked for a great miracle, even if it did seem *small* to some. Yet he knew that the Lord could do it. "Thou art able to show forth great power."

In this prayer we have the picture of a servant of the Lord, effacing himself in sincere humility, while extolling the justice, mercy, and power of the Almighty. It reminds us of Abraham, who, on a notable occasion, in his prayer exclaimed, "Behold, now, I have taken upon me to speak unto the Lord," I,—dust and ashes.

VERSE 6. *The Lord touched the stones.* The prayer of Moriancumer was heard and answered immediately. The Prophet Isaiah, referring to the Millennium and speaking about prayer, says as the word of the Lord: "And it shall come to pass,

finger of the Lord; and it was as the finger of a man, like unto flesh and blood; and the brother of Jared fell down before the Lord, for he was struck with fear.

7. And the Lord saw that the brother of Jared had fallen to the earth; and the Lord said unto him: Arise, why hast thou fallen?

8. And he saith unto the Lord: I saw the finger of the Lord, and I feared lest he should smite me; for I knew not that the Lord had flesh and blood.

9. And the Lord said unto him: Because of thy faith thou hast seen that I shall take upon me flesh and blood; and never has man come before me with such exceeding faith as thou hast; for were it not so ye could not have seen my finger. Sawest thou more than this?

10. And he answered: Nay; Lord, show thyself unto me.

11. And the Lord said unto him: Believest thou the words which I shall speak?

12. And he answered: Yea, Lord, I know that thou speakest the truth, for thou art a God of truth, and canst not lie.

---

that before they call, I will answer; and while they are yet speaking, I will hear" (Isaiah 65:24). God is always ready to help His children, and there is no red tape in the administration of the affairs of His Kingdom.

THE FINGER OF GOD

While the stones were being made luminous by the touch of the Almighty, or were being prepared to become lightbearers, Moriancumer obtained a glimpse of the finger of the Lord. What he saw overwhelmed him. He was struck with fear, and he fell to the earth.

VERSES 7-9. *I knew not that the Lord had flesh and blood. Flesh and blood* is a genuine Hebrew expression for humanity in contrast to divine Existences. We recall our Lord's word to Peter: "Flesh and blood hath not revealed it unto thee, but My Father which is in Heaven," (Matthew 16:27). It is an expression that may be traced to the covenant of God with Noah, when animal blood was said to be the life, or rather the soul (nephesh), the lifegiving principle of living beings. Moriancumer was familiar with this patriarchal concept, and he marveled greatly when the part of the divine person which he saw appeared to be material, flesh and blood, that is, human. Then fear of death added to his weakness. Would the Lord strike him down? (Compare Exodus 33:18-25) The Lord hastened to allay the fears of His servant. He explained to him that what he had seen was in a prophetic vision. "Because of thy faith thou hast seen that I shall take upon Me flesh and blood," some time in the future. Because of his faith, Moriancumer was given a preview of the central fact and main foundation of the *Plan of Salvation,* which the Apostle John states thus: "And the Word was made flesh, and dwelt among us (and we beheld His glory, the glory as of the Only Begotten of the Father,) full of grace and truth" (John 1:14).

VERSE 10. *Show Thyself unto me.* Moriancumer recovered. Then he felt emboldened to ask for a full view of the divine personage Who was speaking to him. It appears from this that Moriancumer, during the first part of the interview, did not see the Lord. He heard His voice. Perhaps not with the outward ear, but in some manner by which we must assume that one spirit communicates with another.

13. And when he had said these words, behold, the Lord showed himself unto him, and said: Because thou knowest these things ye are redeemed from the fall; therefore ye are brought back into my presence; therefore I show myself unto you.

14. Behold, I am he who was prepared from the foundation of the world to redeem my people. Behold, I am Jesus Christ. I am the Father and the Son. In me shall all mankind have light, and that eternally, even they who shall believe on my name; and they shall become my sons and my daughters.

VERSE 13. *The Lord showed Himself.* When Moriancumer had solemnly confessed his implicit faith in the *Divine Word,* he was granted the favor he desired. And not only that, but the entire Plan of Salvation was explained to him.

Because thou knowest these things. The importance of knowledge is here shown in redemption from the Fall; in the return to the Divine Presence, and divine manifestations. This is in accord with modern revelations. "The glory of God is intelligence, or, in other words, light and truth" (Doctrine and Covenants 93:36). Again: "And verily I say unto you, that it is My will that . . . you should obtain a knowledge of history, and of countries, and of kingdoms, of laws of God and man, and all this for the salvation of Zion" (D. and C. 93:53; *See* also 131:6 and 136:32).

VERSE 14. *I am the Father and the Son.* Our Lord, Who, before the earth was created, was prepared to be the Redeemer of His people, here reveals Himself as Jesus Christ, and also as the Father and the Son.

Redemption means, literally, either the repurchase of something that has been sold, by repaying the price (Leviticus 25:25-28), or, the release of what has been impounded, by substituting something else (Leviticus 27:27-31). In the New Testament, redemption stands for the forgiveness of sins (Ephesians 1:7), or, for the deliverance from "vain conversation," which means from former social and useless habits and activities (1 Peter 1:18). The body is said to be redeemed from the grave in the Resurrection (Romans 8:23); and, finally, the Day of Redemption is the day of the deliverance from all evil (Ephesians 4:30). In 1 Timothy 2:5-6, our Lord is said to be both the Mediator, and the ransom (*See* D. and C. 31:13).

Jesus Christ. The first of these two sacred names means Savior (Matthew 1:21). It is the English form of the Name of our Lord. The Hebrew Name is Joshua, an abbreviated form of Jehoshuah (Numbers 13:16).

Christ, the English form of the Greek *Christos,* was originally a title, the equivalent of the Hebrew *Mashiah* which means anointed. Gradually it became, as many other appellatives, a proper name, by which Jesus, the Anointed One, the Messiah, was differentiated from others who were named Joshua, or even Jesus.

The Father and the Son is a phrase that has been regarded as difficult to understand. But the explanation is given in the Doctrine and Covenants 93:4: "The Father because he gave Me of His fulness, and the Son because I was in the world and made flesh My tabernacle, and dwelt among the sons of Men."

We read further:

And I, John, saw that He received not of the fulness at the first, but received grace for grace; and He received not of the fulness at first, but continued from grace to grace until He received a fulness; and thus He was called the Son of God, because He received not a fulness at the first (D. and C. 93:12-14).

15. And never have I showed myself unto man whom I have created, for never has man believed in me as thou hast. Seest thou that ye are created after mine own image? Yea, even all men were created in the beginning after mine own image.

A further explanation of the title *Father,* as applied to the second person in the Godhead, is found in Mosiah 5:7-9: "Because of the covenant ye have made ye shall be called the children of Christ, His sons and daughters; for behold this day He hath spiritually begotten you; for ye say that your hearts are changed through faith in His Name; therefore ye are born of Him and have become His sons and daughters."

Thus, Jesus, the Anointed One, is the Father as well as the Son. (Compare Isaiah 53:10-12)

VERSE 15. *Created after Mine own image.* If, as here stated, all men were created in the beginning, after the image of God, attempts to find room in the account of Creation as recorded in Genesis, for the so-called Darwinian theory of the origin of man, must be given up. In the philosophy of evolution man appears first as a germ, a one-cell organization in the ocean. This creature, origin not accounted for, began to grow and evolve until at first it became a big denizen of the sea; then a land animal, and, finally, man.

In support of this theory—for it is but a theory, notwithstanding the evidence claimed for it—it is generally argued that the human body contains the same kind of matter as other bodies, and that it is, in the beginning similar in form to these in every way or detail. This is quite generally repeated as a valid argument.

And yet, what does it prove? Let us attempt an illustration. On the same piece of ground there may be a modest hut and a pretentious palace. They may have been constructed of the same kind of material—wood, stone, iron, steel, glass, etc.,—but that does not prove that the palace grew, or evolved out of the hut. A plain horse car may be standing at a railroad station by the side of a luxurious Pullman sleeper. There may be a striking similarity in some of the main features of the two vehicles—wheels, axles, windows, seats, doors, etc.,—but that does not prove that they had a common origin. It does prove that the maker intended that the features mentioned perform similar functions in the two structures—wheels to facilitate movement, seats to furnish rest, windows to admit light and air, doors to give egress and ingress. But this similarity in design does not prove identity of origin. The two cars may have been built in the same factory, by the same architects, or one may have come from New York and the other from California, yet each is a separate organization, independent of the other.

Logic leads us to the same conclusion when we consider the similarity of the matter of which animal bodies including the bodies of men are made; or the similarity of purpose of some of the organs of the bodies—eyes to see with, ears to hear with, organs to digest food with, to circulate blood, to utilize air, and so on. As similarities do not prove the Pullman car to have been a horse car at some stage of its existence, and still further back a wheel barrow; neither do they prove that man originally came from an insect.

"In the beginning God created the heaven and the earth" (Genesis 1:1). "All men were created in the beginning after mine own image."

That is more reasonable. It is the revealed word of God.

A word from scientists. Only a short time age, a convention of scientists at Cambridge, England, were told by Oxford professors that after careful examination of a human skull, found in some remote geological formation, human beings 250,000 years ago did not differ materially from modern man. The brain, for instance, had already at that early day assumed the status it has today. Without considering the improbability of the age assigned to the skull—a mere assumption—we naturally ask, if no material change has occurred in the human brain in 250,000 years, how long time has been required for a germ in the ocean to become a statesman, an accomplished musician, an artist of note, or a Shakespeare or George Washington?

Never have I shown Myself to man. In the Gospel of John 1:18, we read: "No man hath seen God at any time; the Only Begotten Son, which is in the Bosom of the Father, He hath declared Him." That is, all manifestations of God to man have been through the Son. Our Lord declares: "He that beholdest Me, beholdeth Him that sent Me (John 12:45). And: "He that hath seen Me hath seen the Father" (Ibid., 14:9). Enoch saw God *face to face* as did Moses (Exodus 33:11), but the Patriarch explains this: "But now my own eyes have beheld God; but not my natural, but my spiritual eyes, for my natural eyes could not have beheld; for I should have withered and died in His presence; but His glory was upon me; and I beheld His face, for I was transfigured before Him." (Pearl of Great Price, Moses 1:2, 11)

The Prophet Joseph Smith, on a beautiful morning early in the spring of 1820, in a secluded grove, where he went and prayed for divine light, saw, after a struggle with the powers of darkness, a pillar of light gradually descending until it rested upon him. The *Shekinah*, the glory of God of the Old Testament sanctuaries (I Kings 8:10-11; 2 Chronicles 7:2-3; Ezekiel 9:3; 43:4) was returning. The Prophet writes: "When the light rested upon me, I saw two personages, whose brightness and glory defy all description, standing above me in the air. One of them spake unto me, calling me by name, and said, pointing to the other—this is My Beloved Son, hear Him." The Prophet further says: "When I came to myself again, I found myself lying on my back, looking up into the heavens" (Pearl of Great Price, Joseph Smith, p. 48). The young prophet had actually been given a vision during a moment of heavenly ecstasy in which he saw the Father and the Son, and heard Them speak.

The Apostle Paul had a somewhat similar experience (2 Corinthians 12:2-4). To him, whether in the body or in the spirit, the third heaven, also called Paradise, was opened, and he heard "unspeakable words, not lawful for a man to utter." St. Paul was transported to the world beyond the veil, while the vision of the Prophet Joseph, as also the manifestations to John on Patmos (Revelation 1:9-10) appeared on this side.

The mission of the Prophet Joseph was to be that of a herald proclaiming the coming of the King of kings to His Millennial Kingdom, for the completion and perfection of the Plan of Salvation, from the power of the adversary and from all evil. The appearance of God, the Father and His Son, Jesus Christ, on this epoch-making occasion in God's Kingdom was fully consistent with its world-wide importance. On the occasion of the baptism of Jesus at the beginning of His earthly mission in the meridian of time, a similar manifestation appeared and a similar testimony was heard.

"Now it came to pass, when all the people were baptized, that, Jesus also having been baptized, and praying, the heaven was opened, and the Holy Ghost descended in a bodily form, as a dove, upon Him, and a voice came out of heaven, Thou art My beloved Son; in Thee I am well pleased." (Luke 3:21-22)

VERSE 16. *Behold, this body, which ye now behold, is the Body of My Spirit.* Redeemer, and he was told that, as our Lord now appeared in the Spirit so He the flesh. This vision passed. What he now saw was the spiritual body of the Moriancumer had been given a prophetic view of the appearance of our Lord in

16. Behold, this body, which ye now behold, is the body of my spirit; and man have I created after the body of my spirit; and even as I appear unto thee to be in the spirit will I appear unto my people in the flesh.

---

would appear in the flesh. Also, that man had been created in the image of this spiritual body.

At the exodus from Egypt, the angel of Elohim went before the Camp of Israel, and when the Egyptians pursued, this divine Personage "removed and went behind them," so that He stood in the fiery cloud between Israel and the pursuers. (Exodus 14:19-20) This Angel of Elohim was Jehovah, for so we read: "And Jehovah went before them by day in a pillar of a cloud, to lead them the way. (Ibid., 13:21)

Jehovah, the great Angel, or Messenger of Elohim, the representative, in other words, of the great Council of Elohim, in which the Plan of Salvation was accepted, and on account of which He was afterwards known as the *Wonderful Counselor,* (Isaiah 9:6) but when Israel, after the many manifestations of His power, turned to the Golden Calf, possibly with ceremonies of which obscene practices formed a part (Exodus 32:25), then He threatened to withdraw entirely. At this critical juncture in the history of Israel, Moses went up on the mountain and pled before Jehovah for Israel, whereupon Jehovah, in answer to His faithful servant, gave him the promise that He would send His angel with him. From this time Jehovah withdrew, and left one of His angels, or representatives, in charge.

Who this angel of Jehovah was, we are not expressly told, but since Daniel says that "the great Prince which standeth for the children of Thy people" is Michael (Daniel 12:1; 10:13 and 21), there can be no harm in the suggestion that Michael, our venerable ancestor, was possibly the angel of Jehovah, who already at this time had performed the mission of which Daniel speaks. But be this as it may, Jehovah withdrew, and as a sign of this, the tent in which religious ordinances were performed and which hitherto had stood in the center of the Camp, was now removed a long distance from it. The cloudy pillar in which the angel of Jehovah manifested his presence, rested there.

A remarkable interview between Moses and Jehovah took place at that tent, away from the Camp. Moses reminded Jehovah that although He had commanded him to be the visible leader of the people, He had not instructed him regarding the journey ahead of them. "Show me now," Moses said, "Thy way." Jehovah answered, "My presence shall go with thee." (Exodus 33:14) That is to say, Jehovah would not entirely abandon the people. He would be near just as Jesus promised to be near His Apostles, even after He departed. In the same sense, Jehovah would be present and manifest Himself from time to time as circumstances required. This promise was fulfilled throughout the entire journey in the wilderness.

After having obtained this promise, Moses said, "I beseech Thee, show me now Thy glory." In answer to that prayer, Jehovah explained to Moses that he could not see His face, but that He (Jehovah) would show him all His goodness and proclaim or explain, His Name to him, and also permit him to see His back as He was passing by a certain place.

This last expression is in all probability a misunderstanding by the translators of the Hebrew word. The word may here mean *behind in point of time, afterwards,* and in that case we may understand the meaning to be Moses was given the privilege of seeing Jehovah in the form in which He *afterwards* would appear in the flesh. This human form, we know was His *glory* for John says: "The Word was made flesh, and dwelt among us, and we beheld His glory (His body) as of the

3. Moroni's Comments.

17. And now, as I, Moroni, said I could not make a full account of these things which are written | therefore it sufficeth me to say that Jesus showed himself unto this man in the spirit, even after

---

Only Begotten of the Father." If we understand the text in Exodus the same way, it is clear. Moses saw Jehovah, just as John saw the bodily form of the Word, all but His face. (*Ibid.*, 33:20-23)

This agrees perfectly with the beautiful narrative in the Book of Ether concerning the interview of the Brother of Jared with our Lord. The Lord showed Himself unto him in the *body of my Spirit*, in the likeness of which He, Jesus Christ, had created man, (Ether 3:14-16) and the Lord said: "The time cometh that I shall glorify My Name in the flesh." (v. 21) That was His *glory*, and that was, we may feel sure, the glory which Moses, as well as the Brother of Jared, saw.

VERSE 17. *Even as He showed Himself unto the Nephites.* Moroni interrupts his narrative for a moment in order to contemplate the wonderful visions which Moriancumer had been given of our Lord, both in His spiritual and His material body as we commonly understand those terms. Now Moroni adds the information that the body in which our Lord manifest Himself to Moriancumer was, both in *manner*, that is to say, functions or acts, and appearance the same as that in which He showed Himself to the Nephites (3 Nephi 11:8-12).

The reality of the human body. In our day and age, at the present stage of development of religious thought, the reason for the importance which Moroni evidently attached to a correct belief in the reality of the human body, including the earthly tabernacle of our Lord, may not be apparent. But when we remember that Christianity during its early days was seriously threatened by a philosophy that denied this reality, we can understand these paragraphs.

According to Platonian philosophy, in the fifth century B.C., reality belongs only to general ideas of objects, such as horse, man, etc., not to individuals, viz., this horse, this man. The latter are not temporary, fleeting copies of the real existences, shadows on the wall, as it were. The species, not the individual, is the real thing. Influenced by such speculations, first the Essenes and then the Gnostics formed some strange ideas. Some of the latter imagined a duality in everything. They believed in two gods, one of which was good, omnipotent, and omniscient, while the other, the demiurge, was weak and imperfect. It was the latter that created the tangible universe and man. Matter was, therefore, imperfect and evil; something from which to be liberated, or saved. And salvation was attained, either by strict asceticism, killing natural desires by not yielding to them, or satisfying them, or, taking an opposite course and creating complete indifference to all earthly pleasures by overindulgence—libertinism. Between the supreme God and the demiurge there was a connecting chain of angelic beings called "principalities and powers," gradually decreasing in perfection and therefore approaching near enough to humanity to serve as mediators between God and man. These are the *fulness*, or *pleroma*, of the Godhead.

In the imagination of some of the early philosophers, there were also two Christs, one material and one spiritual. The latter, they held, came upon our Lord in His baptism and departed from Him before His death. There was, therefore, no resurrection of the body. Others held that the birth, life, and death of our Lord were illusions, imaginary and not real historical facts.

St. Paul brands all such philosophy as *vain deceit*. He warns against an asceticism that exaggerates the importance of abstinence from food and the observance

the manner and in the likeness of the same body even as he showed himself unto the Nephites.

18. And he ministered unto him even as he ministered unto the Nephites; and all this, that this man might know that he was God, because of the many great works which the Lord had showed unto him.

---

of holidays. But he urges a life of righteousness. He warns against making angels the object of worship, because all the fulness of the Godhead—the connecting chain between God and man—dwells in Christ, who is the head of all principalities and powers—all angels, whatever their station in the divine government may be. (See Colossians 2:8-23)

John brands that class of philosophers as *antichrists*, because they deny that Jesus is the Christ, and he says that their appearances indicate *that the end of the world* is near (1 John 2-18-25). St. John also testifies that he and others had seen the Lord, and heard Him, and even handled Him with their hands (1 John 1:1-2). There was no illusion. He was as real in His humanity as in His Godhood.

Dr. Joseph Angus remarks (*Bible-Handbook*, p. 585) that the errors of Gnosticism in its many forms proved more fatal to Christianity than persecution itself. It was the serious consequences foreseen that prompted some of the Apostles, following the inspirations of the Divine Spirit, to turn the full authority of their Priesthood and their holy Apostolic calling against both the heresies and the authors thereof. No doubt Moroni, enlightened by the spirit of prophecy, foresaw the apostasy and its sources, and was thus given to realize the importance of a correct picture of our Lord in His twofold nature, the human and the divine, as well as the true knowledge of the Plan of Salvation. This, it seems, made him pause to contemplate more fully the visions of Moriancumer.*

VERSE 18. *He ministered unto him.* Our Lord ministered unto Moriancumer, as He, centuries afterwards, ministered unto the Nephites (III Nephi Chapters 11-28). He explained to Moriancumer the entire Plan of Salvation, bestowed upon him the power and authority of the Holy Priesthood, and endowed him with the blessings and gifts of the Holy Spirit. The Jaredites were an enlightened people, living in the illumination of the patriarchal religion, as it had been taught to Noah, coming to him from Adam through Enoch, and to them by direct revelations of Himself. There is no reason for the supposition that their civilization was inferior to that of the Assyrians, Babylonians, Sumerians, or Egyptians.

NOTE

*The church fathers who, during the latter part of the second century A.D., formulated the so-called Apostolic Creed, had such antichrists and their destructive heresies in mind. The so-called old Roman text reads, in translation, as follows:

"I believe in God, the Father Almighty;

"And in Jesus Christ, his Only Begotten Son, our Lord, born of the Holy spirit and Mary, the virgin; crucified under Pontius Pilate and buried; on the third day resurrected from the dead, ascended to the heavens, sitteth on the right hand of the Father, whence he cometh to judge living and dead;

"Also in the Holy Spirit, the holy church, the remission of sins, the resurrection of the body, life eternal."

This was the original form. Other phrases were added later, as the war on heresies was continued as the occasion seemed to demand. (See *The Apostles' Creed*, by Dr. Arthur Cushman McGiffert. On the errors of the Essenes and Gnostics, the scholarly notes and dissertations of Bishop J. B. Lightfoot, D.D. can be studied with profit.)

19. And because of the knowledge of this man he could not be kept from beholding within the veil; and he saw the finger of Jesus, which, when he saw, he fell with fear; for he knew that it was the finger of the Lord; and he had faith no longer, for he knew, nothing doubting.

20. Wherefore, having this per-

VERSES 19-20. *Perfect knowledge of God.* In these two paragraphs Moroni stresses the importance of knowledge. It was because of his knowledge that Moriancumer was enabled to receive the divine manifestations. His faith had changed into *perfect knowledge,* and therefore *he could not be kept from within the veil.* (v. 20)

Can God be known? If so, How? No man in his present stage of existence can have *perfect* knowledge of God, if by that phrase is meant the complete, finished cognition of His origin, essence, and attributes. No human being can have so perfect knowledge of anything that there is no more to learn about it. "Now we see through a glass, darkly" (1 Corinthians 13:12), and we presume that the Apostle who penned those words referred to the blurred images reflected in the polished metal plates that served as mirrors in his days, stated an exact fact. All human knowledge is, as yet, imperfect. But if *perfect* in this connection means sure, certain, and therein refers to a conviction of the mind that knows no doubt, then, in that sense, man can know God.

And not only that, man must know God, in order to have Eternal Life, as our Lord Himself declares: "And this is life eternal, that they might know Thee, the only true God, and Jesus Christ, Whom Thou hast sent (John 17:3).

The infinite God, with infinite attributes, is incomprehensible even to the keenest and most logical philosopher, if he depends only on worldly wisdom for his understanding of the Divine. The Infinite cannot be measured with a finite yardstick. ". . . the world by wisdom knew not God" (1 Corinthians 1:21). But the humblest of human beings can be made to realize the reality of the existence of God, and to rejoice in that knowledge. The statesmanship and policy of a king, or the intricate calculations of a mathematician are far beyond the comprehension of a five-year-old child; but the reality of the existence of the king, or the mathematician, and some of their attributes, can be perceived even by the baby in the cradle. This applies also to the existence of God. In His infinite perfections He is beyond human comprehension, but we can know, and if we desire that knowledge, we will know that the existence of God is a reality.

Three philosophical proofs. Theologians at one time, when called upon to give rational reasons for their belief in the existence of God, used to reply with three propositions.

(1) Man, it was argued, had an innate idea of a perfect Being, and, since existence is one attribute without which there cannot be perfection, this Being must exist. The name of Anselm (1033-1109), at one time Archbishop of Canterbury, is prominently connected with this argument which is known as the ontological proof. Descartes, the French philosopher (1596-1650), made use of it in his deductions.

(2) It was argued, next, that if anything exists, there must be a cause of its existence, and a final, self-existing cause. This is known as the cosmological proof. Leibnitz, the German philosopher (1646-1716), in reply to the contention that we know nothing except what we perceive through our senses, summarized this argument in his famous statement, "Nothing if not Intellect itself."[1] Wolff, another German, (1679-1754), popularized the position of Leibnitz on this question.

---

[1] *Nihil nisi Intellectus ipse.*

fect knowledge of God, he could | therefore he saw Jesus; and he
not be kept from within the veil; | did minister unto him.

4. Instructions; the Interpreters.

21. And it came to pass that | Jared: Behold, thou shalt not suf-
the Lord said unto the brother of | fer these things which ye have

---

(3) Wolff also made use of another argument asserting that the countless evidences of design are proof of an intelligent designer, a Creator. This is known as the Theological proof.

These arguments seemed conclusive until Hume, in England, in a philosophical work published in 1779 after the death of its author; and Kant, in Germany, in 1781, denied the conclusions drawn from them. Hume held that the Cause of the universe, and Kant expressed the same thought more strikingly when he said that he could not imagine the Creator saying, "Beside Me there is nothing but that which I have made, but whence did I come from?" or words to that effect.

That may be true, but some deductions from these propositions are not true. If anyone contends that the three famous proofs offered for the existence of the Creator, fail because they do not account for the origin of the divine Maker as well as the works of His hands, the logic of such contention is pretty near the boundary line of absurdity.

Let us imagine ourselves standing near the shore of an ocean beach. Presently a large steamship comes in sight. It draws nearer and nearer. It passes us at a distance of two or three miles. Aided by our spyglasses, we can see the gracefully sloping masts, the brightly painted smokestacks, the bridges, the people moving about on its decks, the immense hull, these with its rows of portholes and perhaps a name in golden letters. Everything we see of this passing object of our observation convinces us that we have before us the creation of an intelligent builder with vast resources at his disposal even if we have never before seen a ship. What we see may not give us any information of the family, the ancestors or countrymen of the builder, or his education, his complexion, or anything else our curiosity might desire to know or find out; but that does not weaken our conclusion that we have seen a great personality embodied in this magnificent creation of modern civilization. There is no room for skepticism as to that. Nor is it reasonable to underrate the value of an argument for the existence of God because it is silent on His divine origin.

"The invisible things of God, His eternal power and Godhead, have been visible from the creation of the world, being understood by the things that are made" (Romans 1:20).

"If there is no God we are not, neither the earth; for there could have been no creation of things, neither to act nor to be acted upon; wherefore all things must have vanished away" (II Nephi 2:13).

(4) *The Dokimological proof.*[2] But if these arguments are not convincing, there is a fourth which we shall call the Dokimological proof until a better name is suggested. Every sincere child of God knows from his own experience that there is a Supreme Being who hears and answers prayer. This is a proposition which everyone can put to the test for himself.

Moriancumer had at one time neglected his prayers habitually. The Lord rebuked him. He repented (Ether 2:14-15). When he resumed his communication with God in regular prayer, his faith and knowledge increased to the extent that he could see the Lord.

---

[2]From "dokimae," (II Corinthians 9:13), translated *experiment, proof, trial.*

seen and heard to go forth unto the world, until the time cometh that I shall glorify my name in the flesh; wherefore, ye shall treasure up the things which ye have seen and heard, and show it to no man.

22. And behold, when ye shall come unto me, ye shall write them and shall seal them up, that no one can interpret them; for ye shall write them in a language that they cannot be read.

VERSES 21-28. *Write these things and seal them up.* This section contains instructions to Moriancumer. He is cautioned against publishing to the world the revelations given to him. He is commanded to place them on record when "ye shall come unto Me," that is, when he was about to die. He was given two stones, by means of which the records would be read in the due time of the Lord. He was now given another vision, this time of the past and the future of the human family. Finally he was directed to put this vision on record with the others, and to place them and the stones, also known as the Interpreters somewhere for safe-keeping until they were to come forth in the due time of the Lord.

VERSE 22. *In a language that they—the Records—cannot be read.* The original Semitic language spoken by Noah and Shem was lost when the Tower was destroyed, except as far it was preserved by Jared and his brother, their families and a few of their friends (Ether 1:35-37). The twenty-four plates must have been written in that vernacular (v. 24). Being lost as a common mode of speech, it could not have been read, particularly in an age when reading was an art, mastered by few.

Semitic languages. These at one time were spoken by inhabitants of Abyssinia, Arabia, Palestine, Phoenicia, Syria, Mesopotamia, parts of Elam, the Nile Valley, Ethiopia, and parts of northern Africa. Arabic, Hebrew, Phoenician, Moabitic, Aramean, Assyrian, Babylonian, Samaritan, Syriac, are all classed as Semitic. A Semitic dialect was at one time the official language of Persia. All these linguistic branches must have had a common stem in a tongue spoken by Noah and Shem. It was also the vernacular of the Jaredites until the dispersion, and of Jared and his friends after that event.

Origin of languages. Some have suggested that words were invented in imitation of such sounds as *hiss, buzz, roar,* etc. Others have thought that languages were developed from interjections, such as, *Oh, alas,* etc. Others think that a gesture language preceded a sound language. But the Scriptures tell us that Adam could speak even before the creation of Eve. He must have been taught to use a highly developed language of none other than his Heavenly Father.

Turn to Genesis 2:19-23. There we read that God brought beasts of the field and fowls of the air before Adam "to see what he would call them." Adam gave them names, but he found no help, meet for him, until Eve had been given being and life. Then he exclaimed, "This is now bone of my bones and flesh of my flesh." He recognized that there was no affinity between him and the brute creation. Here Adam is represented as conversing with his divine Tutor, and as having a vocabulary sufficient for a work on Zoology.

We know not how long a time our venerable ancestor and his wife, Eve, remained in the Garden of Eden, but it is evident that when they entered the world outside they were full equipped, mentally and otherwise, for their earthly mission. They even had a written language and kept a record thereby, a *Book of Remembrance.* This was written by inspiration in the *language of Adam,* which was the tongue

23. And behold, these two stones will I give unto thee, and ye shall seal them up also with the things which ye shall write.

24. For behold, the language which ye shall write I have confounded; wherefore I will cause in my own due time that these stones shall magnify to the eyes of men these things which ye shall write.

25. And when the Lord had said these words, he showed unto the brother of Jared all the inhabitants of the earth which had been, and also all that would be; and he withheld them not from his sight, even unto the ends of the earth.

26. For he had said unto him in times before, that if he would believe in him that he could show

---

spoken by the antediluvian patriarchs presumably down to Noah and his sons (Pearl of Great Price, Moses 6:5-6; 6:46).

VERSES 23-24. *The Two Stones.* These Two Stones, which are also known as the *Interpreters* (Ether 4:5; Mosiah 28:20) and *Urim and Thummim*[3] (Pearl of Great Price, Joseph Smith 2:52; Doctrine and Covenants 17:1) were, as we read here, entrusted into the care of Moriancumer, before he descended from the ever memorable scene of his vision and revelations. They were delivered to him with the admonition that they were to be sealed up, together with the sacred records that were to be kept, and thus be hidden from the eyes of the world, until they, in the due time of the Lord, were to come forth. The purpose of the *Stones* is stated to be to *magnify*, that is to say, to make clear "the things which ye shall write."

According to the Doctrine and Covenants (17:1), the Sacred Instruments deposited in the Hill Cumorah and delivered to the Prophet Joseph, was the Urim and Thummim received by the Brother of Jared on the Mount. When the Prophet Joseph received the *Stones*, September 22, 1827, they were framed in silver bows and fastened to a *breastplate* (Pearl of Great Price, Joseph Smith 2:35). From the Doctrine and Covenants, 130:8-9, where God is said to dwell on a globe which is a Urim and Thummim, and that the Earth is to be sanctified and made immortal— *made like unto a crystal and will be a Urim and Thummim to the inhabitants thereon*—we conclude that that was the nature of the Stones. They were crystals. The Prophet Joseph Smith further adds to our information that the *white stone* mentioned in the Revelation 2:17, will become a Urim and Thummim to each who receives one, and that *a white stone* will be given to everyone who is privileged to come into the Celestial Kingdom. On the stone a new name is written. By this means *things pertaining to a higher order of kingdoms, even all kingdoms, will be made known.*

VERSES 25-28. *All the inhabitants of the Earth.* When Moriancumer had received the Urim and Thummim, the Lord opened his vision, possibly by means of these Stones; and he was shown the human race, past and future, passing as if in a panorama.

Enoch had a similar view of *many generations* upon Mt. Simeon (Pearl of Great Price, Moses 7:2-6, 22-69). Abraham, who received a second Urim and Thummim while he was in Ur, of the Caldees (*Ibid.*, Abraham 3:1), had marvelous visions and revelations concerning the Creation of the Universe, and the intelligences that were organized *before the world was* (*Ibid.*, Abraham 1-28 and

---

[3]Meaning Lights and Perfections.

unto him all things—it should be shown unto him; therefore the Lord could not withhold anything | from him, for he knew that the Lord could show him all things. 27. And the Lord said unto

---

chapters 4 and 5). He was thus prepared for his mission to Egypt (*Ibid.*, 3:15). Moses, too, who may have been the possessor of the same Urim and Thummim that had first been given to Abraham, had similar visions (*Ibid.*, Moses, 1:1-7ff). *He beheld the Earth, yea, even all of it; and there was not a particle of it which he did not behold . . . and he beheld also the inhabitants thereof, and there was not a soul which he beheld not; and he discerned by the Spirit of God. . . And he beheld many lands; and each land was called earth, and there were inhabitants on the face thereof* (*Ibid.*, Moses, 1:27-29).

PRE-EXISTENCE

Ether 3:15-16. This is the only place in the Book of Mormon where pre-existence is clearly spoken of and this was revealed before the organization of the Church, and is a doctrine which was not in possession of the Christian world; hence it shows that it was dictated by a spirit capable of revealing a doctrine unknown to the Christian world. (Orson Pratt, April 13, 1856; *Journal of Discourses*, Vol. 3, p. 352.)

DIVERSITY OF LANGUAGES

The wandering life of the Indians was one of the most powerful causes of the formation of dialects, which was so transformed by time as scarcely to retain a vestige of the mother tongue. The dispersion of the tribes over immense plains and almost inaccessible mountains, the sight of new objects, novel customs, the complete separation, and destruction of all kind of relation with sister tribes were causes more than sufficient to form, in a short time, a multitude of new words, and to produce an idiom which at first view would seem to be entirely distinct from the mother tongue. But the grammatical construction remains an indestructible monument, to attest the affiliation, which no circumstance of time and place can obliterate." (Rivero and Tschudi, *Peruvian Antiquities,* pp. 96-7.)

A COMMON ORIGIN

Mr. T. S. Denison, A.M., in "Mexican Linguistics" expressed the opinion that all American languages have a common origin in some early Old World speech. He maintains that they have retained sufficient vestiges to prove that fact. (*Mexican Linguistics,* p. 10.)

Students of the inspired word of God need no longer fear for their reputation as advanced thinkers, if they accept, for instance, the Biblical account of the creation as true history. For modern, scientific thought goes in that direction. Astronomy, and especially astrophysics, chemistry and experimental physics are changing the concepts of the well-informed, just as the visions, you may say, of Copernicus revolutionized the views, at one time predominant, concerning the place of man and earth in the universe.

Dr. Wayne R. Hales, of the B. Y. U., Provo, Utah, gave an enlightening address on that subject some time ago, to the students. He cited the "tidal theory" of Sir James Jeans of the formation of the earth. He said:

"According to this theory the earth came into being between five and ten million years ago as a result of the orbital intersection of two great suns.

him: Write these things and seal them up; and I will show them in mine own due time unto the children of men.

28. And it came to pass that the Lord commanded him that he should seal up the two stones which he had received, and show them not, until the Lord should show them unto the children of men.

"As the earth mass cooled, successive stages in its development were: (1) the appearance of light through the vapor surrounding the earth; (2) the separation of the atmosphere from condensed waters on the face of the planet; (3) the separation of continents and oceans on the earth and the appearance of plant life; (4) the appearance of sun, moon, and stars, due to the breaking up of thick clouds in the atmosphere; (5) the appearance of fish, reptiles and birds; (6) the appearance of mammals, and, finally, man."

As for the formation of the sun, Dr. Hales said the scientific explanation now is that billions of years ago energy was converted into electrons and protons which combined and formed the sun's mass. The sun has, since, been converting its matter back into energy and radiating it throughout the solar system. "To answer the question, 'Where did the original energy come from?' scientists," Dr. Hales said, "can find no answer except the existence and operation of God." (*Deseret News,* Oct. 19, 1938, p. 18.)

CHAPTER 4

1. *The comments of Moroni are continued throughout this chapter.*

2. *Why Mosiah kept the Record.*

1. And the Lord commanded the brother of Jared to go down out of the mount from the presence of the Lord, and write the things which he had seen; and they were forbidden to come unto the children of men until after that he should be lifted up upon the cross; and for this cause did king Mosiah keep them, that they should not come unto the world until after Christ should show himself unto his people.

2. And after Christ truly had

VERSE 1. *For this cause did King Mosiah keep them.* This Mosiah, the son of King Benjamin, was the last of the kings of Zarahemla, preceding the Judges. He was the translator of the contents of the twenty-four plates of gold which were delivered to him by the hands of Limhi. The translation was made by *the means of those two stones which were fastened into the two rims of a bow.* The stones, we read in the Book of Mormon, *were prepared from the beginning, and were handed down from generation to generation, for the purpose of interpreting languages.* (Mosiah 28:11-14) They were in all probability the stones which were given to Moriancumer, and, later, to the Prophet Joseph by the resurrected Prophet of the Nephites, Moroni.

How did King Mosiah get them?

We turn to the Book of Omni. We read there that during the reign of the first Mosiah, the father of King Benjamin, a large stone with engravings thereon was brought to Zarahemla to the king. The king translated the text thereof *by the gift and power of God,* and found that it contained an *account of one Coriantumr and the slain of his people.* Amaleki, the chronicler, adds the explanation that Coriantumr had been found by people from Zarahemla—perhaps by hunters—and that he had lived with them nine moons (we presume months) of his life.

Coriantumr was the last of the kings of the Jaredites of whom we have any historical record, as Ether was the last of their prophets. He fought his savage enemy, Shiz, at Ramah, until both their armies were annihilated. Then he ended the life of his antagonist. He, himself, was left on the battlefield apparently lifeless. But Coriantumr recovered, and began his pilgrimage which eventually ended in Zarahemla. As the head of the government of the Jaredite Kingdom, he may have had charge of the Urim and Thummim and brought them where King Mosiah at last obtained them, together with the historical stone (Omni 19-22).

LIMHI AND AMMON

In the first part of the Book of Mosiah (8:9-19), an interview between King Limhi and a certain Ammon is recorded. Limhi was the son of King Noah and a grandson of Zeniff. Ammon was a descendant of Zarahemla. During the con-

showed himself unto his people he commanded that they should be made manifest.

3. And now, after that, they have all dwindled in unbelief; and there is none save it be the La-

---

versation which followed their making known to each other the positions each held, Ammon was informed that Limhi had in his possession twenty-four plates of gold filled with engravings, and some other artifacts which must have been left by a people who were destroyed long ago. Limhi asked Ammon if he could interpret an ancient language. Ammon said that he could not, but, he added, the King in Zarahemla, Mosiah, the son of Benjamin, had *wherewith that he can look, and translate all records that are of ancient date.* If this relates to the Urim and Thummim, as it undoubtedly does, it is evident that the two stones were no part of the treasures of Limhi, although he had the Plates, and that King Mosiah had the sacred Instruments, or Interpreters, long before he had received the Plates to interpret.

VERSES 3-7. *All dwindled in unbelief.* In this paragraph Moroni tells us that because the Nephites, the people of Christ, had dwindled in unbelief, and that the Lamanites had rejected the Gospel, he had been instructed of the Lord to hide the sacred relics in the earth; they to come forth again at some future time. These relics were, the *Smaller Plates of Nephi*[1] and Mormon's abridgment of the *Larger Plates of Nephi,* together with some additional writings by both Mormon and his son, Moroni, which included a translation of the Twenty-four gold plates what now is the Book of Ether. There were also what constitutes, we presume, the sealed[2]

---

[1]"And now, I speak somewhat concerning that which I have written; for after I had made an abridgment from the Plates of Nephi, down to the reign of this King Benjamin, of whom Amaleki spake, I searched among the records which had been delivered into my hands, and I found these plates, which contained this small account of the prophets, from Jacob down to the reign of this King Benjamin, and also many of the words of Nephi.

"And these things which are upon these plates pleasing me, because of the prophecies of the coming of Christ; and my fathers knowing that many of them have been fulfilled; yea, and I also know that as many things as have been prophesied concerning us down to this day have been fulfilled, and as many as go beyond this day must surely come to pass—

"Wherefore, I chose these things to finish my record upon them, which remainder of my record I shall take from the Plates of Nephi; and I cannot write the hundredth part of the things of my people.

"But behold, I shall take these plates, which contain these prophesyings and revelations, and put them with the remainder of my record, for they are choice unto me; and I know they will be choice unto my brethren." (Words of Mormon 3-6)

[2]The Prophet writes: "These records were engraven on plates which had the appearance of gold; each plate was six inches wide and eight inches long and not quite as thick as common tin. They were filled with engravings, in Egyptian characters, and bound together in a volume as the leaves of a book with three rings running through the whole. The volume was something near six inches in thickness, *part of which was sealed.* (Italics are Editor's) The characters on the unsealed part were small and beautifully engraved. The whole book exhibited many marks of antiquity in its construction, and much skill in the art of engraving. With the records was found a curious instrument, which the ancients called 'Urim and Thummim,' which consisted of two transparent stones set in the rim of a bow fastened to a breastplate. Through the medium of the Urim and Thummim I translated the record by the gift and power of God."

(Joseph Smith, in a letter to John Wentworth, editor of the *Chicago Democrat,* March 1, 1842. *History of the Church,* Vol. 4, p. 535)

It is supposed by some that the *sealed part* of the plates was two-thirds of the whole, and by others that it was but one-third. Both may be wrong. The above statement by the Prophet is the only declaration we have been able to find that was made by him concerning this particular point. It is alleged by those making that estimate that Elder Orson Pratt so stated it as fact; Elder Pratt was a close associate of the Prophet, and may have gleaned the information from him, but anything authentic could come only from Joseph Smith, himself, and so far nothing has been presented which would truly substantiate any claim.

manites, and they have rejected the gospel of Christ; therefore I am commanded that I should hide them up again in the earth.

4. Behold, I have written upon these plates the very things which the brother of Jared saw; and there never were greater things made manifest than those which were manifest unto the brother of Jared.

5. Wherefore the Lord hath commanded me to write them; and I have written them. And he commanded me that I should seal them up; and he also hath commanded that I should seal up the interpretation thereof; wherefore I have sealed up the interpreters,

according to the commandment of the Lord.

6. For the Lord said unto me: They shall not go forth unto the Gentiles until the day that they shall repent of their iniquity, and become clean before the Lord.

7. And in that day that they shall exercise faith in me, saith the Lord, even as the brother of Jared did, that they may become sanctified in me, then will I manifest unto them the things which the brother of Jared saw, even to the unfolding unto them all my revelations, saith Jesus Christ, the Son of God, the Father of the heavens and of the earth, and all things that in them are.

---

portion of the gold plates that were delivered to the Prophet Joseph Smith by the Angel Moroni;[3] the Urim and Thummim and the Breastplate. These sacred things had long been used by the Church of Christ upon this continent, except, of course, the writings of Mormon and Moroni. All these the Prophet entrusted to the motherly bosom of the earth, there to rest until the Gentiles would repent and exercise faith in the Lord. (v. 7)

Moroni, in this Chapter gives a complete understanding of the conditions that would surround the time when the visions recorded by the Brother of Jared should come to the knowledge of the world. He makes mention of two separate times; the first had already taken place as recorded in verse two. The second is to be as the Voice of the Lord declared it to Moroni and placed on record in verses six and seven.

For emphasis we quote verses four and five of this chapter, and suggest to the

---

[3]Convenient to the Village of Manchester, Ontario County, New York, stands a hill of considerable size, and the most elevated of any in the neighborhood. On the west side of this hill, not far from the top, under a stone of considerable size, lay the plates, deposited in a stone box. This stone was thick and rounding in the middle on the upper side, and thinner towards the edges, so that the middle part of it was visible above the ground, but the edge all around was covered with earth.

Having removed the earth, I obtained a lever, which I got fixed under the edge of the stone, and with a little exertion raised it up. I looked in, and there indeed did I behold the Plates, the Urim and Thummim, and the breastplate, as stated by the messenger. The box in which they lay was formed by laying stones together in some sort of cement. In the bottom of the box were laid two stones crossways of the box, and on these stones lay the plates and the other things with them.

I made an attempt to take them out, but was forbidden by the messenger, and was again informed that the time for bringing them forth had not yet arrived, neither would it, until four years from that time. . .

(Joseph Smith, Pearl of Great Price, vv. 51-53, p. 53)

At length the time arrived for obtaining the plates, the Urim and Thummim, and the breastplate. . .

(*Ibid.*, v. 59, p. 54)

student that in its connection he will read verses 23 to 25 of Chapter 12 of this Book. "Behold, I have written upon these plates the very things which the Brother of Jared saw; and there never were greater things made manifest than these which were made manifest unto the Brother of Jared. Wherefore the Lord hath commanded me that I should seal them up; and He also hath commanded that I seal up the interpretation thereof; wherefore I have sealed up the Interpreters, according to the commandment of the Lord." (Ether 4:4-5)

Moroni was bowed down with a burden of care. He had seen his people, the Nephites, the people of Christ, destroyed. All about him was death and nothing appeared to ameliorate the gloom that hovered over all. The Sun shone brightly but the day was dark. Far reaching lands and fertile fields, that in times past had yielded bounteous crops to the labor of the husbandman, were now desolate. The ramparts of cities, once the gardens of their citizens, had been turned into battle-grounds where unburied bodies lay seething in their own filthiness.

As it was in the days before the ministry of the resurrected Redeemer, the Lamanites again chose apostate Nephites to lead their armies.[4] The hatred these apostate Nephites had of their former brethren was intense; their spite was keen and inexhaustible, and of all the passions that occupy the human heart, apostate ill-will is the most bitter and malignant. They left no stone untouched or unturned that they might throw at the crumbling bulwark and battlements of the Christian Religion. They hunted like wild beasts the few remaining Saints who still took upon themselves the Name of Christ, and who would not deny their belief in His Majesty. Wasted lands and ruined cities bore mute evidence of the barbarity of the Lamanite horde that swept over the face of the earth.

3. *Moroni quotes our Lord.*

Moroni, we may feel sure, was about to despair. However, the Lord, seeing his distress, sought to comfort him. With the faith and courage that comes to one after a life of service to the Master, Moroni's heart and mind had become attuned to the whisperings of that *Still Small Voice* which comes from the Father to lead and to guide and to warn of things to come. He, almost overwhelmed with sadness, and notwithstanding the sorrow in his heart, perceived a Voice. "A pleasant Voice, as if it were a whisper"; the Voice of One from On High, Who is mighty and powerful; Whose Voice is unto the ends of the Earth, even the Voice of Jesus Christ: "Come unto Me." (vv. 13 and 14)

Moroni listened attentively to the Voice, and we, too, hear it through him.

---

[4]And thus did he appoint chief captains of the Zoramites, they being the most acquainted with the strength of the Nephites, and their place of resort, and the weakest parts of their cities; therefore he appointed them to be chief captains over his armies. (Alma 48:5)

And it came to pass that the Lamanites came with their thousands; and they came into the Land of Antionum, which is the land of the Zoramites; and a man by the name of Zerahemnah was their leader.

And now, as the Amalekites were of a more wicked and murderous disposition than the Lamanites were, in and of themselves, therefore, Zerahemnah appointed chief captains over the Lamanites, and they were all Amalekites and Zoramites.

And this he did that he might preserve their hatred towards the Nephites, that he might bring them into subjection to the accomplishment of his designs. (Alma 43:5-7)

And they were inspired by the Zoramites and the Amalekites, who were their chief leaders, and by Zerahemnah, who was their chief captain, or their chief leader and commander; yea, they did fight like dragons, and many of the Nephites were slain by their hands, yea, for they did smite in two many of their head-plates, and they did pierce many of their breast-plates, and they did smite off many of their arms; and thus the Lamanites did smite in their fierce anger. (*Ibid.*, 44)

Not a voice like rushing mighty waters, not like thunder upon the distant mountain tops. But a voice like the calm of eventide with healing in its wings. Not in these exact terms, but with a meaning plain that all may understand: "The words of your prophets are the words of 'My servants whom I have sent unto you to declare good tidings.' " (Helaman 5:29) " 'Their words are My words, 'For I am He Who speaketh.' " (v. 8)

In no uncertain terms, but in plainness, that we may quickly comprehend, the Lord, Himself, verifies as His own, the words of His servants. And whether or not we believe their words, at the last day all will know "It is I that speaketh." (v. 10)[5]

And furthermore, the Lord promises that whosoever believeth the words which He has spoken by the mouth of His servants, "him will I visit with the manifestations of My Spirit, and he shall know and bear record. For because of My Spirit he shall know that these things are true; for it persuadeth men to do good." (v. 11)

The Voice of the Lord, Jesus Christ, in His own beautiful but simple words, proclaims the *summum bonum* of all existence, or in other words, the supreme or highest good from which all our blessings come: "Good cometh of none save it be of Me." (v. 12)[6]

We may understand this to mean that not only does good come from Him in a personal manner or relation, but that belief in Him causes men to do only that which is good. In this way *good cometh of Him.*[7]

Some people have the idea that God created evil since they say He created all things, and that by overcoming evil we progress. That is only partly true. We may progress by doing better that which is good. God did not create evil! It, as an opposite to good, always existed.[8]

---

[5]For my soul delighteth in plainness; for after this manner doth the Lord God work among the children of men. For the Lord God giveth light unto the understanding; for He speaketh unto men according to their language, unto their understanding. (II Nephi 31:3)

[6]Wherefore, all things which are good cometh of God; and that which is evil cometh of the devil; for the devil is an enemy unto God, and fighteth against Him continually, and inviteth and enticeth to sin, and to do that which is evil continually. (Moroni 7:12)

And behold, there were divers ways that He did manifest things unto the children of men, which were good; and all things which are good cometh of Christ; otherwise men were fallen, and there could no good thing come unto them. (*Ibid.*, 7:24)

[7]And now, my beloved brethren, and also Jew, and all ye ends of the earth, hearken unto these words and believe in Christ; and if ye believe not in these words believe in Christ. And if ye shall believe in Christ ye will believe in these words, for they are the words of Christ, and He hath given them unto me; and they teach all men that they should do good. (II Nephi 33:10)

And they all cried with one voice, saying: Yea, we believe all the words which thou hast spoken unto us; and also, we know of their surety and truth, because of the Spirit of the Lord Omnipotent, which has wrought a mighty change in us, or in our hearts, that we have no more disposition to do evil, but to do good continually. (Mosiah 5:2)

For behold, the Spirit of Christ is given unto every man, that he may know good from evil; wherefore, I show unto you the way to judge; for every thing which inviteth to do good, and to persuade to believe in Christ, is sent forth by the power and gift of Christ; wherefore ye may know with a perfect knowledge it is of God. (Moroni 7:16)

[8]For it must needs be, that there is an opposition in all things. If not so, my first-born in the wilderness, righteousness could not be brought to pass, neither wickedness, neither holiness nor misery, neither good nor bad. Wherefore, all things must needs be a compound in one; wherefore, if it should be one body it must needs remain as dead, having no life neither death, nor corruption nor incorruption, happiness nor misery, neither sense nor insensibility. (II Nephi 2:11)

And to bring about His eternal purposes in the end of man, after He had created our first parents, and the beasts of the field and the fowls of the air, and in fine, all things which are created, it must needs be that there was an opposition; even the forbidden fruit in opposition to the tree of life; the one being sweet and the other bitter. (*Ibid.*, 2:15)

GOOD

Are Good—

Jacob	5:36	Nevertheless I know that the roots are good
	42	Trees of my vineyard are g. for nothing
	48	Branches . . . overcome the roots which are g.?
Omni	1:25	Languages, and in all things which are good
Moroni	7:5	If their roots be g. then they are g. also
	12	All things which are g., cometh of God
	24	All things which are g., cometh of Christ

Do Good—

2 Nephi	33:4	For it persuadeth them to do g.
	10	They teach all men that they should do g.
Jacob	2:19	Seek them, for the intent to do g.
Mosiah	5:2	To do evil, but to do g. continually
Alma	12:31	Whether to do evil or to do g.
	39:12	Command thy children to do g., lest
	41:7	Own judges whether to do g. or do evil
	14	Judge righteously, and do g. continually
	63:2	And he did observe to do g. continually
Helaman	12:4	Quick to do iniquity, and how slow to do g.
	14:31	And ye can do g. and be restored unto
3 Nephi	12:44	Do g. to them that hate you
Ether	4:11	For it persuadeth men to do g.
	12	Whatsoever thing persuadeth men to do g.
	8:26	That they may be persuaded to do g.
Moroni	7:6	A man being evil cannot do . . . g.
	10	A man being evil cannot do . . . g.
	13	Inviteth and enticeth to do g. continually
	13	Thing which inviteth and enticeth to do g.
	16	Everything which inviteth to do g.
	17	For he persuadeth no man to do g.

Good Thing—

1 Nephi	17:25	It must needs be a g. thing for them
Alma	34:39	For behold, he rewardeth you no g. thing
Moroni	7:19	If ye will lay hold upon every g. thing
	20	That ye can lay hold upon every g. thing?
	21	Whereby ye may lay hold on every g. thing
	22	There should come every g. thing
	24	There could no g. thing come unto them
	25	They did lay hold upon every g. thing
	28	In him, will cleave unto every g. thing

Which is Good—

2 Nephi	2:5	They perish from that which is g.
	26:33	He doeth that which is g. among the children
	28:16	And revile against that which is g.
	20	To anger against that which is g.
Jacob	5:32	And there is none of it which is g.
Omni	1:25	There is nothing which is g. save it
Alma	41:3	Be restored unto that which is g.
	13	G. for that which is g.

Helaman	5:7	That ye should do that which is g.
	7:26	Has lifted you up beyond that which is good
	14:31	Be restored unto that which is g.
	31	Or have that which is g. restored unto
Moroni	7:6	A man being evil cannot do that which is g.
	10	A man being evil cannot do that which is g.
	14	Or that which is g. . . . to be of the devil
	26	Ask the Father in my name, which is g.
	9:19	Delight in everything save that which is g.

Is Good—

2 Nephi	9:29	But to be learned is g.
Jacob	5:61	Which natural fruit is g.
	75	The natural fruit, that it is g.
Alma	5:40	Whatsoever is g., cometh from God
	32:28	Or that the word is g., for it beginneth
	30	You must needs say that the seed is g.
	31	Are ye sure that this is a g. seed?
	32	If a seed groweth it is g.
	33	Ye must needs know that the seed is g.
	35	And whatsoever is light, is g.
	35	Therefore ye must know that it is g.
Moroni	10:6	Whatsoever thing is g., is just and true
	6	Nothing that is g. denieth the Christ

The Good—

2 Nephi	2:30	And I have chosen the g. part
	17:15	Know to refuse the evil and to choose the g.
	16	Know to refuse the evil and choose the g.
Jacob	5:45	They have overcome the g. branch
	59	That the g. may overcome the evil
	65	According to the strength of the g.
	66	According as the g. shall grow
	66	Until the g. shall overcome the bad
	77	Then will I cause the g. and the bad
	77	The g. will I preserve unto myself
	6:7	Ye have been nourished by the g. word
	8	Deny the g. word of Christ, and the
Alma	5:38	That the good shepherd doth call you
	38	Not hearken unto the voice of the g. shepherd
	38	Ye are not the sheep of the g. shepherd

Was Good—

1 Nephi	18:4	My brethren beheld that it was g.
Jacob	5:17	Fruit. And he beheld that it was g.
	20	Fruit, and he beheld also, that it was g.
	75	Of the vineyard saw that his fruit was g.
Mosiah	9:1	When I saw that which was g. among
Alma	11:21	That he might destroy that which was g.
	32:36	Experiment to know if the seed was g.
Helaman	16:22	The people against that which was g.
Ether	10:17	Corom did that which was g. in the sight
	19	Lib also did that which was g. in the sight

Were Good—

Alma	3:26	Their works, whether they were g., or
	41:3	And if their works were g. in this life
	3	And the desires of their heart were g.
Helaman	5:6	Said, and also written, that they were g.
Moroni	7:24	He did manifest things . . . which were g.

Good—

2 Nephi	2:11	Holiness nor misery; neither g. nor bad
	23	Doing no g., for they knew no sin
	3:24	Whether they be g., or whether they be
	5:30	G. in my sight, for the profit of thy people
	15:20	Wo unto them that call evil g., and g.
	25:8	Wherefore, for their g. have I written
	27:14	As many witnesses as seemeth him g.
Jacob	4:11	And obtained a g. hope of glory in him
	5:25	This I have planted in a good spot of
	34	Thou beholdest that they are yet g.
	43	I did plant in a g. spot of ground
Mosiah	3:24	Whether they be g., or whether they be evil
	12:16	Mayest do with him as seemeth thee g.
	21	The feet of him that bringeth g. tidings
	21	That bringeth g. tidings of g.
	15:14	Who have brought g. tidings of g.
	18	The feet of him that bringeth g. tidings
	16:3	Devilish, knowing evil from g.
	10	Whether they be g. or whether they be
	11	If they be g., to the resurrection of end
	18:28	Free will and g. desires towards God
	24:13	Lift up your heads and be of g. comfort
	16	Be of g. comfort, for on the morrow I come
	27:23	Bidding them be of g. comfort
	37	They did publish g. tidings of g.
Alma	1:1	Having warred a g. warfare, walking
	13	A man who has done much g. among
	29	And all manner of g. homely cloth
	3:26	Whether it be a g. spirit or a bad one
	11:44	Whether they be g. or whether they be
	13:3	Therefore they having chosen g.
	17:11	That ye may show forth g. examples
	31	My brethren, be of g. cheer and let us
	21:5	Are not this people as g. as thy people?
	32:28	If it be a true seed, or a g. seed
	28	It must needs be that this is a g. seed
	32	But if it groweth not, behold it is not g.
	39	This is not because the seed was not g.
	37:37	And he will direct thee for g.
	39:1	Has he not set a g. example for thee?
Alma	39:7	If it were not for your g.
	12	Command thy children to do g.
	40:13	They chose evil works rather than g.
	41:5	Or g., according to his desires of g.

	14	Ye shall have g. rewarded unto you again
	48:16	In doing g., in preserving his people
Helaman	5:2	More numerous than they who chose g.
	29	I have sent unto you to declare g. tidings
	8:7	Let this man alone, for he is a g. man
	12:26	They that have done g., shall have everlasting
3 Nephi	1:13	Lift up your head and be of g. cheer
	3:9	The works thereof I know to be g.
	12:13	The salt shall be thenceforth g. for no
	45	The sun to rise on the evil and the g.
	14:11	Being evil know how to give g. gifts unto
	11	Father who is in heaven give g. things
	17	Every g. tree bringeth forth g. fruit
	18	A g. tree cannot bring forth evil fruit
	16:15	Savor, which is thenceforth g. for nothing
	20:40	The feet of him that bringeth g. tidings
	40	That bringeth g. tidings unto them of g.
	26:4	Judged of their works, whether they be g.
	5	If they be g., to the resurrection of everlasting
	27:14	Judged of their works, whether they be g.
	28:30	Unto whatsoever man it seemeth them g.
Ether	4:12	G. cometh of none, save it be of me
	12	I am the same that leadeth men to all g.
	9:23	And did administer that which was g.
	10:16	And he did live to a g. old age
	11:4	He lived to a g. old age and begat Shiblom
Moroni	6:4	And nourished by the g. word of God
	7:5	Know them; for if their works be g.
	10	Neither will he give a g. gift
	11	A bitter fountain cannot bring forth g.
	11	Neither can a g. fountain bring forth bitter
	10:1	I, Moroni, write somewhat as seemeth me g.
	18	That every g. gift cometh of Christ
	25	For there shall be none that doeth g.
	25	If there be one among you that doeth g.
	30	And lay hold upon every g. gift

GOODLY

| 1 Nephi | 1:1 | I, Nephi., having been born of g. parents |
| Mosiah | 18:7 | There were a g. number gathered |

GOODNESS

Goodness of God—see Goodness of God.

Goodness—

1 Nephi	1:1	Had a great knowledge of the g.
	14	Thy power, and g., and mercy are over
2 Nephi	1:10	Brought by his infinite g. into this
	4:17	The great g. of the Lord in showing me
	9:10	O how great the g. of our God
	26:28	They should not partake of his g.?
	33	Come unto him, and partake of his g.

8. And he that will contend against the word of the Lord, let him be accursed; and he that shall deny these things, let him be accursed; for unto them will I show no greater things, saith Jesus Christ; for I am he who speaketh.

9. And at my command the heavens are opened and are shut; and at my word the earth shall shake; and at my command the inhabitants thereof shall pass away, even so as by fire.

10. And he that believeth not my words believeth not my disciples; and if it so be that I do not speak, judge ye; for ye shall know that it is I that speaketh, at the last day.

11. But he that believeth these things which I have spoken, him will I visit with the manifestations of my Spirit, and he shall know and bear record. For because of my Spirit he shall know that these things are true; for it persuadeth men to do good.

12. And whatsoever thing persuadeth men to do good is of me; for good cometh of none save it be of me. I am the same that leadeth men to all good; he that will not believe my words will not believe me—that I am; and he that will not believe me will not believe the Father who sent me. For behold, I am the Father, I am the light and the life, and the truth of the world.

13. Come unto me, O ye Gentiles, and I will show unto you the greater things, the knowledge which is hid up because of unbelief.

14. Come unto me, O ye house of Israel, and it shall be made manifest unto you how great things the Father hath laid up for you, from the foundation of the world; and it hath not come unto you, because of unbelief.

15. Behold, when ye shall rend that veil of unbelief which doth cause you to remain in your awful state of wickedness, and hardness of heart, and blindness of mind, then shall the great and marvelous things which have been hid up from the foundation of the world from you—yea, when ye shall call upon the Father in my name, with a broken heart and a contrite spirit, then shall ye know that the Father hath remembered the covenant which he made unto your fathers, O house of Israel.

Jacob	5:59	May take strength because of their g.
Mosiah	4:11	Or if ye have known of his g.
	11	His g. and long suffering towards you
	27:22	See and know of the g. and glory of God
Alma	19:6	Which was a marvelous light of his g.
	24:7	God has in g. sent these our brethren
	34:4	Ye may try the experiment of its g.
Helaman	12:1	That the Lord in his great infinite g.
	6	Notwithstanding his great g. and his
Mormon	1:15	And know of the g. of Jesus
Moroni	8:3	Through his infinite g. and grace

16. And then shall my revelations which I have caused to be written by my servant John be unfolded in the eyes of all the people. Remember, when ye see these things, ye shall know that the time is at hand that they shall be made manifest in very deed.

17. Therefore, when ye shall receive this record ye may know that the work of the Father has commenced upon all the face of the land.

18. Therefore, repent all ye

VERSES 16-17. *Revelations by My servant John.* Moroni here predicts the unfolding of the Revelations by St. John, the beloved Apostle, as a sign of the approaching end of one dispensation and the beginning of another. "Remember," he says, "When ye see these things—that is the Revelations of John—and when ye shall receive this record—the Book of Ether—ye may know that the work of the Father has commenced upon all the face of the land." We note that the Prophet now addresses both the Gentiles and the House of Israel, and invites them to accept the Gospel in order that their knowledge of God and spiritual things may increase. (vv. 13-14)

This prophecy concerning the unfolding of the Revelations of John has been fulfilled in our day and age. About March 1, 1832, the Prophet Joseph Smith, who at that time lived in Hiram, Portage County, Ohio, received a marvelous "Key" to the Revelation by John. He and Sidney Rigdon had been studying the Scriptures since some time in December, 1830, when the latter was instructed by revelation (Doctrine and Covenants, 35:20) to act as amanuensis to the Prophet, and it was while they were thus engaged that the unfolding took place.

The *Key* to Saint John's Revelations, as given to the Prophet Joseph (*Ibid.*, 77), embraces only the first eleven Chapters of the Book. These form one continuous link of visions concerning "the things which are, and the things which shall be hereafter" (Revelation 1:19). The spiritual conditions of the Church at the time of the close of the first century A.D. are depicted in letters to the churches in Asia Minor (Chapters 2:1-3:22). These are a revelation concerning *the things which are.*

The scene now changes from Earth to the sanctuary in Heaven. There the Apostle had a view of *the things which must come to pass hereafter.* First he saw God, the Father, sitting upon His throne, surrounded by representatives of the entire Creation. There were twenty-four Elders, representing the Church; seven burning lamps, representing the "seven Spirits of God";[9] there was a *sea of glass,* representing the Earth, in its sanctified, immortal, eternal state; there were four *beasts,* or rather *living creatures,* representing "Heaven, the Paradise of God, the happiness of man, and of beasts, and of creeping things, and of fowls of the air, that which is spiritual being in the likeness of that which is temporal." (*Ibid.*, 77:1-2) They are the Cherubim of Ezekiel (Ezekiel 10:1-22), which he saw at the River Chebar. In the Revelation by John, these living creatures glorify God continually, saying, "Holy, holy, holy, is the Lord God Almighty, which was and which is and which is to come"; and when they give honor and glory to God, they are joined by the twenty-four Elders; and unitedly they exclaim, Worthy art Thou, our Lord and our God, to receive the glory and the honor, and the power, for Thou didst create all things, and because of Thy will they were, and are and were created. (See Revelation 4:1-11)

In the next Chapter we read the account of the vision of John, of a Book written on both sides and sealed with seven seals. This Book contained "the revealed will, mysteries, and works of God; the hidden things of His economy concerning this

---

[9]Meaning we believe, the Holy Ghost. The word *seven* always stands for something complete, perfect.

Earth during the seven thousand years of its continuance, or its temporal existence"; each seal representing a thousand years. (Doctrine and Covenants, 77:6-7). The Lamb, the Son of God, receives the Book from the hands of His Father, whereupon the Elders, representing the Church, the angels, of which there are thousands upon thousands; and every created thing join in worshiping Him, as well as the Father, saying, Unto Him that sitteth on the throne, and unto the Lamb, be the blessing, and the honor, and the glory, and the dominion, for ever and ever. And the four living creatures said, *Amen*. And the Elders fell down and worshiped. (*See*, Revelation 5:12-13) That the Lamb was given the Book, to break the seals and unfold the roll, signified that our Lord was made ruler of human history, as the King of kings and the Lord of lords.

The breaking of the seals begins in Chapter 6. The sealing of 144,000 of the Tribes of Israel enumerated, and the worship of an innumerable number of all nations are seen in Chapter 7. (*See*, Doctrine and Covenants, 77:8-11) In Chapters 8 and 9 events are shown that belong to the sixth millennium, immediately preceding the beginning of the seventh, which is the era of the Reign of our Lord upon the earth (*Ibid.*, 77:12-14). In the 10th Chapter a mighty angel with a little book makes his appearance. This is evidently an outstanding feature of the history of the time of the end. The "little book" is "a mission and an ordinance for him (the angel) to gather the Tribes of Israel." "Behold, this is Elias, who, as it is written, must come and restore all things." (*Ibid.*, 77:14)

"That great Prophet, Apostle, and martyr, Joseph Smith, was the Elias, the Restorer, the presiding messenger, holding the keys of the dispensation of the fulness of times,[10] Yes, that extraordinary man . . . was the chosen vessel to be a messenger in the spirit and power of Elijah, to prepare the way of the Lord! For behold! He will suddenly come to His Temple." (Parley P. Pratt, *Key to Theology*, p. 79)

Concerning the *Little Book*, See, also, *An Introduction to the Study of the Book of Mormon*, p. 258. The Book of Mormon is, preeminently, a document authorizing the *Gathering of Israel*.

In the last paragraph of the 10th Chapter of this Revelation, the Apostle John is told: "Thou must prophesy again before many peoples, and nations, and tongues and kings," referring to the part he, together with Peter and James, was assigned in the foundation of the Church of Jesus Christ of Latter-day Saints.

The main feature of the 11th Chapter is the testimony of the Two Witnesses, who will perform a mission among the Jews, "after they are gathered and have built the City of Jerusalem in the land of their fathers." (Doctrine and Covenants, 77:15)

This ends the main part of the Book of Revelation. The *Key* in the Doctrine and Covenants also ends with this Chapter.

The second portion of the Book contains the following additional features, placed there by the inspired author, himself: A vision of a woman and her child, persecuted by a dragon, but miraculously saved (v. 12); a *beast* persecuting the Saints (v. 13); the Lamb (Son of God) on Mount Zion with 144,000 worshipers (v. 14); seven last plagues (v. 15); seven vails of wrath and the Battle of Armageddon, before the coming of the Lord (v. 16); the judgment of a woman on a scarlet-colored beast (v. 17); the fall of Babylon (v. 18); the union of the Lamb and the Saints (v. 19); the Millennium (v. 20); a New Heaven and a New Earth (v. 21); and *Paradise Restored* (v. 22).

These additions were made by the Apostle John, himself, by inspiration, in order to make his Revelation a complete and perfect picture of the history of the

---

[10]Fulness of times is, we understand, the end of the Roll, the Seventh Seal, the Seventh Millennium.

race. Any unauthorized elimination of some of its contents, or any additions thereto from uninspired apocalyptic literature would destroy the unity of the plan, and, by distorting it; distract from its value. Hence the solemn danger signal: "If any man shall add unto these things, God shall add unto him the plagues that are written in this book; And if any man shall take away from the words of the book of this prophecy, God shall take away his part out of the Book of Life, and out of the Holy City, and from the things which are written in this book." (Revelation 22:18-19)

THEORIES ON THE REVELATION

There are, in the main, three theories concerning the time in history, to which the various visions and revelations in the book refer.

The Preterist Interpretation. According to this, most of the contents of the book refer to events in the early days of the Apostolic Church. Grotius, Wetstein, Eichhorn, are among the advocates of this view.

The Historical Interpretation. Others, particularly Protestants, regard the book as a prophetic history of the Church and the world, from the days of the Apostles to the end of time. Among the advocates of this view are, Mede, Sir Isaac Newton, Vitringa, Bishop John Newton, and Dr. Alexander Keith.

The Futurist Interpretation. According to this theory, the greater part of the prophetic contents of the book, if not all of it, will be fulfilled during the last days, before the second advent of our Lord. Among the exponents of this view are Maitland and Burgh.[11]

The explanation of the Prophet Joseph Smith. By this we mean the definition in the Doctrine and Covenants, Section 77, revealed to the Prophet in 1832.

According to these inspired Key-Words, the sealed scroll contained the "revealed will, mysteries and works of God," during seven thousand years of the *temporal existence* of the Earth. The first seal contained the history and revelations of the first one thousand years, the second of the second thousand, and so on until the seventh. During these ages a conflict is raging between the forces of good and of evil. The people of God are suffering oppression again and again, but the outcome of each conflict is a triumphant victory of truth over falsehood, righteousness over sin. Persecuting Rome falls; Jerusalem, where also their Lord was crucified." (Revelation 11:9) is destroyed by an earthquake (v. 13); antichristian Babylon is *thrown down* as a millstone cast into the sea (*Ibid.,* 18:21). Finally, every enemy of the Son of God will be subjected, willingly or unwillingly, to His sovereign rule.

Applying this interpretation, the prophecies in the Book of Revelation, as the events of history, repeat themselves. The denunciations pronounced against Babylon may apply to any other city, to Jerusalem, to pagan Rome, to a persecuting city that has flourished in any age, as well as to the ancient center of civilization on the banks of the River Euphrates. The angel with the little book of Revelation 10, may represent the Prophet Joseph Smith in our age, as well as the Apostle John in his time. The woman with the infant, Chapter 12, may symbolize the Church of Jesus Christ of Latter-day Saints, and not only the first Apostolic Church. For the Latter-day Saints, too, found a refuge in the wilderness under the protecting shelter of the "two wings of a great Eagle" (*Ibid.,* 12:14).

The Doctrine and Covenants has a double interpretation of prophecies. In Section 88, the sounding of seven trumpets is the sign of the Second Advent of our Lord and the first resurrection and judgment (vv. 92-106). Then there is an interval of the Millennium, at the end of which seven angels again sound their trumpets,

---

[11]Dr. Joseph Angus, *Bible Handbook,* pp. 642-643

before the very last battle between the Hosts of Heaven under Michael, the Arch-
angel, and the armies of hell, commanded by the adversary (vv. 108-116), "when
they shall no more see death." Here it is evident that the events symbolized by
the sounding of the seven trumpets in Revelation 8:7-21 and 11:15-19 are repeated
first at the time of the Second Advent and then at the time of the final victory
of our Lord over all enemies, including sin and death.

The Author. It is generally understood and agreed upon among Bible students
that *St. John the Divine*, the author of the Revelation, was the Apostle John, *whom
Jesus loved* (John 21:20). This Apostle was, as far as can be ascertained from the
records, a son of Zebedee and Salome, a sister of the mother of Jesus (Matthew 27:56
and Mark 15:40), and therefore a cousin of our Lord. James, the brother of John,
was also a prominent Apostle.

The Title. "The Revelation of Jesus Christ, which God gave unto Him, to
show His servants things which must shortly come to pass." (Revelation 1:1) When
the Apostles on one occasion asked the Master to tell them something about *the end
of the world,* (Matthew 24:3) He enumerated some of the signs, but concerning
the time He added, "Of that day and that hour knoweth no man, no, not the angels
which are in Heaven, neither the Son, but the Father" (*Ibid.*, 24:36; Mark 13:32;
Acts 1:6-8). Now the Father had given His Son these revelations for the special
purpose of imparting to His people the knowledge needed for their comfort in times
of trial. Our Lord promised through the Prophet Moroni (Ether 4:16), that John
would commit the revelations to writing, and that they would be further unfolded
at the time of the end of the dispensation immediately preceding His Second Advent.

One of John's first visions. The initial vision of the Revelation is that of
Seven Candlesticks, representing an equal number of churches in Asia Minor. A
supernatural Being is seen walking among them. He is, John says, "like unto the
Son of man." He is clothed in a garment reaching the feet. He wears a golden
girdle around his chest. His hair is white as wool, or as snow, and his eyes are
as a flame of fire. The description reminds us of the appearance of the *Ancient of
Days* in Daniel 7:9, who, the Prophet Joseph Smith says, is Michael, or Adam.[12]
The Apostle was so strongly affected by this vision that he fell at his feet as dead
(Revelation 1:17).

It is sometimes assumed that this supernatural Being was our Lord Jesus Christ.
But the text does not say so. The glorious messenger represented our Lord, *"the
First and the Last, He that liveth and was dead and Who liveth for evermore; He
Who hath the keys of the grave and death."* He spoke for Him, and the message
he brought was from Him. But as for further identity, John says he was *like unto
the Son of man.* It is true, this title was conferred upon the Second person in the
Godhead, or was properly assumed by Him (Daniel 7:13; Matthew 8:24; 9:6; 24:30
and many more passages). For as our first ancestor, Adam, was the representative
of the entire human race, and as such is the MAN, so Jesus, the Savior of MAN,
became the Second Adam, and such is the representative of the entire race (I Corinthians 15:45-47). He bore the likeness of Adam, the representative of MAN.[13]

We are inclined to the view that the Supernatural Being who appeared in the

---

[12]Daniel speaks of the Ancient of Days. He means the oldest man, our father Adam
(Michael). He will call his children together and hold a council with them, to prepare them
for the Son of Man. He (Adam) is the father of the human family, and presides over the
spirits of all men; and all that have the keys must stand before him in this grand council.
This may take place before some of us leave this stage of action." (*Journal of Discourses,*
Volume 6, p. 238)

[13]The expression *Son of Man* occurs about a hundred times in the prophetic Book of
Ezekiel. *Son* in the Hebrew sometimes means an individual of a class, and is so understood
in Ezekiel. It is the same as *man.*

initial vision of this book was the Holy Spirit, and not the Son of God, Who afterwards appears as a Lamb standing as though it had been slain (Revelation 5:6). Our reason for this suggestion is a very obvious one, that this messenger instructs John to end all the dictated letters to the churches thus: *He that hath an ear, let him hear what the Spirit saith unto the churches.* The natural inference is that, while the message comes from the Son, the Messenger is the Spirit. If this interpretation is correct, the Holy Spirit appeared in this vision as he made himself known to the young Prophet Nephi, who says: I spake to him as a man speaketh; for I beheld that he was in the form of a man; yet, nevertheless, I knew that it was the Spirit of the Lord; and He spake unto me as a man speaketh with another (I Nephi 11:9-12; compare 10:11).

Beginning of history. The student of the predictions and prophetic visions concerning the seven millenniums, or seven thousand years, should be cautioned against regarding these figures as proving that the Earth was created about four thousand years before our era; that, in other words, the total age of our orb now (1960) is only about 5960 years. There is, as far as we know, no support of such a notion anywhere in the Sacred Literature of the world. On the contrary, the Scriptures give us to understand that that time is but a brief period of the life of our earthly habitation.

In the Doctrine and Covenants, Section 77:6-7, we read as follows:

"What are we to understand by the book which John saw, which was sealed on the back with seven seals?

"We are to understand that it contains the revealed will, mysteries, and works of God; the hidden things of His economy concerning this earth during the seven thousand years of its continuance, or its temporal existence."

"What are we to understand by the seven seals with which it was sealed?

"We are to understand that the first seal contains the things of the first thousand years, and the second also of the second thousand years, and so on until the seventh."

Temporal existence we understand to mean *being*, or existence in time. We may express this thought somewhat differently, and say that the prophecies do not concern themselves with geological ages, except as far as they recognize God as the Creator and Ruler of all existence. They deal with history and historical facts, or periods. We read again from the Doctrine and Covenants, Section 77:12, concerning the seven trumpets:

"We are to understand that as God made the world in six days and on the seventh day He finished His work, and sanctified it and also formed man out of the dust of the earth; even so, in the beginning of the seventh thousand years will the Lord God sanctify the earth, and complete the salvation of man, and judge all things, and shall redeem all things except that which He hath not put into His power, when He shall have sealed all things; and the sounding of the trumpets of the seven angels, are the preparing, and finishing of His work, in the beginning of the seventh thousand years;—the preparing of the way before the time of His coming."

Thus the limits of the prophetic vision are clearly defined. It is, as it were, only a week, from Sabbath to Sabbath, in the life of the Earth.

Chronological tables compared. As is well known, the genealogical records of Genesis begin with Adam, the first man, about 4000 B.C., as calculated by Bishop Usher. These are the Hebrew records. The tables in the Samaritan version of the Bible, and the seventy translators differ somewhat from the Hebrew figures, but we need not enter in that here. If we now add the 1960 years of our era to the 4000 preceding years, we have a total 5960 years as the age of the human race. If, further, we understand that each 1000 years represent one prophetic day, we find ourselves now living very near the close of the sixth day, there being only 40 common years before the seventh millennium, that is to see the Second Advent of our Lord.

We are not intending this as prediction; much less as an inspired prophecy; we are only trying to point out an unavoidable conclusion from the extant records, provided they have come to us as they were originally written, and provided also that our interpretation of them is correct.

Egyptian records are interesting for the sake of comparison, since Moses had his first education in Egypt. Manetho, an Egyptian historian (323-283 B.C.) allows, we are told,[14] 3555 Egyptian, or 3553 Julian years from Menes, the first ruler in Egyptian annals, until the end of the 30th dynasty, 340 B.C. add the 1960 of our era to the 3553 of Menes, we have a total of 5853 years as the age of history. This is remarkably close to the Hebrew 5960 years from our first ancestor, Adam.

MOSIAH I

Mosiah resided in the Land of Nephi and lived there during the latter half of the third century before Christ. Whether he was originally a prophet, priest or king, the historian (Amaleki) does not inform us. Most certainly he was a righteous man for the Lord made choice of him to guide the obedient Nephites from their choice country to a land that he would show them.

The causes that led the Lord to make this call upon the Nephites are not stated but some of them can be easily surmised. Among such we suggest that:

The aggressive Lamanites were constantly crowding upon them, ravaging their more remote districts, entrapping and enslaving the inhabitants of the outlying settlements, driving off their flocks and herds and keeping them in a constant state of anxiety and dread which hindered their progress and stayed the growth of the work of God. The Lord therefore led them to a land of peace.

Again, this course of events continued for so long a period, had caused much hard-heartedness and stiff-neckedness in the midst of the Nephites. Some of the people had remained righteous, some had grown very wicked. To separate these classes the Lord called the faithful and obedient to follow Mosiah to another land.

For a third reason there was a portion of the house of Israel a few hundred miles to the north entirely unknown to their Nephite brethren. These people had sunk very low in true civilization, they were so degraded that they denied the being of their Creator, they had had many wars and contentions among themselves, they had corrupted their language, had no records nor scriptures and were altogether in a deplorable condition. To save and regenerate this branch of God's covenant people Mosiah and the Nephites were led to the place where they dwelt.

The statement made by Amaleki regarding this great migration under Mosiah is brief. We are altogether left to our imagination to picture the scenes that occurred at this division of a nation. Nor can we tell how many, preferring home, kindred and friends and the endearments and associations of their native land, faltered and tarried behind, while the faithful started on their journey northward into the untrodden wilderness. Nor are we informed what afterwards became of those who allowed the allurements of the world to prevail. It is most probable that they united with the Lamanites, were absorbed into that race and like them became darkened, bloodthirsty and savage.

The Nephite evacuation of the cities built in the land of Nephi no doubt had a beneficial effect on those portions of the Lamanite race that took possession of them. They thereby became acquainted with some of the comforts and excellencies of civilization and though very slow to learn, their experience at this time laid the foundation for a slight advance of the arts of peace in their midst.

Mosiah gathered up the willing and obedient and as directed by the Lord,

---

[14]Victor Rydberg.

started on the journey. Whither they were going they understood not, only they knew that the Lord was leading them. With preachings and prophesyings they crossed the wilderness and passed down into the land of Zarahemla.

On the west bank of the river Sidon the people of Mosiah found a populous city, of whose existence they had never before heard. Its people were a semi-civilized and irreligious race, speaking a strange language and with many habits and customs different from those of the newcomers.

The meeting must have been a perplexing one to both people, brought face to face but unable to understand each other by reason of their different modes of speech. We often read in history of the irruption of an inferior or more barbarous race into the domains of a more highly civilized one but it is seldom, as in this case, that the superior race moves in a body, occupies the country and unites with the less enlightened people. It is probable that the first feelings of the old settlers were akin to dismay as they learned of the hosts of the invaders that were marching upon them but these feelings were soon soothed and an understanding arrived at by which the two peoples became one nation. We are forced to the conclusion that this arrangement could not have been affected without the direct interposition of heaven by and through which both peoples were brought to a united purpose and common understanding.

When the Nephites began to comprehend the language of their new fellow citizens they found that they were the descendants of a colony which had been led from Jerusalem by the hand of the Lord in the year that that city was destroyed by the king of Babylon (say B.C. 589). At this time their king or ruler was named Zarahemla (about B.C. 200). The reason assigned for their departure from the worship of the true God, their degradation and the corruption of their language was that their forefathers brought with them from their ancient home in Palestine no records or copies of the holy scriptures to guide and preserve them from error in their isolated land of adoption.

When the two races joined it was decided that Mosiah should be the king of the united people though the Nephites were then the less numerous. This arrangement probably grew out of the fact that though fewer in numbers they were the more civilized and also being worshipers of the God of Israel they would not willingly submit to be ruled by those who had no knowledge of His laws.

The education of the people of Zarahemla to the standard of the Nephites and the work of harmonizing the two races were not the task of an hour. It required much wisdom, patience and perseverance. Mosiah gave stability to the new kingdom by his own virtues and wise example, by the just laws he established and by placing the service of the Lord before all earthly considerations. It is evident that he built a temple in the new land as its existence is particularly mentioned in the days of his son, King Benjamin and as the people observed the law of Moses in the matter of sacrifices and offerings a temple would be one of their very first necessities. But to the forms, types and ceremonies of the Mosaic law were added gospel principles with a clear and definite understanding of the coming and divine work of the Messiah. Mosiah was not only a divinely inspired leader and king but he was also a seer. While reigning in Zarahemla a large engraved stone was brought to him and by the gift and power of God he translated the engravings thereon. They gave an account of the rise, fall and destruction of the great Jaredite nation from the days of its founders to the time of their last king Coriantumr, who himself was discovered by the people of Zarahemla and lived with them nine moons. When Mosiah died he was succeeded by his son Benjamin.

MOSIAH II

The third king of the Nephites in the Land of Zarahemla where he was born B.C. 154; he was consecrated king by his father Benjamin, B.C. 124 and died in Zarahemla, B.C. 91, aged 63 years. He came to the throne under most happy circumstances, he had the full confidence of his subjects, who were a righteous, God-fearing people, the Lamanites were at peace with the Nephites and internal development and prosperity characterized the condition of his kingdom. Individually he proved to be one of the greatest and best of kings; his whole energies were devoted to the good of his people, who loved him with an intensity of affection scarcely equaled in the annals of any race. In the fourth year of his reign the expedition under Ammon started which resulted in the return to Zarahemla of nearly all the living descendants of the company that left under Zeniff to re-occupy the land of Lehi-Nephi. The leader of one of these companies was Alma, the elder, whom Mosiah called to take charge of the church in Zarahemla. Soon after the arrival of these fugitives from the Land of Nephi, Mosiah gathered all the people together and had them made acquainted with the vicissitudes and sorrows through which the newcomers had passed since their fathers left Zarahemla. Also taking advantage of the presence of so many of his subjects he addressed them on such matters as he deemed necessary and desirable. At his request Alma also taught them. When assembled in large bodies Alma went from one multitude to another preaching repentance and faith in the Lord; afterwards, by Mosiah's direction, he went through the land organizing and establishing churches and ordaining priests and teachers over every church. Thus were seven churches established at this time in the Land of Zarahemla.

In the course of years many of the rising generation gave no heed to the word of God. These were mostly such as were too young to enter into covenant with the Lord at the time that Benjamin anointed Mosiah to be his successor. Not only did they themselves reject the doctrines of the atonement, the resurrection and other gospel principles but they led away many who were members of the Church and sorely persecuted those who remained faithful to God and His laws. Encouraged by the fact that four of Mosiah's sons and one of Alma's were leaders in this crusade they paid no attention to the national law which guaranteed freedom of conscience to all men alike. By divine interposition, through a holy angel, these young men were turned from the error of their way and afterwards became strong pillars in the church and messengers of salvation to both Nephite and Lamanite. For the four sons of Mosiah (named Aaron, Ammon, Omner and Himni) not content with their zealous labors among their countrymen proposed to go and labor among the Lamanites. The good king, like many of his subjects, did not favorably regard this proposal. He feared for the lives of his sons but having inquired of the Lord and received assurances of heavenly protection he gladly let them go.

Mosiah now felt that it was time that the question of the succession to the throne should be settled. In his magnanimity he sent among the people to learn whom they would have for their king. The people chose his son Aaron but Aaron would not accept the royal power, his heart was set upon the conversion of his fellow-men to the knowledge of the gospel. This refusal troubled the mind of Mosiah, he apprehended difficulties if Aaron at some future time should change his mind and demand his rights. Mosiah therefore issued another address in which he proposed to retain the kingdom during the remainder of his life after which the Nephites should be governed by judges elected by themselves. In other respects also Mosiah consented to newly arrange the affairs of the people and if we may so

ends of the earth, and come unto me, and believe in my gospel, and be baptized in my name; for he that believeth and is baptized shall be saved; but he that believeth not shall be damned; and signs shall follow them that believe in my name.

19. And blessed is he that is found faithful unto my name at the last day, for he shall be lifted up to dwell in the kingdom prepared for him from the foundation of the world. And behold it is I that hath spoken it. Amen.

---

express it, to codify the laws. This code became the constitution of the nation under the rule of the Judges which limited the powers of the officials, and guaranteed the rights of the people. This compilation was acknowledged by the people whereupon the historian remarks "Therefore they were obliged to abide by the laws which he had made" and from that time they became supreme throughout the nation. It is stated in another place that this change was made by the direct command of Jehovah. But besides being a king Mosiah was also a seer. The gift of interpreting strange tongues and languages was his. By this gift he translated from the twenty-four plates of gold, found by the people of King Limhi, the record of the Jaredites. No wonder that a man possessed of such gifts, so just and merciful in the administration of the law, so perfect in his private life, should be esteemed more than any man by his subjects and they waxed strong in their love towards him. As a king he was a father to them but as a prophet, seer and revelator he was the source from whence divine wisdom flowed unto them.

His sons having started on their missions to the Lamanites (B.C. 91) Mosiah gave the sacred plates and the associate holy things into the care of the younger Alma and the same year passed away to the rest of the Just.

CHAPTER 5

1. Instructions to Translators Concerning Sealed Portion—2. Three Witnesses.

This Chapter is one of the last contributions to the Book of Mormon. It was added by Moroni to the record he received from his father, Mormon, after the battle between the Nephites and the Lamanites at Cumorah, which record he completed and hid in the famous Hill (Mormon 8:4-14).

1. *Instructions to translators.*

1. And now I, Moroni, have written the words which were commanded me, according to my memory; and I have told you the things which I have sealed up; therefore touch them not in order that ye may translate; for that thing is forbidden you, except by and by it shall be wisdom in God.

2. And behold, ye may be privileged that ye may show the plates unto those who shall assist to bring forth this work;

2. *Three witnesseses.*

3. And unto three shall they be shown by the power of God; wherefore they shall know of a surety that these things are true.

Verse 1. *The things which I have sealed up.* Authentic descriptions of the original Book-of-Mormon Plates note the fact that a considerable part of the golden record was sealed. Martin Harris so informed Professor Charles Anthon, New York, in their strange interview in 1828. In this Chapter Moroni furnishes the interesting information that he had written the words commanded him, from memory, referring possibly, more especially, to Chapters 3 and 4; and that the things he had told from memory had been sealed up. These things, consequently, formed part of the sealed portion of the Plates.

I have told you. This may indicate that the wonderful story of the interview of Moriancumer, the Brother of Jared, with the Lord on the mountain, as we can read it in the Book of Ether, was part of a sermon of Moroni at some public assembly before the final conflict at Cumorah.

Touch them not. Moroni addresses this admonition to future translators. They must leave the sealed portion alone, until otherwise directed by the Lord. There must be some strong reason for this precaution. Our surmise is that the exceedingly glorious manifestations of God on Mount Shelem, translated into imperfect human language, would have been incomprehensible to the world at the time of the coming forth of the Book of Mormon, and that ignorance and bigotry at that time would have martyred the Prophet Joseph long before the completion of his mission on Earth if these visions had been put into print.

Verse 2. *Ye may show the Plates.* Nevertheless, Moroni says, ye may be privileged to show the Plates to certain friends. This was also necessary as a corroboration of the testimony of the Prophet.

Verses 3-4. Moroni here predicts that three witnesses will be selected to view the Plates by the power of God. They will thereby be competent to confirm the

4. And in the mouth of three witnesses shall these things be established; and the testimony of three, and this work, in the which shall be shown forth the power of God and also his word, of which the Father, and the Son, and the Holy Ghost bear record—and all this shall stand as a testimony against the world at the last day.

5. And if it so be that they repent and come unto the Father in the name of Jesus, they shall be received into the kingdom of God.

6. And now, if I have no authority for these things, judge ye; for ye shall know that I have authority when ye shall see me, and we shall stand before God at the last day. Amen.

---

testimony of the Prophet Joseph Smith. Moroni was familiar with the prediction in II Nephi 27:12-14, concerning the Three Witnesses, and he corroborated this prophetic utterance by revealing his own inspired vision of the future.[1]

THE THREE WITNESSES

The translation of the Book of Mormon was completed in June 1829. Intimate friends of the Prophet had been given to understand that three witnesses, according to the record itself, would get the privilege to see the original plates (II Nephi 27: 12; Ether 5:3, 4), and to testify to their actual existence, as revealed "by the grace of God"; also to the accuracy of the translation. Naturally, Martin Harris, Oliver Cowdery and David Whitmer, who, at various times, had befriended the Prophet, when he needed friends, were anxious to be selected for that mission. They all made it a subject of prayer, and the answer came on June 29, 1829, in a revelation recorded in the Doctrine and Covenants, Section 17. A short time previously, it had been intimated to David Whitmer, in a revelation, that he might be called upon to be a witness to the world (Section 14:8).

A few days after the revelation, Section 17, had been received, the Prophet Joseph, Oliver Cowdery, David Whitmer and Martin Harris went to a secluded place in the woods, where they engaged in prayer. To begin with they felt no response. Martin Harris, listening to the voice of his own conscience, withdrew from his brethren, greatly distressed. The three renewed their petitions. Almost immediately, a brilliant light shone above them, and a heavenly messenger descended and stood before them. He had the Book of Mormon plates in his hands and turned, leaf after leaf. To David Whitmer he said, "David, blessed is the Lord, and he that keeps his commandments." Then a voice coming from the light above them said: "These plates have been revealed by the power of God, and they have been translated by the power of God. The translation of them which you have seen is correct, and I command you to bear record of what you now see and hear."

Shortly afterwards, Martin Harris, who had been joined by the Prophet, had a similar manifestation, whereupon he arose and cried out in joy, "'Tis enough! Tis enough! Mine eyes have beheld! Mine eyes have beheld!"

This is, briefly, the plain story of the calling of the three witnesses. Is there any rational explanation of it, except that it is true? Can it be fiction? Was the angel an impostor? Was the light a fake? Would a trick have been convincing to these three men, or to any of them?

---

[1]For detailed accounts of the Three Witnesses, *See, Essentials of Church History*, pp. 72-80, Joseph Fielding Smith. Also, *An Introduction to the Study of the Book of Mormon*, pp. 47-66, Janne M. Sjodahl.

The messenger who appeared must have been a supernatural being. A friend of Joseph, playing that part, would have been known to the others, too. They would have detected the fraud immediately. An unscrupulous stranger, who might have been induced to take a role in a tableau vivant of this nature, would not have kept his secret long, when unimpeachable damning testimony to that fact might have brought him a fortune from adversaries of the Prophet. Advocates of the impossible theory of fraud, if there are any such left, ignore the light, the fervent prayers, the peculiar experience of Martin Harris, and the unfeigned joy of the four friends after the vision.

It has been the boast of so-called sleight-of-hand performers that they can duplicate every trick of spiritists, no matter how astounding; but here is a plain divine manifestation of which no human art, or ingenuity, can furnish an imitation.

But, What about the Witnesses? Did they not apostatize and repudiate their testimonies?

Never!

Two of them parted company with the Prophet for a short time, and one for the rest of his life, but none of them ever denied his testimony, or the divine calling of the Prophet Joseph.

"So it was with David Whitmer until his death. He believed that Joseph had been led astray, first, into receiving the Melchizedek Priesthood as well as the Aaronic Priesthood. That he received the Aaronic Priesthood and was ordained under the hand of John the Baptist he admitted and believed, but he denied any ordination under the hands of Peter, James and John to the Melchizedek Priesthood, and consequently he went to work and organized a church and a presidency after the order of the Aaronic Priesthood. But never, up to the time of death, did he deny his testimony as one of the three witnesses, and in his dying words he declared that his testimony contained in this book"—the Book of Mormon—"is true." (*Gospel Doctrine,* by President Joseph F. Smith, p. 590.)

Oliver Cowdery. "He left the Church because he lost the love of truth; and after he had traveled alone for years, a gentleman walked into his law office and said to him, 'Mr. Cowdery, what do you think of the Book of Mormon now? Do you believe that it is true?' He replied, 'No, sir, I do not!' 'Well,' said the gentleman, 'I thought as much; for I concluded that you had seen the folly of your ways, and had resolved to renounce what you once declared to be true.' 'Sir, you mistake me; I do not believe that the Book of Mormon is true; I am past belief on that point for I know that it is true, as well as I know that you now sit before me.' 'Do you still testify that you saw an angel?' 'Yes, as much as I see you now and I know the Book of Mormon to be true.'" (*Discourses of Brigham Young,* Selected by Dr. John A. Widtsoe, p. 168)

Martin Harris moved to Clarkston, Cache County, Utah, where he passed away on July 10, 1875, in full fellowship with the Church. In a letter to President George A. Smith, dated July 9, that year, Martin Harris Jr. wrote:

"He was taken ill a week ago yesterday with some kind of stroke. * * * He has continued to talk and testify to the truth of the Book of Mormon, and was in his happiest mood when he could get somebody to listen to his testimony. * * * The last audible words he has spoken were something about the three witnesses to the Book of Mormon.' (*Introduction to the Study of the Book of Mormon,* p. 60)

CHAPTER 6

1. *A Miraculous Voyage*—2. *The People Became Numerous*—3. *Orihah Appointed King.*

1. *A miraculous voyage.*

1. And now I, Moroni, proceed to give the record of Jared and his brother.

2. For it came to pass that the Lord had prepared the stones which the brother of Jared had carried up into the mount, the brother of Jared came down out of the mount, and he did put forth the stones into the vessels which were prepared, one in each end thereof; and behold, they did give light unto the vessels.

3. And thus the Lord caused

After the Lord had prepared the Stones, Moroni interrupted, at Ether 3:16, his abridgment of the translation of the Book of Ether made by King Mosiah (Mosiah 28:13; Ether 4:1). He did so in order to insert his own commentaries.[1] In this chapter he resumes his rendition of Ether's narrative.

VERSES 1-12. *They got aboard of their barges, and set forth into the sea.* This is Ether's account of the miraculous voyage of the Jaredites from their port of embarkation to some part of the American Continents. There were eight vessels (Ether 3:1); they were lighted by means of luminous stones; they were driven by a furious wind toward the Promised Land; sometimes they were in the depths of the sea; divine services were held every day and every night, continuously, judging from the information recorded in verse 9: "The Brother of Jared did sing praises unto the Lord, and he did thank and praise the Lord all day long; and when the night came, they did not cease to praise the Lord." As the fire on the altar of burnt-offerings, during the Mosaic economy, was kept burning continually because it had come from Heaven (Leviticus 9:24), so the praises of the Jaredites to God kept ascending day and night, naturally under the direction and supervision of the Brother of Jared.

Dancing. Let us here note, in passing, that although songs of praise are mentioned as the main feature of the divine services of the Jaredites, it is almost certain that the rhythmical movement called *dance* accompanied their worship. Primitive peoples knew how to express their emotions—joy or sorrow, love or hatred—by means of gestures and movements. Egyptians, Greeks, Romans, all had their sacred dances which were performed on special occasions. In all probability, dancing was originally religious worship, although it gradually degenerated into worldly pastime, and even into unmitigated profanity. Among the Jews, during the Mosaic order of things, it certainly was a ceremony by which the people intended to show their loyalty to God,[2] and to praise Him for favors and mercies they had received. This is apparent from these quotations:

"And Miriam the prophetess, the sister of Aaron, took a timbrel in her hand; and all the women went out after her with timbrels and with dances. And Miriam answered them, Sing ye to the Lord, for He hath triumphed gloriously; . . ." (Exodus 15:20-21)

---

[1]The Book of Ether, as we have it, may have been, originally, a lecture on the Twenty-four Plates, delivered by Moroni before the conflict at Cumorah. That would account for the interpolations.

[2]Or to some pagan deity.

stones to shine in darkness, to give light unto men, women, and children, that they might not cross the great waters in darkness.

4. And it came to pass that when they had prepared all manner of food, that thereby they might subsist upon the water, and also food for their flocks and herds, and whatsoever beast or animal or fowl they should carry with them—and it came to pass that when they had done all these things they got aboard of their vessels or barges, and set forth into the sea, commending themselves unto the Lord their God.

5. And it came to pass that the Lord God caused that there should be a furious wind blow upon the face of the waters, towards the promised land; and thus they were tossed upon the waves of the sea before the wind.

6. And it came to pass that they were many times buried in the depths of the sea, because of the mountain waves which broke upon them, and also the great and terrible tempests which were caused by the fierceness of the wind.

7. And it came to pass that when they were buried in the deep there was no water that could hurt them, their vessels being tight like unto a dish, and also they were tight like unto the ark of Noah; therefore when they were encompassed about by many waters they did cry unto the Lord, and he did bring them forth again upon the top of the waters.

8. And it came to pass that the wind did never cease to blow towards the promised land while they were upon the waters; and thus they were driven forth before the wind.

9. And they did sing praises

"And David danced before the Lord with all his might . . . so David and all the House of Israel brought up the Ark of the Lord with shouting and with the sound of the trumpet." (II Samuel 6:14-15)

"Praise ye the Lord . . . Praise Him with the timbrel and the dance; praise Him with the stringed instruments and organ." (Psalm 150:1-4)

The Indians have always been noted for dancing, as they understand the terpsichorean art, and to this day some of them are still practicing the rhythmic movement of their bodies as a religious performance. In the *American Anthropologist* for April and June, 1923, there are interesting notes on *Two Pueblo Feasts* by Esther S. Goldfrank on the reverence paid to St. Joseph and St. Elizabeth. Bancroft, in *Native Races,* describes dancing by natives in widely separated localities, both the religious, dignified kind, and the degenerated variety. Referring to the first-mentioned class, he says that the dances were portraying love, jealousy, hatred, and friendship; "men and women dance in honor of the spirit of the sea." Among the Veeards, he says, "When the dance is concluded, an orator pronounces a thanksgiving oration. The Cahrocs have a similar festival which they call 'The Feast of Propitiation.' The chief personage of the day is called 'The Charega,' which is the appellation of their deity."

Recent instances of Indian religious dances. Newspapers often note the holding of dance festivals by the Indian tribes of North America. One such is recorded to have been effected by the Hopi Indians of Arizona on August 26, 1934. The Indians danced and prayed for rain. Hundreds of visitors, curious to see the result, con-

unto the Lord; yea, the brother of Jared did sing praises unto the Lord, and he did thank and praise the Lord all the day long; and when the night came, they did not cease to praise the Lord.

10. And thus they were driven forth; and no monster of the sea could break them, neither whale that could mar them; and they did have light continually, whether it was above the water or under the water.

11. And thus they were driven

---

gregated. Dispatches from Oaraibi, Arizona, the following day related that a thunderstorm had broken the drought, and that the Indians and the tourists were watching the rain with mounting enthusiasm and relief. On July 6, 1936, something similar happened. A dispatch from Ganada, Arizona, said that rains had drenched the Tohatchi and Fluted Mountains, and that showers watered fifteen millions of acres in answer to the dancing and supplications of the native Navajo medicinemen.

Origin of the religious dance. This peculiar feature of Indian culture is, we believe, and as we see it, an inheritance from their Asiatic forebears. We know from Ether 8:11, that the Jaredites were familiar with dancing, and that some of the followers of Lehi in the ship they constructed at Irreantum blasphemously combined dancing with drunkenness and other forms of debauchery (I Nephi 18:9). From the Book of Mormon it is, therefore, evident that the leaders of both these lines of immigration brought the religious dance with them to the Promised Land.

A verifying tradition. Elsewhere we have called attention to a Navajo Indian tradition which seems to verify and corroborate the accounts of Nephi as regards dancing. Here we desire to give further details concerning that tradition, as kindly furnished us by Elder J. Fred Evans, of Council Bluffs, Iowa, in a letter dated November 3, 1938. He says:

"I have checked up on the reference in Brasseur de Bourbourg's 'Quatre Lettres sur le Mexique,[3] published in Paris, in 1868. On page 401 he gives us a translation of several native Indian documents comprising 46 pages, and entitled 'Corroborating Documents.' No. 1, 'History of the Mexican Nation,' manuscript in the Nahuatl language of the year 1576, comes from the collection of Boturini.

"On page 403 Brasseur de Bourbourg translates this native Indian document thus:

"*Mexican History.*[4] This is the beginning of the arrival of the Mexicans from the place called Aztlan. It was through the midst of the waters that they made their way to this place. There were four tribes. While enroute they rowed on the ships. On the way they built their ships at a place called, the cave of Quinevayan. From this place came eight tribes.

"Here was the development of smelting by fire. They came from their home toward the rising sun, from the place called, 'On the shore of the sea.' For it was on the shore by the sea that the ore, smelted by the fire, was brought to this place, without being very heavy. On the way they smelted the ore by means of the heat of the water. On the way they built their ships, launching them in the water, at the place called, The Cave of the Earth, whence they embarked, at the same place from which came the eight ships made by the heat."

This is an exceedingly interesting tradition, and, if the document that contains it is genuine, is as important as it is instructive.[5] But the comments by the learned abbe, particularly on *rowed*, are equally striking. He writes, p. 403:

---

[3]Four Letters on Mexico.
[4]The translation from the French is by Elder Evans.
[5]Brasseur de Bourbourg (1840-1874) was a French abbe' and archaeologist. He served in his ecclesiastical calling in Quebec and Boston. Finally he went as a missionary to Mexico, and while there he wrote his, *Ancient Monuments of Mexico.*

forth, three hundred and forty and four days upon the water.

12. And they did land upon the shore of the promised land. And when they had set their feet upon the shores of the promised land they bowed themselves down up-

on the face of the land, and did humble themselves before the Lord, and did shed tears of joy before the Lord, because of the multitude of his tender mercies over them.

"Aztlan, name given by the traditions to the country that was thought to be the primeval home of the Mexicans, and that I long believed to be Asia.

"They rowed, *macevaya*, translated ordinarily 'to dance,' 'to do penance,' etc., but no where by the word *row*, that I have used here."

As is apparent, several particulars in this document have a striking resemblance to certain historical facts recorded in the Book of Mormon. For instance:

1. Two immigrations seem to be indicated, one consisting of four, and one of eight tribes.

2. They came from the same place, or home, Aztlan (Asia), situated toward the *rising sun*, the east.

3. In a camp called, *On the Shore of the Sea*, they procured ore for ship-building. Compare Lehi on the shore of Irreantum (I Nephi 17:5, 9-11, and 16), where it is recorded that Nephi procured ore he needed by smelting; also Ether 2:13 and 3:1, where we read about the Jaredites at the Camp Moriancumer, by the *great sea which divideth the land*. It was there that the leader of the little colony melted out of rocks he gathered on Mt. Shelem the sixteen stones he needed for purposes of illumination.

4. Enroute, the tradition says, the pilgrims *rowed*, or as Abbe' Brasseur de Bourbourg explains against his own conviction, *danced* on the ships.

5. The document translated by the Abbe' seems to have preserved features of the history of the Jaredites and the Lehites and joined both sets together into one tradition. This is what might be expected, since the Twenty-four Plates of the Jaredite historians and the records of the Nephites were kept together for centuries by the same custodians, in common depositories. That, too, is corroborative of the Book of Mormon.

VERSE 11. *Long Voyage.* The Jaredites were 344 days crossing the water. The Ark of Noah sheltered its tenants for one year and eleven days (Genesis 7:11 and 8:14). The inference is that the barges crossed the ocean at a parallel, where the "sea that divideth the lands" is wider than the Bering Sea, also known as the Sea of Kamchatka.

VERSE 12. *And they did land.* Where they landed is a geographical question that must be left unanswered as yet. In the *Story of the Book of Mormon* by one of the authors hereto (President George Reynolds of the First Council of Seventy) says that "it is generally understood" it was south of the Gulf of California and north of the Isthmus of Panama. That is somewhere on the west coast of Southern Mexico or Central America. Before this theory is dismissed, it should be remembered that the Jaredites came here about 4000 years ago (Usher's chronology), when some of the after-effects of the last glacial period may still have been lingering along our west coasts, with floating icebergs and raging new storms. The Jaredites were looking for a land, *choice above all the lands of the earth.* (Ether 1:42) That was the promise made to them. But they would not have found such a place in the far north at that time in the age of the earth; nor in the extreme south. But

2. The people become numerous.

13. And it came to pass that they went forth upon the face of the land, and began to till the earth.

14. And Jared had four sons; and they were called Jacom, and Gilgah, and Mahah, and Orihah.

15. And the brother of Jared also begat sons and daughters.

16. And the friends of Jared and his brother were in number about twenty and two souls; and they also begat sons and daughters before they came to the prom-

---

wherever the debarkation took place, their fondest expectations were realized, for on the shore they "shed tears of joy before the Lord, because of the multitude of His tender mercies."

However, the landing place is not nearly as important as the fact that they landed. They came from somewhere. They did not grow spontaneously on American soil, as maintained by some. They came from some center of population in Asia. They are an important branch of the human family. We have endeavored, elsewhere, to show that they were Hebrews, in the wider meaning of that term, inasmuch as they were descendants of Joktan, the son of Eber (or Heber), and the younger brother of Peleg, the ancestor of Abraham, in whose days (Peleg's) the Earth was divided between the nations (Genesis 10:32). They came here by Divine appointment, and under Divine protection. That is the important information conveyed by the Book of Ether.

VERSE 13. *They began to fill the earth.* The new country was, as it were, hospitably waiting for their arrival. Its virgin soil was prepared to yield its abundant wealth to the industrious husbandman.

The importance of early agriculture in this part of the world, and the success it achieved, can best be judged from the fact that the world is indebted to the Indians for a number of useful plants, such as potatoes, tomatoes, corn or maise, and others; and they knew the sedative effect of such plants as tobacco and datura, in advance of medical science.[6]

VERSE 14. *Jared had four sons.* Their names seem to indicate kinship to the Semitic Language. *Jacum* may be related to the Hebrew *Jakim* (I Chronicles 8:19; 24:12), signifying one who is raised up by the Lord; it evidently comes from the verb, *kum,* to stand up. It may also be related to *khamamu,* which is said to mean to hold, to fix, to grasp, and in Babylonian to fix the laws, to lead, to govern (H. F. Lutz, Kingship in Babylonia, Syria, and Egypt; *American Anthropologist,* October and December, 1924).

Gilgah may be a variant of Gilgal, which means a wheel, or a circle. It was the place where the Israelites made their first camp in Palestine, after having crossed the Jordan and occupied Jericho. It was there that they set up twelve stones, possibly in a circle, forming a stonehenge in memory of that great event in Israelitish history (Joshua 4:19-20; 9:16; 10:6-7). *Maha* may be the mahan of the Pearl of Great Price (Moses 5:31. *See* comments under Ether 2:13). *Orihah* is, undoubtedly, the same as Urijah (2 Kings 16:10-12), meaning *the* light of the Lord.

---

[6]There can be no question as to the early use of antiseptics and narcotics by the Zuni.... The Zuni rain priests administer *Datura meteloides* that one may become a seer, and the Zuni *doctor* gives the root of the plant to render his patient unconscious while he performs simple operations—setting fractured limbs, etc. (Matilda Coxe Stevenson, *Ethnobotany of the Zuni Indians,* Smithsonian Institution, p. 41.)

ised land; and therefore they began to be many.

17. And they were taught to walk humbly before the Lord; and they were also taught from on high.

3. Orihah appointed King.

19. And the brother of Jared began to be old, and saw that he must soon go down to the grave; wherefore he said unto Jared: Let us gather together our people that we may number them, that we may know of them what they will desire of us before we go down to our graves.

20. And accordingly the people were gathered together. Now the number of the sons and the

18. And it came to pass that they began to spread upon the face of the land, and to multiply and to till the earth; and they did wax strong in the land.

daughters of the brother of Jared were twenty and two souls; and the number of sons and daughters of Jared were twelve, he having four sons.

21. And it came to pass that they did number their people; and after that they had numbered them, they did desire of them the things which they would that they should do before they went down to their graves.

VERSE 21. *They did number the people.* There must have been a considerable number of people at this early time, toward the end of the first generation. The increase of the Children of Israel in Egypt during four generations may be referred to for the sake of comparison. It is, of course, mostly indefinite. The number of persons who went with Jacob to the Land of Goshen was seventy (Genesis 46:26), or seventy-five (Acts 7:14). They sojourned in the Land of the Pharaohs 400 (Genesis 15:13; Acts 7:6), or 430 years (Exodus 12:40). At the time of the Exodus, they numbered 600,000 men capable of marching (Exodus 12:37-38). It has been estimated, as pure guesswork, that two million souls left Egypt under Moses, considering the probable number of old men, women and children, together with a *mixed multitude* of Egyptians who had joined the refugees (Exodus 12:38), glad to escape their taskmasters.

The figures upon which to venture an estimate of the total number of Jaredites at this time are also very indefinite. The Brother of Jared, his wife and twenty-two children; Jared, his wife and twelve children; their friends who numbered twenty-two or eleven couples with say, forty children between them—make a hundred souls in all comprising the original company. If we now assume that they multiplied at a rate similar to that of the Israelites in Egypt, the total number of Jaredites at the end of the first generation must have been considerable. A guess as to number would be however of little value. But the total, whatsoever it was, made a census desirable, and necessitated a popular decision as to what form of government to adopt for the benefit of all.

VERSE 22. *A king desired.* In this section we find an illustration of democratic government. Jared and his Brother were advocates of democracy in all its forms, and therefore ruled in that manner. At the end of their careers, when they expected to be released from their earthly missions, they turned their God-given authority over to the people. They did not claim it as theirs, to bequeath to their heirs.

22. And it came to pass that the people desired of them that they should anoint one of their sons to be a king over them.

23. And now behold, this was grievous unto them. And the brother of Jared said unto them: Surely this thing leadeth into captivity.

24. But Jared said unto his brother: Suffer them that they may have a king. And therefore he said unto them: Choose ye out from among our sons a king, even whom ye will.

25. And it came to pass that they chose even the firstborn of the brother of Jared; and his name was Pagag. And it came to pass that he refused and would not be their king. And the people would that his father should constrain him, but his father would not; and he commanded them that they should constrain no man to be their king.

Democracy is generally understood to mean *rule of the people,* as opposed to monarchy, *the rule of one,* or aristocracy, rule of the *nobility,* oligarchy, *the rule of a few,* and we may add, mobocracy, the *rule of the mob.* American democracy is representative; that is to say, it is the rule of the people, by the people, for the people, by their chosen representatives.

The principle of democracy is as old as the human race. It is older than any political form of government. When our Heavenly Father turned this earth over to our first ancestors as their residence, He endowed them with sovereignty over the entire creation thereof, for themselves and their descendants, to have and to hold during their earthly existence, because they were created in His image, His likeness. (Genesis 1:26-28) "Have dominion," He said, "over the fish of the sea, and over the fowl of the air, and over every living thing that moveth upon the earth." That was the Divine Magna Carta that gave all human beings a share in the proper management of the earth's bounties, and the responsibility accompanying proprietorship; as well as an inalienable right to the pursuit of the enjoyment of life and happiness. That is the essence and also the origin of democracy. The two Jareds understood this principle. They proved that by their anxiety to have an expression of the popular will on the government, the executive offices of which would soon be vacant.

VERSES 23-27. *Orihah selected.* The Brother of Jared felt sorrowful for the people who accompanied him and Jared, because of their choice. As a seer he saw a dark picture of strife and loss of freedom in a future time. Jared, less spiritually minded, joined the majority. But the sons of the Brother of Jared refused to accept the office of kingship. Three sons of Jared also declined. Finally, the youngest of Jared's own sons, Orihah, accepted. He was anointed King. (v. 27)

That *he was anointed* indicates that the office was considered sacred. Probably the religious functions of the head of the young state were the most important. That became the case in Assyria, where the king claimed to be a high-priest and a mediator between Heaven and Earth. Also in Babylonia, where kings regarded themselves as the sons of God in a special sense, a doctrine that found its way into Egypt, and also later on, into Peru.

There is nothing objectionable in the *title* king, itself. It all depends on the personality of the incumbent. Our Lord is a King, even, the King of kings, and His sovereignty is the completion of the Plan of Salvation. Melchizedek was a king (Genesis 14:19), but he was a king of righteousness as well as King of Peace

26. And it came to pass that they chose all the brothers of Pagag, and they would not.

27. And it came to pass that neither would the sons of Jared, even all save it were one; and Orihah was anointed to be king over the people.

28. And he began to reign, and the people began to prosper; and they became exceedingly rich.

29. And it came to pass that Jared died, and his brother also.

30. And it came to pass that Orihah did walk humbly before the Lord, and did remember how great things the Lord had done for his father, and also taught his people how great things the Lord had done for their fathers.

(Hebrews 7:1-2). Moses made provision for the position of king in his Hebrew state. He says:

"When thou art come unto the land which the Lord thy God giveth thee, and shalt possess it, and shalt dwell therein, and shalt say, I will set a king over me, like as all the nations that are about me; thou shalt in any wise set him king over thee, whom the Lord thy God shall choose." (Deuteronomy 17:14-15)

One of such a king's duties was to read the word of God, especially the Law, every day (*Ibid.*, 17:18-20), "that his heart be not lifted up above his brethren." The first three kings of Israel, Saul, David, and Solomon, were all selected by divine guidance. As kings, they were the representatives of God, although the human frailty often made them seem unfit for the position.

VERSES 28-30. *The Reign of Orihah.* Orihah's reign was long, and materially prosperous. The Sacred Record says "his days were exceeding many." He walked in humility before the Lord, remembering, and teaching the people to remember, the great wonders and blessings of God in the past.

VERSE 29. *Jared died.* This verse notes that Jared died, also his brother. On the death of the Brother of Jared—Gard—see an Indian legend in a paper on the Nephites in COMMENTARY ON THE BOOK OF MORMON, Volume I.

FOUR GROUPS OF INDIANS

The following classification of the American Indians (aborigine) is credited to Dr. Roland Dickson of Harvard University. He finds four main groups:

1. The Eskimos of North America, and the tribes in the southern part of South America, related to the peoples of the Arctic Regions of Europe and Asia.

2. Another group related to the dark-complexioned inhabitants of the Pacific Islands.

3. Representatives of a third group are found west of the Rocky Mountains, on the shores of the Gulf of Mexico and in the Amazon-Orinoco region of South America.

4. A fourth group, related to the peoples of western and central Asia and eastern Europe, is supposed to be peopling Alaska, northwestern Canada, Mexico, Central and South America.

Students of anthropology may find it interesting to compare these subdivisions with the Jaredites, Mulekites, Nephites, and Lamanites of the Book of Mormon.

PAGAG

The eldest son of the Brother of Jared. When it was decided to establish a monarchy on the new land to which the Lord had led the Jaredites, Pagag was the first choice of the people for king. But he resolutely refused the honor, sensing, perhaps, the evils which would follow the adoption of this form of government. The people desired that his father should compel him to be king, but he would not do so and commanded that they should constrain no man to be their king. The result was that all Pagag's brothers and three of the four sons of Jared followed his example and when chosen refused to accept the proffered dignity; at last, Orihah, the fourth son of Jared accepted. Nothing more is said of Pagag in the Book of Mormon but from his action in this matter we judge him to have been a wise and God-fearing man. (Ether 6:25)

JACOM

The eldest son of Jared, the father of the Jaredite Race. Jacom, with others, was offered the kingly authority by the people but refused that honor. His name is mentioned only once in the Book of Mormon. (Ether 6:14)

GILGAH

One of the four sons of Jared (his name is given the second place). He was in all probability born in Asia before his father and associates commenced their wonderful journey to the Land of Promise. All we know of him is that when the Jaredites desired a king, he was one of those to whom this honor was offered, and who refused. From the general summary given us of the character of the people of that generation, we have every reason to believe he was a righteous man.

CHAPTER 7

1. *Orihah, Kib, Corihor, Shule, Noah, Cohor, Nimrod.*

1. And it came to pass that Orihah did execute judgment upon the land in righteousness all his days, whose days were exceeding many.

2. And he begat sons and daughters; yea, he begat thirty and one, among whom were twenty and three sons.

3. And it came to pass that he also begat Kib in his old age. And it came to pass that Kib reigned in his stead; and Kib begat Corihor.

4. And when Corihor was thirty and two years old he rebelled against his father, and went over and dwelt in the land of Nehor; and he begat sons and daughters, and they became exceeding fair; wherefore Corihor drew away many people after him.

5. And when he had gathered together an army he came up unto the land of Moron where the king dwelt, and took him captive, which brought to pass the saying of the brother of Jared that they would be brought into captivity.

6. Now the land of Moron, where the king dwelt, was near the land which is called Desolation by the Nephites.

VERSES 1-2. *Orihah.* Orihah, in his office, was true to the character indicated by his name, the *Light of the Lord.* He ruled as a wise and righteous judge, not as a self-seeking monarch. He was happy in his family life as well as in his public administration, for he became the father of twenty-three sons, and eight daughters.

VERSE 3. *Kib was the last born of the sons of Orihah.* He succeeded his father in the office of king. It may seem strange that the succession should go to the youngest son, but that also was the case in the selection of David to succeed Saul, the first king of Israel. David was the youngest of the eight sons of Jesse. (1 Samuel 6:6-13) In the family of Jacob, the patriarch, Joseph the next youngest of twelve boys, became the most prominent. We believe it is the rule, barring the exceptions that prove the rule, that children born of mature, not to say old, parents, come into the world better equipped mentally than the children of immature fathers and mothers. The brief story of Orihah illustrates the fact that righteous and wise leadership is the channel through which come the divine blessings that reach the people.

VERSES 4-6. *Corihor.* Corihor was a son of Kib, and at the age of thirty-two decided to drive his father from the throne and take his place. With this object in view he fled from the Land of Moron, where the king dwelt, to the Land of Nehor. Here he established a family, and by the aid of feminine charms and, we may suppose, brilliant social functions, he gathered around him a considerable following. At the head of an armed force he then invaded the Fatherland and made the royal family prisoners of war. As a genuine usurper he destroyed the liberty of the people. Thus

7. And it came to pass that Kib dwelt in captivity, and his people under Corihor his son, until he became exceeding old; nevertheless Kib begat Shule in his old age, while he was yet in captivity.

8. And it came to pass that Shule was angry with his brother; and Shule waxed strong, and became mighty as to strength of a man; and he was also mighty in judgment.

9. Wherefore, he came to the hill Ephraim, and he did molten out of the hill, and made swords out of steel for those whom he had drawn away with him; and after he had armed them with swords he returned to the city

Nehor and gave battle unto his brother Corihor, by which means he obtained the kingdom and restored it unto his father Kib.

10. And now because of the thing which Shule had done, his father bestowed upon him the kingdom; therefore he began to reign in the stead of his father.

11. And it came to pass that he did execute judgment in righteousness; and he did spread his kingdom upon all the face of the land, for the people had become exceeding numerous.

12. And it came to pass that Shule also begat many sons and daughters.

13. And Corihor repented of the many evils which he had

the prophecy of the Brother of Jared concerning the loss of liberty under a monarchial form of government (Ether 6:23) came true.

Moroni (v. 6) adds what may be called a marginal reading, or gloss, explaining that the Land of Moron was near, probably bordered on, the Land which the Nephites knew as the Land Desolation.

VERSES 7-22. *Shule, Noah, Cohor, Nimrod.* The story of Shule is one of revolutions and radical changes. Corihor had, it appears, united the two countries of Moron and Nehor, the latter being the land where his wife's family resided (v. 4). Also, he had moved the Capital of Moron to the City of Nehor, and here his father, Kib, was a prisoner of war.

In his advanced age, while he was in captivity, Kib became the father of a boy whom he named Shule, a word which in all probability is related to the Hebrew *shaal,* meaning to ask for, and therefore, meaning, a son asked for, a child of prayer.

Years later, when Shule was old enough to take an interest in public affairs, he felt that it was his calling to force his brother to change his unnatural conduct. He began by gathering together, at a Hill called Ephraim,[1] a number of malcontents. There they armed themselves with swords made of steel,[2] "molten out of a hill." Properly equipped, they attacked the usurper in the City of Nehor, deposed him and restored the kingdom to their aged father who had been legally elected king.

---

[1]*Ephraim,* meaning a place that brings fruit, or that grows.
[2]*Steel,* or hardened iron, is, of course, a product of modern industry. Whether it was in use as far back as the time of Jared, we know not. The steele mentioned here may, or may not, have been specially treated iron. According to Moses, Tubal-cain, son of Lamech, was an instructor of expert workers in *brass and iron* (nechushet ubarsel, Genesis 4:22). In the very early days, copper (nechuset) and bronze were used for many purposes in the place of iron which was introduced later. The passage in Job (28:12) *molten out of stone,* refers to the smelting of copper ore. The word *brass* is frequently used in the Old Testament for copper. The ordinance (Numbers 31:22-23) prescribes that metals taken in war, including

done; wherefore Shule gave him power in his kingdom.

14. And it came to pass that Corihor had many sons and daughters. And among the sons of Corihor there was one whose name was Noah.

15. And it came to pass that Noah rebelled against Shule, the king, and also his father Corihor, and drew away Cohor his brother, and also all his brethren and many of the people.

16. And he gave battle unto Shule the king, in which he did obtain the land of their first inheritance; and he became a king over that part of the land.

17. And it came to pass that he gave battle again unto Shule, the king; and he took Shule, the king, and carried him away captive into Moron.

18. And it came to pass as he was about to put him to death, the sons of Shule crept into the house of Noah by night and slew him, and broke down the door of the prison and brought out their father, and placed him upon his throne in his own kingdom.

19. Wherefore, the son of Noah did build up his kingdom in his stead; nevertheless they did not gain power any more over Shule the king, and the people who were under the reign of Shule the king did prosper exceedingly and wax great.

20. And the country was divided; and there were two kingdoms, the kingdom of Shule, and the kingdom of Cohor, the son of Noah.

21. And Cohor, the son of Noah, caused that his people should give battle unto Shule, in which Shule did beat them and did slay Cohor.

22. And now Cohor had a son who was called Nimrod; and Nimrod gave up the kingdom of Cohor unto Shule, and he did gain favor in the eyes of Shule; wherefore

---

Kib, however, feeling the weight of years, and the effect of his captivity, declined the responsibility, and placed the reigns of government in the steady hands of his son's rule. Shule was a righteous judge, and again the people prospered. He also led a happy life and was blessed with many sons and daughters. But his happiest day was, undoubtedly, that on which he could welcome his repentant brother, Corihor, to the family circle and entrust him with some office of responsibility and influence.

Corihor had many children. Two of his sons, Noah and Cohor, rebelled against King Shule, their uncle, and Corihor, their father. Noah was the leader of the secession. Soon he had all his brothers and many of the people on his side. Then he began hostilities. Success seemed to follow his banners. He gained control over the government of the land of their first inheritance. Next, the King, Shule, fell into the hands of Noah and was carried, a captive, into the Land of Moron. However, that was the end of the career of Noah. He was slain by the sons of Shule, who was set free and again established on the throne in his own kingdom.

---

brass and iron, *must go through fire,* in order to be clean. Perhaps we are willing to admit that the people of the early ages of the stone or bronze age, knew more about metals than we are able to credit. The encyclopedias tell us that iron and steel were obtained anciently by mixing ore and charcoal in a fire and a blast applied to obtain the necessary high temperature. (See, *An Introduction to the Study of the Book of Mormon,* pp. 74-76, Janne M. Sjodahl)

Shule did bestow great favors upon him, and he did do in the kingdom of Shule according to his desires.

2. Prophets, repentance, and peace.

23. And also in the reign of Shule there came prophets among the people, who were sent from the Lord, prophesying that the wickedness and idolatry of the people was bringing a curse upon the land, and they should be destroyed if they did not repent.

24. And it came to pass that the people did revile against the prophets, and did mock them. And it came to pass that king Shule did execute judgment against all those who did revile against the prophets.

25. And he did execute a law

But there were now two kingdoms; Shule was acknowledged ruler of one, and Cohor, the son of Noah, of the other. The people of Shule prospered exceedingly, with the result that Cohor, when he again began hostilities, was defeated and slain.

Cohor had a son whose name was Nimrod. He took a course different from that of his father. He voluntarily gave up his office to Shule. Thus the breach between the two countries was healed and peace was established.

VERSES 23-27. *Shule's last days.* The rest of the story of Shule is soon told. During his reign prophets appeared who warned the people against wickedness and idolatry. This would indicate that the king no longer officiated in spiritual functions, but that the office of the prophet had been separated from that of the king as it was in the days of Israel during the time of Samuel, the Prophet and Saul, the first King of the covenant people. It seems that when a government deteriorates and inclines toward autocracy, it necessarily leaves the Priesthood standing outside of its calculations. God can always find a prophet fit to be a king, but seldom a king qualified for the office of a prophet.

As is usually the case, the prophets of God met with the opposition of the wicked, because they spoke the truth. But the king protected them and made religious persecution a crime. Protected by law, the prophets delivered their message with great power. The people repented. Family life, a sure indication of the moral and social status of a people, flourished. The last paragraph in this chapter concerning Shule is a beautiful tribute to his memory: "And there were no more wars in the days of Shule; and he remembered the great things that the Lord had done for his fathers in bringing them across the great deep into the promised land; wherefore he did execute judgment in righteousness all his days."

VERSES 23-24. *Idolatry.* On a certain level of culture, men and women feel the need of some visible form before which to pay homage to the Deity. They make themselves images, and their worship becomes *idolatry*, in the strict sense of that word. At another stage worshipers turn to the Sun, the Moon, the stars, as the life-giving and sustaining agents of the Infinite God, worthy representatives of His almighty power and boundless wisdom. This, too, becomes idolatry in the wider meaning of that term. Sometimes idolatry refers to the strange efforts of mortals to win the favor of evil powers by prayers and sacrifices. These powers are then represented by images of loathsome snakes and terrible dragons. And then again, idolatry may consist in homage to false concepts of God, causing one to "walk in his own way, and after the image of his own god, whose image is in the likeness of the world, and whose substance is that of an idol, which waxeth old and shall perish in Babylon, even Babylon the great which shall perish. (Doctrine and Covenants, 1:16)

It is a noteworthy fact that the Greeks, in their seeming insignificant country, as to area, developed an entirely different idea of the Deity. While other nations depicted the divine images, or beings, as bulls, lions, eagles, bears, and even snakes, or, at least made beasts their symbols, Greek poets and artists vied with each other in efforts to give their gods the most perfect, the most beautiful form in nature, the human figure, with the result that not only Greek sculpture, but other branches of art also produced inimitable patterns, almost unapproachable in latter years. The statue of Zeus by Phidias (about 500 B.C.) was ordered by Pericles to beautify Athens by public works. Among his creations were Pallas Athena, and the collossal statue of Zeus. Of the latter it has been said that it stands alone and has never been equalled. It was forty feet high, seated upon a throne made of cedar, inlaid with gold, ebony and ivory, and was studded with precious stones. The temple that was the palace of this deity was sixty-eight feet high, ninety feet wide, and two hundred-thirty feet long. The facial features of the statue, it is said, reflected power, majesty, wisdom, and goodness, and as a work of art it was admired by all. It was by means of such works that the Greek civilization rose to the highest level of which it was capable. It was by such means that it became the inspiration of the entire Roman civilization.

But where did the Greeks get the inspiration to clothe God in human form? Where did the Greek poets learn the great truth that man is the offspring of God?[3] The answer is, that the Hellenes were living not far from Palestine, and that they may have obtained many valuable truths from that country, as well as merchandise. The description of the throne of Zeus, for instance, reminds one of the account of the throne of Solomon in 1 Kings 10:18-20. But we believe that Paul's answers to the questions were satisfactory.

The great Apostle to the Gentiles came, on his second missionary journey, to Athens. While there he was given an opportunity to address a select audience of philosophers on Mars Hill. His discourse was possibly the most eloquent and logical that was ever delivered by him. Unfortunately, he was interrupted by a very polite mob, and did not finish.

He began by refuting the charge that he was trying to introduce *strange gods*. He was not, he said. He had noticed an inscription on one of their altars, "To the Unknown God." That he said, was the God he preached. To quote: "What therefore ye worship in ignorance, this set I forth unto you. The God that made the world and all things therein, He, being the Lord of heaven and earth," etc. (Acts 17:22-23)[4]

The *Unknown God* was the God of Creation, the Lord of the Heavens and the Earth, and the eyes, ears, hands, mouth, etc., so happily adapted by Greek genius to their idea of the divine, was Hebrew. It could have come from no other source. But, is that not anthropomorphism? Possibly. But what then? Is there anything more perfect, more beautiful, more miraculous, in all nature than a human being free from blemishes? What else is there to which a Divine Person, who has given us permission to call Him, Father, can be compared? The fact is, that God, in Whose image we are created, is the true God, and that the Greeks accepted the idea under Hebrew

[3]Paul says in his argument before the philosophers at Athens that certain also of your poets have said, *For ye are also his offspring* (Acts 17:28). This is supposed to be a quotation from the Stoic poet Aratus. But if St. Paul is exact in his language, more than one poet must have held the same view of the relationship between God and man.

[4]Learned theologians have suggested that the *Unknown God* was some bad underground demon whose name was never mentioned in polite society; but the application of the Apostle of his discovery of the altar and the inscripion thereon makes that explanation absurd. Paul was not the messenger of a demon.

throughout all the land, which gave power unto the prophets that they should go whithersoever they would; and by this cause the people were brought unto repentance.

26. And because the people did repent of their iniquities and idolatries the Lord did spare them, and they began to prosper again in the land. And it came to pass that Shule begat sons and daugh-

ters in his old age.

27. And there were no more wars in the days of Shule; and he remembered the great things that the Lord had done for his fathers in bringing them across the great deep into the promised land; wherefore he did execute judgment in righteousness all his days.

---

influence, which at one time was strong enough at Athens to leave an altar to the *Unknown God*. Further, that the most advanced civilization in the world traces its origin back to this so-called anthropomorphic concept of God. To Greek philosophers, whether Epicurians or Stoics, Platonists or followers of Aristotle, the true God was both unknown and unknowable, for "the world by wisdom knew not God." (1 Corinthians 1:21) God is known only through revelation.

VERSES 25-27. *Religious Liberty.* Shule established religious liberty by law, as did the framers of the American Constitution, by withholding from the Congress the authority to make laws respecting an establishment of religion, or prohibiting the free exercise thereof, and reserving that prerogative to the people. (Amendments, Art. 1) He made it lawful to hold minority opinions on religious questions and to express them in public, naturally with due regard to the rights of others, and without disturbing the public peace. There can be no greater boon to a nation than such freedom. Saint Paul assures the Corinthians (2 Corinthians 3:17) that the Lord, the real Ruler, is the Spirit, and that *were the Spirit of the Lord is, there is liberty.* The law of liberty is the rule where the Spirit of the Lord rules.

This freedom does not mean liberty to do anything but that which is right. It is not liberty to do wrong. (Romans 14:13-17; 1 Corinthians 7:22-24; 1 Peter 2:16)

The religious legislation of Shule made any outburst of hostility against the divine prophets illegal. It branded acts of intolerance as crimes. Thus the prophets were protected in the deliverance of their messages. Law can do no more, without depriving God's children of their free agency. What to believe and how to worship, are matters not of law; they are manifestations of an intelligent understanding of religion and a firm conviction which are obtained only in secret and sacred communion with God, and a conscientious performance of duty.

MORON, LAND OF

The Land where the Jaredites made their first settlements was north of the Land called Desolation by the Nephites, and consquently in some part of the region which we know as Central America. It appears to have been for a lengthy period, if not during the whole of their existence, the seat of government, the residence of the reigning monarch, and the center of Jaredite civilization. In the numerous fratricidal wars that disgraced the annals of the race, Moron was, more than any other land, the chief seat of war; for here the revolutionists attacked the King, and when successful drove him thence.

HILL EPHRAIM

A hill mentioned in the Book of Ether (7:9) from which Shule obtained iron ore with which to make swords to arm his followers in their efforts to replace his father, Kib, on the throne. We judge this hill to be located in Central America, as it is no great distance from the Land of Moron, afterwards called Desolation.

CORIHOR

Corihor was a Jaredite prince, the son of Kib, and grandson of Orihah, the first king of that people. Corihor was the first who raised the standard of revolt, which revolt caused much bloodshed in the midst of the Jaredite people. When Corihor was thirty-two years old he rebelled against his father, and went from Moron and established himself in the Land of Nehor. There he drew many to him; when strong enough he invaded the Land of Moron, took the king, his father, captive, and reigned in his stead. After many years, Shule, a son born to Kib while he was in captivity, drove Corihor from the throne and replaced their father thereon. After this, Corihor appears to have been loyal to his father and to his brother, Shule, who succeeded Kib. For this loyalty and devotion Corihor was placed in authority in the nation's councils, but one of his sons, named Noah, proved to be a traitor, and rose up in rebellion against Shule and Corihor, and eventually obtained possession of the kingdom.

NOAH

Noah was an early Jaredite leader and the son of Corihor, and the father of Cohor. Noah rebelled against King Shule and against his own father, drawing from their allegiance to them, all his brothers and many of the people. When sufficiently strong he attacked and defeated Shule, and took possession and reigned over the Land of the Jaredites' first inheritance, probably Moron (near to the Land known to the Nephites as Desolation). A second time he attacked Shule, he defeated and captured him and carried him to Moron. It was Noah's intention to put Shule to death, but before he carried out his plan to do so, some of Shule's sons crept into the house of Noah by night and slew him. They then broke down the door of the prison in which their father was confined, liberated him, and restored him to the throne, while Cohor reigned over that portion of the land originally conquered by his father, Noah.

COHOR

Cohor was one of the earliest Jaredites. He was the son Corihor, the son of Kib, the son of another Corihor who was the son of Jared who came forth from the Tower. He was associated with his brother, Noah, in a rebellion against King Shule, who was their uncle, though possibly their junior in years as he was born when his father, Kib, was very aged. The rebellion of Noah, Cohor, and their associates was partly successful, the country was divided into two kingdoms and Noah reigned in Moron, the Land of the Jaredites' first inheritance. Cohor is mentioned but once by name in the Book of Ether.

COHOR, THE NEPHEW OF THE PRECEDING

Cohor was the son of Noah, the son of Corihor. He succeeded his father as King of the Land of Moron. Making war with Shule, the King of the other portion of the country, Cohor was defeated and slain. He was succeeded on the throne by his son Nimrod, who, apparently deeming Shule the rightful monarch of the country, gave up any claims to the Kingdom to him; thus once more and again uniting the entire Jaredite people in one nation under one King.

NIMROD

Nimrod was an early Jaredite Prince, the son of Cohor. In his days the Kingdom was a divided one, Shule reigning over one portion and Cohor over the other. Cohor, desiring to obtain undivided dominion, gave battle to Shule, defeated and slain. Nimrod, recognizing the superior rights of Shule, surrendered the region his father had ruled over to that monarch. For this act and for his faithful allegiance, Nimrod found favor in the eyes of Shule, and he had authority given unto him to do "according to his desires," in the latter's Kingdom.

CHAPTER 8

1. *Omer, Jared, and Akish.*

1. And it came to pass that he begat Omer, and Omer reigned in his stead. And Omer begat Jared; and Jared begat sons and daughters.

2. And Jared rebelled against his father, and came and dwelt in the land of Heth. And it came to pass that he did flatter many people, because of his cunning words, until he had gained the half of the kingdom.

3. And when he had gained the half of the kingdom he gave battle unto his father, and he did carry away his father into captivity, and did make him serve in captivity;

4. And now, in the days of the reigns of Omer he was in captivity the half of his days. And it came to pass that he begat sons and daughters among whom were Esrom and Coriantumr;

5. And they were exceedingly angry because of the doings of Jared their brother, insomuch that they did raise an army and gave battle unto Jared. And it came to pass that they did give battle unto him by night.

6. And it came to pass that when they had slain the army of Jared they were about to slay him also; and he plead with them that they would not slay him, and he would give up the kingdom unto his father. And it came to pass that they did grant unto him his life.

7. And now Jared became exceeding sorrowful because of the loss of the kingdom, for he had set his heart upon the kingdom and upon the glory of the world.

8. Now the daughter of Jared being exceeding expert, and seeing the sorrows of her father, thought to devise a plan whereby she could redeem the kingdom unto her father.

9. Now the daughter of Jared

VERSES 1-19. *Jared rebelled.* There is tragedy in this section of Jaredite history. Omer, the fifth descendant of the first Jared, saw a time of strife, bloodshed, and almost incredible wickedness. His reign was actually the beginning of the end.

Jared II was the son of Omer. Not satisfied with his position as a prince, he became possessed by an uncontrollable craving for more power and glory, and set about to dethrone his father. As a beginning he went to the Land of Heth. Here he began his agitation for followers and, by means of the contemptible tricks known to deceivers of the easy-going masses, including, no doubt, tom-toms, feasts, and above all, bold misstatements concerning the past and present and hypocritical promises for the future, he succeeded in securing fifty percent of the voters of the kingdom for his plans. People do forget that one who is a traitor to his own kin, cannot be trusted to be loyal to either God or anybody else.

was exceeding fair. And it came to pass that she did talk with her father, and said unto him: Whereby hath my father so much sorrow? Hath he not read the record which our fathers brought across the great deep? Behold, is there not an account concerning them of old, that they by their secret plans did obtain kingdoms and great glory?

10. And now, therefore, let my father send for Akish, the son of Kimnor; and behold, I am fair, and I will dance before him, and I will please him, that he will desire me to wife; wherefore if he shall desire of thee that ye shall give unto him me to wife, then shall ye say: I will give her if ye will bring unto me the head of my father, the king.

11. And now Omer was a friend of Akish; wherefore, when Jared had sent for Akish, the daughter of Jared danced before him that she pleased him, insomuch that he desired her to wife. And it came to pass that he said unto Jared: Give her unto me to wife.

12. And Jared said unto him: I will give her unto you, if ye will bring unto me the head of my father, the king.

13. And it came to pass that Akish gathered in unto the house of Jared all his kinsfolk, and said unto them: Will ye swear unto me that ye will be faithful unto me in the thing which I shall desire of you?

14. And it came to pass that they all sware unto him, by the God of heaven, and also by the heavens, and also by the earth, and by their heads, that whoso should vary from the assistance which Akish desired should lose his head; and whoso should divulge whatsoever thing Akish made known unto them, the same should lose his life.

15. And it came to pass that thus they did agree with Akish. And Akish did administer unto them the oaths which were given by them of old who also sought power, which had been handed down even from Cain, who was a murderer from the beginning.

16. And they were kept up by

Having secured a following, Jared now attacked his father with a military force. The king, unaware and unprepared, or perhaps unwilling to see his natural son slain, was captured and made a prisoner of war.

But the apparent success of Jared did not last. Two younger sons of Omer, Esrom and Coriantumr, raised an army, defeated Jared in battle and threatened to end his life. At this turn of his fortune, he proved himself a craven at heart, as tyrants generally are. He begged that his worthless life be spared. His pitiful pleas were granted, and their father, Omer, was again seated on the throne.

Jared was still a rebel. The advantages he possessed as a prince seemed to be insignificant when compared with his boundless ambitions. He became gloomy and morose, and, no doubt, made life miserable to his family.

Jared had a daughter who is described as exceedingly expert; that is, clever and well informed. Also, she was exceedingly fair, the Sacred Record informs us. When she learned the cause of her father's trouble, she made an astounding proposition.

the power of the devil to administer these oaths unto the people, to keep them in darkness, to help such as sought power to gain power, and to murder, and to plunder, and to lie, and to commit all manner of wickedness and whoredoms.

17. And it was the daughter of Jared who put it into his heart to search up these things of old; and Jared put it into the heart of Akish; wherefore, Akish administered it unto his kindred and friends, leading them away by fair promises to do whatsoever thing he desired.

18. And it came to pass that they formed a secret combination, even as they of old; which combination is most abominable and wicked above all, in the sight of God;

19. For the Lord worketh not in secret combinations, neither doth he will that man should shed blood, but in all things hath forbidden it, from the beginning of man.

2. *Moroni warns all the world against secret combinations.*

20. And now I, Moroni, do not write the manner of their oaths and combinations, for it hath been made known unto me that they are had among all people, and they are had among the Lamanites.

21. And they have caused the destruction of this people of whom I am now speaking, and also the destruction of the people of Nephi.

22. And whatsoever nation shall uphold such secret combina-

She suggested a banquet in honor of a friend named Akish. At that function, she said, she would dance and display her feminine charms. The guest of honor would, perhaps, be fascinated and would desire her for a wife. Jared could then ask for his father's head as the price of the bride.

Akish was an old friend of the house, perhaps a trusted confederate in the first rebellion. The *expert* daughter may have had a secret, tender, reason for her own villainous plot.

The preparations for the murder of Omer were carefully designed and very elaborate. Akish founded a secret society, the members of which were held together by contempt for, and repudiation of, all moral law and order, it being understood that they were at liberty to murder and rob, to lie and to welter in the malodorous pools of passion, while at the same time, they were bound by oath on the pain of death, not to reveal the crimes of their fellow-criminals. He, naturally, felt sure that the prospect of plunder in the royal house would, under the circumstances, appeal to these licensed assassins. Akish got the daughter for wife. Jared got the throne, but not his father's head.

VERSES 20-26. *They are had among the Lamanites.* All associations with rituals and signs of recognition not made public are not criminal, nor condemnable. Only those which, behind a veil of secrecy commit crimes and formulate plans against their fellows, the legally established state, or any lawfully existing institution. Such societies are the enemies of mankind.

American Indians still have societies which may be called secret insofar as they

tions, to get power and gain, until they shall spread over the nation, behold, they shall be destroyed; for the Lord will not suffer that the blood of his saints, which shall be shed by them, shall always cry unto him from the ground for vengence upon them and yet he avenge them not.

23. Wherefore, O ye Gentiles, it is wisdom in God that these things should be shown unto you, that thereby ye may repent of your sins, and suffer not that these murderous combinations shall get above you, which are built up to get power and gain— and the work, yea, even the work of destruction come upon you, yea, even the sword of the justice of the Eternal God shall fall upon you, to your overthrow and destruction if ye shall suffer these things to be.

24. Wherefore, the Lord commandeth you, when ye shall see these things come among you that ye shall awake to a sense of your awful situation, because of this secret combination which shall be among you; or wo be unto it, because of the blood of them who have been slain; for they cry from the dust for vengeance upon it, and also upon those who built it up.

25. For it cometh to pass that whoso buildeth it up seeketh to overthrow the freedom of all lands, nations, and countries; and it bringeth to pass the destruction of all people, for it is built up by the devil, who is the father of all lies; even that same liar who beguiled our first parents, yea, even that same liar who hath caused man to commit murder from the beginning; who hath hardened the hearts of men that they have murdered the prophets, and stoned them, and cast them out from the beginning.

---

have initiation ceremonies with which only the members thereof are acquainted. Such ceremonies they observe regularly, but no strangers, and in some cases, no women, are permitted to attend.

Murderous combinations. Moroni carefully explains the nature of the associations he condemns. They are, he notes, combinations organized for the selfish purpose of concentrating *power and wealth* in the hands of the organizers. Furthermore, they are persecutors and murderers of the Saints of God. And what is more, they are the destroyers (we are quoting Moroni) of the *freedom of all lands, nations, and countries*. Note that Moroni is speaking of murderous organizations in general, but he has one special association in mind to which he refers to in verse 24: "Wherefore the Lord commandeth you, when ye shall see these things come among you that ye shall awake to a sense of your awful situation, because of this secret combination which shall be among you."

Associations such as those herein described must necessarily destroy the influence of the Saints and good religion everywhere in order to gain their object, which is to fasten the chains of serfdom on the limbs of their fellowmen. Moroni correctly states that such organizations are the instruments in the hands of the *father of all lies*, who, from the beginning, *caused man to commit murder*. (Compare the Pearl of Great Price, Moses 4:3-4) "Wherefore, because that satan rebelled against Me, and sought to destroy the agency of man, which I, the Lord God had given him, and also, that I should give unto him Mine own power; by the power of

26. Wherefore, I, Moroni, am commanded to write these things that evil may be done away, and that the time may come that Satan may have no power upon the hearts of the children of men, but that they may be persuaded to do good continually, that they may come unto the fountain of all righteousness and be saved.

Mine Only Begotten, I caused that he be cast down, and he became satan,[1] yea, even the devil,[2] the father of all lies, to deceive and to blind men, and to lead them captive at his will, even as many as would not hearken unto My voice."

CORIANTUMR, THE SON OF OMER

Coriantumr, the son of Omer, was a Jaredite Prince, who was born while his father was held in captivity by his brother, Jared. When Coriantumr grew to manhood he became exceedingly angry at the course pursued by Jared, and together with another brother, Ezrom, he raised an army and made an unexpected night attack upon the military forces of Jared in which the latter was almost entirely destroyed. They then restored their father, Omer, to the throne.

KIMNOR

Kimnor was one of the early Jaredites. He is simply known to us as the father of Akish, the friend of King Omer.

ESROM

Esrom was a son of the unfortunate Jaredite King, Omer, and was born to him while he was held in captivity by the King's son, Jared. Esrom and his brother, Coriantumr, growing exceedingly angry at the treatment received by their father, raised an army and made a night attack upon the forces of the usurper in which they gained a complete victory; Jared's army being destroyed and he, himself, taken prisoner. Esrom and his associates then replaced their father upon the throne. In the rebellion of Akish, it is said that the Lord was merciful to Omer, and also to his sons and daughters who did not seek his destruction. It is therefore, altogether probable that if Esrom still lived, he accompanied his father in his exile to the distant Land of Ablom.

JARED

One of the most unscrupulous and bloodthirsty of the ancient Jaredites. In early life he rose in rebellion against Omer, his father, eventually dethroned him and held him a captive for many years, while he (Jared) occupied the throne. Some of Omer's younger sons, incensed at the treatment to which their father was subjected, raised an army and totally routed the forces of the usurper. Jared was taken prisoner and only saved his life by humble submission to his father. At first he kept his promise but his ambition would not remain dormant. He sighed and wearied for the kingly authority until his unrest became marked by all. He had a daughter who shared her father's feelings and at her instigation he sent for a friend of Omer's named Akish through whom he hoped to regain the throne. An entertainment of some kind, by which Jared's daughter could be introduced, was

---

[1]An adversary, opposer.
[2]An accuser, one who slanders another for the purpose of injury. The Hebrew for devil is, saweer, meaning hairy. The satyr of Greek mythology.

given. By pre-arrangement with her father she danced before Akish and so exhibited the beauties of her person and the graces of her movements that he became desperately enamored of her. As she anticipated, Akish asked Jared to give her to him as a wife. The latter consented but on most revolting conditions. The father and daughter had planned that the price of her hand was to be the head of her grandfather, the king. Did ever ambition conceive a more unnatural crime? Akish, though a friend of Omer, consented to the proposed terms and to help him in his treason Jared suggested to him, again at the instance of his daughter, the plans and oaths common among the antediluvians, originally used by Cain, by which the wicked accomplished their vile and bloody purposes. He consented, Omer was driven from the throne, though by God's mercy his life was spared; Jared was again proclaimed king and Akish became his son-in-law. Soon the latter coveted the royal dignity; possibly the woman who plotted the death of her grandfather was willing to sacrifice her father also that she might be queen; such a supposition is not improbable. At any rate Jared was slain on his throne while giving audience to his people by some of the members of the secret society of assassins that he had been the means of calling into existence and Akish reigned in his stead.

AKISH

Akish was one of the most cruel and subtle of the early Jaredites. Nothing more is known of his descent than that he was the son of one, Kimnor. The history of Akish is one with which are associated deeds of cruelty, treachery, and iniquity, that are scarcely paralleled in the annals of any nation.

When the Jaredites first reached this continent they were a righteous, God-fearing, though somewhat an unstable people. They, however, made one great mistake; they desired to be ruled by a king. Their prophet-leaders told them that this thing would lead them into captivity, but they insisted and Orihah, the youngest son of Jared, was chosen as their first monarch. The words of their prophets were quickly fulfilled, and bloodshed and internal commotions soon disgraced the history of this favored people. Orihah was succeeded by Kib, who was dethroned by Corihor, but was afterwards restored. In the succeeding reign, that of Shule, the Kingdom was rent in twain, but when he died he was succeeded by his son, Omer, who, we have reason to believe was a good man. The example of the kings and princes had thus far, as a rule, been pernicious and tended to encourage the people to live lives of wickedness.

Omer had a son named Jared; an ambitious, unscrupulous man. He rebelled against his father, and by his flatteries induced half of the people to join his standard. He established himself in a Land named Heth, and when he felt sufficiently strong he gave battle to and defeated the forces of his father whom he took prisoner and held him in captivity; and it is said that Omer remained in this condition half of his days. So long, indeed, was the time that Jared kept him prisoner that sons begotten by him during his captivity grew up to manhood before he was released. Two of these sons, named Esrom and Coriantumr, became very angry at the way their father was treated and they raised an army and attacked their brother, Jared, by night. This attack appears to have been an utter surprise to Jared for his army was entirely destroyed, and he, himself, would have been slain had he not humbly pleaded with his brothers that his life might be spared; he promising that he would surrender the Kingdom to his father. On these conditions his life was granted him.

Now Jared, though he had made this promise when his life was in peril, still longed for the glories and power of the kingly authority and his sorrow and unrest could not be hid from those near him. Among those who noticed his deep-seated grief was a daughter who was exceedingly fair and was apparently as unscrupulous as her father. Whether it was because she really had great affection for him, or, like him, languished for the pomp and magnificence of the court life she no longer possessed that caused her to submit to him a plan by which he might regain the Kingdom cannot be said. Perhaps, also, she may have loved the man whom she suggested as the instrument to be used in the fulfillment of her ambition— possibly all three, for our motives are seldom single; our actions, in other words, are generally the result of a combination of motives.

The young lady's plan was this: She reminded her father that when their ancestors came across the great waters they brought with them records of the doings of mankind in the ages before the flood. And in these records was an account of how men, by secret plans and combinations, obtained kingdoms and great glory. She suggested that her father acquire a knowledge of these unholy methods and use them to regain the throne. She further proposed that he send for a friend of Omer's, named Akish, the son of Kimnor, and she, being graceful as well as beautiful, would dance so entrancingly before him that he would desire her to wife. If she did not love Akish, she simply sold herself to gratify her father's and possibly her own ambition.

Her advice was listened to; her suggestions were carried out. The old oaths and bloody mysteries were searched out, the plan was laid, Akish was invited, the suggested dance danced, Akish's passions were inflamed, and the maiden asked in marriage. The proposal was received with favor, but terrible conditions were attached, such that would have appalled any honorable man. It was that Akish obtain the head of Jared's father, Omer, the King, and to enable him to carry out this murderous design, Jared proposed that he, himself, administer to his friends, the old oaths that had come down from the days of Cain, the first murderer.

Akish accepted this terrible responsibility. He gathered his associates at the house of Jared and there made them all swear by the God of Heaven and by the Heavens, by the Earth, and by their heads, that whoso should vary from what he desired, should lose his own head, and whoso should divulge whatever he made known should lose his life. He then submitted plans to them which they accepted. The plot was so far successful that they overthrew the Kingdom of Omer, but did not succeed in obtaining his head. For the Lord was merciful to Omer, and warned him in a dream to depart out of the land. So, taking those who were faithful to him, he traveled for a great distance until he reached the shores of the Atlantic Ocean. There he and his companions tarried until the course of events permitted him to return.

Omer being driven from his Kingdom, Jared was appointed King, and his daughter was given to Akish to wife. But this did not satisfy Akish. He had learned the power of these secret combinations, and now determined to use them for his own ends. He aspired to the throne, and made up his mind to murder his father-in-law. So he assembled his followers, instructed them in his wishes and Jared was slain by them as he sat upon his throne giving audience to the people; a case of poetical retribution which, though often found in fiction, is seldom met with in real life. Akish was now made King and under his cruel rule wickedness became almost universal. The secret societies by which he obtained power had corrupted the hearts of nearly all the people. As well may be supposed with such a condition of society his throne was not a stable one. He became jealous of one of his sons. What cause, if any, he had therefor, we are not told, but he shut him up in prison and slowly starved him to death. This cruel act greatly incensed another of Jared's sons, named Nimrod, and he, gathering a few followers, fled to the Land of Ablom where Omer dwelt.

Now Akish had other sons and though they had sworn to support him in all his doings they were not true to their oaths. They found that the hearts of the

Jaredites were consumed with the love of gain, and they bribed the greater portion of the people to join them in a revolt against their father. So corrupt had the people become that their extinction appears to have been the only remedy; they would not repent, they seem to have reached the point where human wickedness cannot pass.

A war of the most horrible character broke out, which lasted for several years, and ended when nearly every soul was slain. Of the Kingdom of Akish, for which he had sinned so much, there remained but thirty souls. All the rest—men, women, and children, had been swept by bloody hands into untimely graves. The people of Akish having been thus destroyed, Omer, with his friends, returned from his exile and reigned over the feeble remnant of a wasted people.

CHAPTER 9

1. *The Story of Akish and Omer, Continued*—2. *Emer Anointed King*—3. *Coriantum Succeeds Emer*—4. *Com Reigns in His Stead*—5. *Heth Dethrones and Kills His Father.*

1. *The story of Akish and Omer continued.*

1. And now I, Moroni, proceed with my record. Therefore, behold, it came to pass that because of the secret combinations of Akish and his friends, behold, they did overthrow the kingdom of Omer.

2. Nevertheless, the Lord was merciful unto Omer, and also to his sons and to his daughters who did not seek his destruction.

3. And the Lord warned Omer in a dream that he should depart out of the land; wherefore Omer departed out of the land with his family, and traveled many days, and came over and passed by the hill of Shim, and came over by the place where the Nephites were destroyed, and from thence eastward, and came to a place which was called Ablom, by the seashore, and there he pitched his tent, and also his sons and his daughters, and all his household, save it were Jared and his family.

VERSES 1-13. *They did overthrow the Kingdom.* With the aid obtained from the secret combinations which they had established, Akish and his followers usurped the government, but Omer escaped with his life.

VERSE 3. *Omer departs.* Akish had promised to give Jared, Omer's son, his father's head in exchange for his daughter's hand in marriage. But Omer, the royal parent of Jared, was warned in a dream and fled the intended assassins. He took with him his loyal sons and daughters to a place called Ablom by the seashore. They reached this refuge by traveling many days. They passed the Hill Shim, where Amaron later deposited "all the sacred engravings concerning the Nephites." (Mormon 1:3) They also passed the Hill Cumorah in the Land Cumorah, where Mormon concealed the sacred plates after having made a synopsis of them for the benefit and blessing of future generations. (Mormon 6:1-15)

Prehistoric Americans were good travelers and covered vast areas of country during their nomadic excursions, although they had no, what to us, are rapid means of transportation. This seems to verify the accounts in the Book of Mormon of its people making long treks over little-known terrain. Certain impressions known as *footprints*, have long been puzzling scientists. They are found in some ancient lime formations, and of them, Mr. David I. Bushnell, a Smithsonian ethnologist, now offers the explanation that they are the work of former Indians. He has traced these footprints all the way from the falls in the James River, Virginia, to the foothills of the Rocky Mountains. They are, he says, always found near water, and he believes that they were hewn in the rock by nomadic tribes to indicate to others who might come the same way, that near such a print, they would find a watering place. If this explanation is correct, we may conclude that the American aborigines were good travelers, and the records of the Book of Mormon concerning great journeys become quite intelligible.

4. And it came to pass that Jared was anointed king over the people, by the hand of wickedness; and he gave unto Akish his daughter to wife.

5. And it came to pass that Akish sought the life of his father-in-law; and he applied unto those whom he had sworn by the oath of the ancients, and they obtained the head of his father-in-law, as he sat upon his throne, giving audience to his people.

6. For so great had been the spreading of this wicked and secret society that it had corrupted the hearts of all the people; therefore Jared was murdered upon his throne, and Akish reigned in his stead.

7. And it came to pass that Akish began to be jealous of his son, therefore he shut him up in prison, and kept him upon little or no food until he had suffered death.

8. And now the brother of him that suffered death, (and his name was Nimrah) was angry with his father because of that which his father had done unto his brother.

9. And it came to pass that Nimrah gathered together a small number of men, and fled out of

---

VERSE 4. *Anointed by the hand of wickedness.* Jared became king. He was even anointed, but by the *hand of wickedness,*—some kind of blasphemous ceremony in initiation of the sacred ordinance.

Anointing with sacred oil is a very ancient rite. It is depicted on early Egyptian monuments. Kings were called the *anointed of the gods.* Those who held the Priesthood were confirmed in their office with the application of sacred oil. Jacob poured consecrated oil upon the stone pillow at Bethel, consecrating it to God. (Genesis 28:10-19)

Jared gave his daughter to Akish for wife. But that was a union without divine blessing and without the sanction of the Priesthood. It did not bring happiness.

VERSE 5. *Jared slain.* A subordinate place in the wicked government did not satisfy Akish. His ambition was to be king. Murder was to him a means to an end. So he hired assassins, belonging to his secret society. They slew Jared while he was seated upon his royal throne, and Akish was then anointed king. That was retribution. The arch-assassin now became the ruler.

It may be observed here that criminals never quite trust each other. A criminal does not trust, much less love, a partner in sin. He views him with contempt, knowing that he is as contemptible as he himself is. Respect, friendship, brotherly love, are gorgeous and fragrant flowers which thrive only in a soil of truth and righteousness; they need the sunshine of humble communion with God, and a good conscience.

Nemesis on the track of Akish. Akish, suspicious of his own son, imprisoned him and caused him to starve to death. A brother of the victim, Nimrah, gathered a small company of men and fled to Ablom, where Omer, the rightful King, lived in exile. In the meantime, other sons of Akish gained the confidence of the people. A civil war, which raged in murderous fury for years, broke out. At the end of the slaughter which took place, the kingdom was almost depopulated. Akish must have been slain in that conflict. The exiles in Ablom returned to their inheritances, and Omer again reigned as king.

the land, and came over and dwelt with Omer.

10. And it came to pass that Akish begat other sons, and they won the hearts of the people, notwithstanding they had sworn unto him to do all manner of iniquity according to that which he desired.

11. Now the people of Akish were desirous for gain, even as Akish was desirous for power; wherefore, the sons of Akish did offer them money, by which means they drew away the more part of the people after them.

12. And there began to be a war between the sons of Akish and Akish, which lasted for the space of many years, yea, unto the destruction of nearly all the people of the kingdom, yea, even all, save it were thirty souls, and they who fled with the house of Omer.

13. Wherefore, Omer was restored again to the land of his inheritance.

14. And it came to pass that Omer began to be old; nevertheless, in his old age he begat Emer; and he anointed Emer to be king to reign in his stead.

2. Emer anointed king.

15. And after that he had anointed Emer to be king he saw peace in the land for the space of two years, and he died, having seen exceeding many days, which were full of sorrow. And it came to pass that Emer did reign in his stead, and did fill the steps of his father.

16. And the Lord began again to take the curse from off the land, and the house of Emer did prosper exceedingly under the reign of Emer; and in the space of sixty and two years they had become exceeding strong, insomuch that they became exceeding rich—

17. Having all manner of fruit, and of grain, and of silks, and of

---

VERSES 14-15. *Emer made king.* Omer began to feel the weight of many years, and anointed his last born son, Emer, to fill his place. Two years afterwards Omer passed away in peace.

It is not easy to imagine human beings as depraved as Jared and Akish; so utterly devoid of conscience and human instincts. But more recent history knows similar character. The assassination of Licinius, the brother-in-law and political rival of Constantine (306-337 A.D.), is branded as an "atrocious and unprovoked breach of faith" by this famous potentate, who is also charged with the murder of his own son, Crispus, who, his father thought, had won too great a degree of popular favor.[1]

VERSES 16-20. *Prosperity under Emer.* It is said of Emer, that he walked in the steps of his father, and that the people prospered. Peace always means prosperity to a nation, while war means financial as well as moral and intellectual ruin. History is decisive on that point. We read that the Jaredites under Emer had an

---

[1]*See*, Gibbon's portrait of Emperor Phocas, whose few years of murder and tyranny ended in the shameful death of a criminal, in the year 630 A.D. (*Decline and Fall of Rome*, Vol. 4, p. 454)

fine linen, and of gold, and of silver, and of precious things;

18. And also all manner of cattle, of oxen, and cows, and of sheep, and of swine, and of goats, and also many other kinds of animals which were useful for the food of man.

19. And they also had horses, and asses, and there were elephants and cureloms and cumoms; all of which were useful unto man, and more especially the elephants and cureloms and cumoms.

---

abundance of fruit, grain, silks, fine linen, gold, silver, oxen, cows, sheep, swine, goats, horses, asses, elephants, cureloms, and cumoms, *all of which were useful to man, and more especially the elephants and cureloms and cumoms.*

Such assets as those here enumerated were *useful*. They, and not money, are the real wealth of a nation. Money is only a medium of exchange, convenient but not absolutely necessary. But if there were no food, no clothing, no needful commodities and luxuries to exchange, money would be useless. The Jaredites under Emer had all these things, they had the real wealth.

VERSES 17-19. *Precious things and animals.* Students of the Book of Mormon will agree that these verses constitute one of the few difficult passages in that volume, as long as recognized authorities on early American culture insist that the aborigines of these continents had neither silk, nor oxen, cows, or sheep, except the wild mountain variety; and certainly no horses until the arrival of the Spaniards; and no elephants. There seems to be a serious discrepancy between the statement of Moroni and the findings of science. But we have no doubt that there is a satisfactory answer or explanation of the seeming contradiction, if it can be found, by which the difficulty may be removed. As to what that explanation is, we can, as yet, offer only a few suggestions.

Silks and fine linen. The Jaredites came from Asia, presumably across China, the reputed home of the silk industry. Just when that occupation began is uncertain. A Chinese tradition says that the wife of Emperor Hoan-ti started it in the year B.C. 2609. That would be before the time of Noah, in Ussher's chronology. As far as tradition goes, there is no reason for believing that silk was unknown to Jared and his Brother. If they did not have silk worms, or eggs of the mother insect, as well as swarms of bees (Ether 2:3), they more than likely had silk in the form of skeins, or woven fabrics, or both, in abundance.

However, the reading in our text is *silks,* in the plural. That is best understood as a collective noun, *silk goods,* analogous to, for instance, silver-ware, glassware, etc. If so understood, it means not only genuine silk, but any article resembling that material, soft, glossy, and elegant enough to be used as a substitute for it. That is the literal meaning of silks even today. Every one knows that our markets are flooded with elegant silks which are nothing better than the mercerized imitation of the genuine fabric. The spinners and weavers of the Jaredites would have produced such woven materials as soon as the country became settled for peaceful industrial pursuits.

Lehi and his family, who emigrated from Jerusalem about 600 B.C., must have known both the material and the Hebrew name for it (meshi, Ezekiel 16:10, 13). In all probability, King Solomon, who had commercial connections with many faraway countries, imported silk from eastern Asia. In the prophecies of Isaiah (B.C. 811-750) reference is made to the land of the Sinim (Isaiah 49:12), generally understood to mean China. If the Hebrews at that time traded with eastern Asia, they certainly

20. And thus the Lord did pour out his blessings upon this land, which was choice above all other lands; and he commanded that whoso should possess the land should possess it unto the Lord, or they should be destroyed when they were ripened in iniquity; for upon such, saith the Lord: I will pour out the fulness of my wrath.

21. And Emer did execute judgment in righteousness all his days, and he begat many sons and daughters; and he begat Coriantum, and he anointed Coriantum to reign in his stead.

---

imported silk among other luxuries.[2] And the conclusion appears reasonable, that Moroni, who was a student of Isaiah, and knew the traditions of his ancestors from Lehi, had knowledge of silk, as handed down from generation to generation. He might, therefore, naturally and very properly, have called the fine fabrics of the Jaredites, silk.

That the American Indians of later times were unsurpassed masters in the fine art of producing cloth of cotton or wool, will not be disputed by any well-informed Americanist.

Our text, as we understand it, does neither prove, nor disprove, the opinion that the Indians anciently had the genuine Chinese silk cloth. It leaves that question open for future discoveries. It does inform us that the Jaredites were acquainted with that kind of material, and that they became experts in manufacturing imitations of it.

Fine Linen. This may have been material a shade coarser than the silk, and yet fine, as compared to the linen in common use.

Cattle, Oxen, Cows, Sheep. Scholars who are committed to the theory that man in America, and elsewhere, gradually rose from a brute beginning to the level of savagery, then to that of barbarism, and finally, to the dizzy heights of civilization, must of necessity deny the occurrence of civilized pursuits among the American aborigines as far back as four thousand years ago.[3]

But if we accept the Book of Moses as the word of the Lord, we cannot admit that the Jaredites came here as savages. They had a certain degree of civilization, in some respects more advanced then we moderns, in our haughty estimation of ourselves, care to express. They knew something about agriculture when they selected the fertile Plain of Shinar, in Mesopotamia as their home. They knew how to burn

---

[2]There is no *a priori* improbability in regarding the name Sinae as referring to the inhabitants of Eastern Asia in the time of Isaiah * * * for it is certain that at that time an inland commercial route connected the extreme east with the west, and that traffic was maintained on the frontier of China between the Scytians and the Sinae, in the manner that is still followed by the Chinese and the Russians at Kiachta. If any name for these traders traveled westward, it would probably be that of the Sinae. (Sinim, *Smith's Bible Dictionary*)

[3]Bancroft, speaking of the skill of Indians of later periods in manufacturing cloth, says: "The Zapotecs, Miztecs, Mayas, and others, since the conquest, have long been justly celebrated for the manufacture of cotton stuffs, a fact that is all the more surprising when we consider the very imperfect implements they possessed with which to perform the work. Burgoa speaks of the excellence and rich quality of their manufactures in cotton, silk and gold thread, in 1670, and Thomas Gage, writing about the same time, says 'it is rare to see what works these Indian women will make in silk, such as might serve for patterns and samplers to many schoolmistresses in England.' All the spinning and weaving is done by the women." (*Native Races*, Vol. 1, p. 657) I suspect that the silk mentioned was not all the Chinese output. And I believe that what the Indians could do in 1670, the Jaredites could do.

According to the chronology of Bishop Ussher, Peleg and Joctan lived B.C. 2247. Add 1960 A.D., the present year, and we get the date of the migration of Jared, the son of Joctan. 4207 years ago.

and make bricks and to build cities with towers.[4] They were astronomers, and they must have had some knowledge of geography to have been able to travel as they did. They had, above all, the religious knowledge that enabled them to hold communion with God and to receive revelations. That alone placed them well within the boundaries of civilization. And because they were a civilized race, the statement of Moroni, if correctly understood, is far from incredible.

When the Jaredites came here they found a variety of animals.

The musk ox. In the extreme north the musk ox roamed; an animal that still is of importance in the Arctic Regions.

The Caribou. Farther south, the American reindeer, commonly known as the caribou, must at that time have been plentiful. During historic times that animal has been found inhabiting the wooded districts of Canada and adjacent parts of the United States. In northern Europe the reindeer serve their owners, chiefly Laplanders, as both cows and horses. They give rich milk. They furnish meat, clothing, bones for tools, etc., and they are an invaluable means of speedy transportation. If the caribous of antiquity were anything like their now-known European kindred, and if Jaredite hunters succeeded in capturing and domesticating some, they would certainly have found them as valuable to their national prosperity as we do the cattle.

The Bison. Farther south the bison, or American buffalo, was grazing, in immense herds, on the plains between the Mississippi and the Rockies, from Canada to New Mexico. The buffalos, or rather bisons, are indigenous to America. As close relatives of the ox family they may properly be regarded as cattle. They certainly were useful animals. They provided juicy meat, including the pemmican, indispensible to hunters and explorers. They gave fat and tallow for various uses; skins for leather, clothing, tent covers, canoes, etc., and hair of which to manufacture material for cloth. The Jaredites may have kept small herds of them for domestic purposes, as we now do on reservations in several places, in order to save the species from extinction. Such herds would account for the oxen and cows mentioned in the Book of Ether.

Sheep. The Jaredites may not have had the merino, as bred and developed in later times in Spain, France and the United States. But they must have come across the Rocky Mountain sheep, generally known as the Bighorn. Varieties of this animal inhabited the western mountain regions from Alaska and the shores of the Bering Sea in the north to Mexico in the south. To what extent the Jaredites utilized these animals we do not know, but they must have been known by this enterprising people.

Under "Mexico" in *Encyclopedia Britannica*, the author relates that one of the ancient Aztecs, in a prayer, called the attention of his god, Tezcatlipoca, to the fact that he had sacrificed a sheep to the deity. The author thought that Spanish influence was in evidence in the use of the word "sheep," but Mr. Denison, who quotes the *Britannica* article, says the Aztecs appear to have had a name for sheep always, and that in the prayer mentioned a wild sheep may have been meant. He also mentions that bones of the Canadian sheep have been found in Arizona ruins.[5]

The Peccary. This animal, resembling the swine family, is about three feet long, with fewer teeth than the boar or pig. One variety has been found from Arkansas

---

[4]Called *Ziggurat* by the Sumerians. There was a great Ziggurat in the City of Ur, where Abraham lived. It was built, no one knows how long ago. Probably shortly after the dispersion. These towers had a religious character. They were built in terraces, representing the realm of the dead, the Earth and the Heaven. In the language of Genesis concerning the Tower of Babel, "whose top may reach into Heaven" (Genesis 11:14), the top represented Heaven. It was the place of worship of the builders; their temple, where they received revelations from on high. Or, rather, that was the intention of the religious leaders of the people.

[5]T. S. Denison, "Mexican Linguistics," pp. 23, 24

in the north to Patagonia in the South. A larger variety is said to be found in Central America and South America as far south as Brazil. Peccaries may have been the "swine" of the Jaredites. That would account satisfactorily for the name in our text.

However, that the Jaredite people, Semitic descendants, had swine is surprising. During the Mosaic dispensation those kind of animals were unclean, because they do not ruminate. Noah, the father of Shem, knew this division of living creatures to be a divine arrangement, for the Lord commanded the patriarch to save both clean and unclean beasts from destruction in the flood (Genesis 7:2, 8). In view of the Mosaic Law concerning unclean animals (Leviticus 11:7, 8), which, undoubtedly, was patterned after a previous patriarchal statute, the mention of swine among the edible animals of the Jaredites is unexpected.

But, probably, these pilgrims from Asia, during their wanderings through uninhabited deserts, could not always select their food with strict regard to legal rules of fitness. Probably they were under the necessity, frequently, to live on whatever they could find. Thus, the regulations observed when they lived in settled communities, may have been set aside by the force that is said to "know no law," and when they, finally, after years of traveling, formed settlements in the new country, some laws and rules, once deemed important, may never again have been enforced, even if they were not entirely forgotten. Such cases might be found even in the history of the immigrations into the United States in our own day.

Goats. The Rocky Mountain goat is an animal about the size of a large sheep. It has a coat of long, soft and warm, white hair, and an undercoat of fine wool. Domesticated, the goat is a useful animal. The wild species live in family groups on high mountain sides, where only experienced mountaineers can follow them. Jaredites had evidently captured some of them.

Many other kinds of Animals. Among these may be mentioned the deer, the moose or American elk, the bear, the beaver. The Jaredites must have found these and many other useful species. There were, besides, birds, migratory as well as permanent inhabitants of forests and canyons; fish in the streams and lakes and in the waters of the oceans, and shellfish and mussels in great abundance, as shown by the shellheaps on the coasts around the American continents, and in some places inland. Dogs are not mentioned among the assets of the people, but they must have had those faithful friends of man. They may even have brought dogs with them from their home land.

Horses. As a contribution to the discussion of Jaredite culture, it may be mentioned that press dispatches dated June 13, 1936, announced the discovery, by explorers, of a cave under a ledge in the mountains near Albuquerque, New Mexico, in which there were a hearth of stone, a flint tool and bones of prehistoric animals, such as horses, camels and mastodons, which, scientists say, disappeared from this continent thousands of years ago. A conservative conclusion from these and similar finds is, according to Dr. D. D. Brand, head of the anthropology department of the University of New Mexico, that so-called pleistocene animals; that is to say, animals that lived during the glacial period, may actually have continued their existence for some time after the withdrawal of the great ice sheets which marked the end of the pleistocene period. If this logical conclusion obtains confirmation, we may suppose that some of the horses of the previous ages survived and were found by man during historic times. The Jaredites may on that theory, have had horses. The equines, as other early living creatures, may not have become totally extinct until after the dawn of historic times. The Jaredites, we know, destroyed their own culture during historic times, and came near enough to exterminating each other. Some domesticated animals may have shared their fate. On March 21, 1938, the Associated Press announced that explorers in Death Valley had come across footprints of camels, pigs, one-toed horses and wading birds. Not even a guess was offered concerning the probable remoteness of the time at which those marks were placed where now found.

Asses. We need not say a great deal about those useful creatures here. The Jaredites had the animals known in the wild state as asses, and, domesticated, as donkeys, even if we do not know how they got them.

To those who insist that donkeys were unknown in America during the early years of the Jaredites, we offer the suggestion that the small horses may have reminded them of the asses of their own country. The two branches of the equine family are closely related and resemble each other very much. This resemblance may have suggested the name for the small horses. In that case, the asses would be the same as our "ponies."

Elephants. While Dr. John A. Widtsoe, the Apostle, was presiding over the European mission, he received a clipping from the Sheffield, England, "Weekly Telegram," of Nov. 4, 1933, in which the statement was made that there were pictures of elephants among Maya pictographs, which must have been carved by Asiatics who knew the Asiatic elephant. The paper asked, "How did these people cross the ocean? Was a native boat journey of two thousand miles possible?"

Well, a Chinese historian, writing in the 7th century of our era, states that a Chinese expedition long ago discovered a country 20,000 *li*[6] to the east of Tahan, which was called Fusang. Tahan, says Bancroft,[7] is generally supposed to be Kamchatka, and Fusang the northwest coast of America, California or Mexico. The story is, of course, not accepted as true. It has a great many fantastic details. But it is by no means impossible that, hidden among the embellishments, there is a modicum of historic facts. And they may point to the possibility of migrations over eastern Asia of people who carried to America the knowledge of both elephants, horses and other animals. About three thousand years ago, during the time of King Solomon, the oceans were highways, on which Hebrew and Phoenician navigators may have reached America and visited the islands on their perilous course.

Marquis de Nadaillac says that among the ornaments of a certain wall at Uxmal, an ancient Maya city, were details supposed to be elephant-trunks. This, he says, would be a curious fact, if true. For the elephant was certainly not living in America at the time of the erection of the monuments of Uxmal.

It all depends. The Mayas, according to some authorities, entered Yucatan during the 6th century A.D., from Guatemala, Mexico and British Honduras. If the ornaments in question are of a later date, the elephants may have been extinct when the frieze of which they form a detail was fashioned. But even in that case, Maya artists would have known elephants by hearsay, just as educated people in our day know something about mastodons and dinosaurs, although they may never have seen one, not even in a museum. But if the structures of Uxmal, which for centuries have been only ruins, are pre-Mayan, elephants may still have inhabited favorable localities in America, when those buildings were new. Giants from prehistoric times may still have swung their long muscular noses, their "big sticks," fuzzily warning enemies of danger.

The Mastodon. This extinct animal is known to have survived into the historical period. According to Mr. M. R. Harrison, curator of the Los Angeles Museum, the earliest inhabitants of California, the "Folsom" people, hunted both bisons and mammoths, the latter being also known as extinct elephants. Obsidian spearheads

---

[6]A "li" is supposed to equal a third of a mile.
[7]*Native Races,* Vol. 5, p. 33.

3. *Coriantum succeeds Emer.*

22. An after he had anointed Coriantum to reign in his stead he lived four years, and he saw peace in the land; yea, and he even saw the Son of Righteousness, and did rejoice and glory in his day; and he died in peace.

23. And it came to pass that

---

and knives, we are informed, have been found among bones of those extinct animals on the shores of a pond in Clear Lake Park, where the people mentioned seem to have had a favorite camp.

Cureloms. We note that the animals enumerated are divided into three classes:

(1) Cattle, oxen, cows, sheep, swine and goats, and also many other kinds "were useful for the food of man."

(2) Horses, asses, elephants, cureloms and cumoms "were useful unto man," but not for food.

(3) Elephants, cureloms and cumoms were "more especially" useful.

The elephant is a marvelously intelligent creature, and if the question is of transportation, or the carrying of burdens, or even of military service in primitive warfare, he cannot be surpassed, when properly trained. But what of the cureloms and cumoms?

There is a Hebrew verb, "garal," meaning to roll forth, or, roll off (a burden, for instance). The Semitic or Jaredite ancestor of that word may have been, "karal," having the same meaning. Curel or Kurel can have been formed from karal, to denote an animal with a characteristically rolling motion, such as the camel has. The sounds represented by g and k are interchangeable, or the letters are. The motion of the camel, the "ship of the desert," is peculiar. When walking, he lifts both feet simultaneously, first on one side and then the other, causing a rolling motion unpleasant to those not accustomed to it. The "om" in curel-om we consider a plural termination, as "im" in the Hebrew. Curel-om would, according to this conjecture, mean camels. The South American llama belongs to the camel family. The curel-om of the Jaredites may have been relatives of those proud-looking and useful creatures if not their ancestors.

Cumoms. If we eliminate the American plural "s" and understand the "om" to be equivalent to the Hebrew plural "im," the word in the singular would be "cum." But the Hebrew "kum" means to rise up, to stand up.[8] It may be for either friendly or unfriendly purposes. The bear shows that characteristic. He rises up on his hind legs to fight an enemy, and also, at least in zoological gardens, to beg visitors for tidbits. Being a hibernating animal, he goes to sleep in the fall and rises in the spring as from the dead. Bears may possibly be the cum-om of the Book of Ether,[9] because of these peculiarities. Their skins would certainly be "more especially" useful in areas where the summers are hot but the winters cold.

VERSE 22. *Son of Righteousness.* This is one name of the Son of God, denoting a divine attribute. The Prophet Malachi (4:2) refers to Jesus as the "Sun of Righteousness," to express His equality with the Father. Speaking of the Lord's day, the Hebrew prophet says it shall burn up all the proud and all that do iniquity; they

---

[8]Comp. "Talitha cumi," damsel arise!" (Mark 5:41)

[9]When the Lord had formed every beast of the field, he brought them before Adam "to see what he would call them." And whatsoever Adam, naturally after careful observation of their characteristics called them, that became their name. (Genesis 2:19) The Hebrew name for bear is, "dob." But that, it is said, refers only to the species peculiar to Syria.

Coriantum did walk in the steps of his father, and did build many mighty cities, and did administer that which was good unto his people in all his days. And it came to pass that he had no children even until he was exceeding old.

24. And it came to pass that his wife died, being an hundred and two years old. And it came to pass that Coriantum took to wife, in his old age, a young maid, and begat sons and daughters; wherefore he lived until he was an hundred and forty and two years old.

4. Com Reigns in his Stead.

25. And it came to pass that he begat Com, and Com reigned in his stead; and he reigned forty and nine years, and he begat Heth; and he also begat other sons and daughters.

5. Heth Dethrones and Kills his Father.

26. And the people had spread again over all the face of the land, and there began again to be an exceeding great wickedness upon the face of the land, and Heth began to embrace the secret plans again of old, to destroy his father. 27. And it came to pass that

shall be stubble; but unto those who fear the Lord's name, "shall the Sun of Righteousness arise with healing in His wings." Malachi seems to have borrowed a figure of speech suggested by the winged sun in Egyptian mythology, especially the Osiris myth; and in other eastern religions featuring sun worship. The Jews at the time of Malachi must have been familiar with those religious concepts and symbols. Moroni here uses an original name, Son of Righteousness, which reminds us of Jeremiah 23:6: "And this is the name whereby He shall be called, THE LORD OUR RIGHTEOUSNESS." This is His name. The Sun of Righteousness is only the symbol of the Name. Commentators have suggested that the expression of Malachi does not refer to the Lord, or any other person, but to a principle. In the text before us it is made clear that the Son of Righteousness is none other than our Lord, Jesus Christ, Himself.

Verse 23. *The Reign of Coriantum.* The king walked in the footsteps of his father Emer. He built many mighty cities, and devoted his entire life to the welfare of the people. His wife passed away at the age of 102 years. Coriantum, although having reached a high age, married a young girl and became the father of several children. His biographer gives the impression that his second marriage prolonged his life. Moroni says, "Wherefore he lived until he was 142 years old." (v. 24)

Verse 25. *Com.* One of his sons, Com, probably the youngest, succeeded him.

Verses 26-35. *Heth.* One of the sons of Com was named Heth, a noun that means "terror." It was the name of the progenitor of the Hittites, the children of Heth, in Genesis, who were the inhabitants of Palestine during the time of Abraham. Ephron, of whom the Patriarch bought the field of Machpelah, with the cave in which he interred the remains of his wife Sarah, was a Hittite. (Genesis 23:1-20)[10]

---

[10]At the time of Joshua, northern Palestine was part of a Hittite empire which the Lord gave to the children of Israel. (Joshua 1:4)

he did dethrone his father, for he slew him with his own sword; and he did reign in his stead.

28. And there came prophets in the land again, crying repentance unto them—that they must prepare the way of the Lord or there should come a curse upon the face of the land; yea, even there should be a great famine, in which they should be destroyed if they did not repent.

Heth, the son of Com, was what his name signified, a terror. He joined some criminal, secret organization, murdered his father and usurped his office. (v. 27)

The wickedness of the king had its corrupting influence on the people. His subjects imitated him. Lawlessness in high places is particularly contagious. As a rule, the moral status of a nation is at the level of the leading and ruling classes. The Jaredites under Heth became as wicked as he was.

The Lord sent prophets, or missionaries, who called upon them to repent and who predicted a great famine if they persisted in wrong-doing. They rejected the message and persecuted, and even killed, the messengers, at the instigation of the king. (vv. 28, 29)

The famine came. God withheld rain. The gardens and fields became parched. Water supplies dried up. Prosperous farms were desolated by the scorching rays of the sun. Trees died. Nowhere any cooling shade. Hot sandstorms added terror to other calamities. People perished by famine. Some were killed by the poisonous reptiles that multiplied in the deserted land. Domestic animals, being without the wanted human care and protection, followed their instinct and began a gradual trek southward toward the country of Zarahemla, away from the burning desert and the loathesome snakes. But many of these perished on the road. Some reached the land southward. (vv. 30-32)

Time passed. The snakes disappeared from the land still occupied and multiplied along the main roads of traffic, where they became a deadly menace to traders and travelers. The country became isolated as well as desolated. The inhabitants hunted carcasses of animals that had been killed by snakes, and when that source of food had been exhausted, death seemed to be the only alternative. (vv. 33, 34)

Then the people repented. They turned to the Lord. He sent rain. The country was resurrected to life and became prosperous again. (v. 35)

The apostate Jaredites may, possibly, have turned to serpent worship in their blind efforts to escape God. That may have been one tenet of their secret society. If so, the punishment by snakes was a method of divine instruction as well as retribution. It proved to the people that the death-dealing reptiles were anything but divine, and that God in Heaven is the supreme Ruler in the world.

The children of Israel had, at one time, a similar demonstration in the wilderness. At Mt. Horeb they became rebellious and accused Moses of having led them out into a desert to perish of hunger. Then their camp became infested by serpents which killed many of the agitators. The people were frightened and turned to God. Moses was instructed to make a serpent of brass and raise the image up on a pole. Anyone who was wounded would be healed by looking at this brazen figure.

Many of the Israelites, no doubt, had the eastern idea that the serpent had healing power. Among Assyrians, Chaldeans, Egyptians, Phoenicians and others, the serpent was supposed to bring health and good fortune. Moses by directing the wounded to look upon the brazen image hanging lifeless on a pole, demonstrated that healing comes from God, by faith, not from contact with a coiling reptile. (Numbers 21:4-9) The vindication of the supremacy of God, we think, was the object

29. But the people believed not the words of the prophets, but they cast them out; and some of them they cast into pits and left them to perish. And it came to pass that they did all these things according to the commandment of the king, Heth.

30. And it came to pass that there began to be a great dearth upon the land, and the inhabitants began to be destroyed ex-ceeding fast because of the dearth, for there was no rain upon the face of the earth.

31. And there came forth poisonous serpents also upon the face of the land, and did poison many people. And it came to pass that their flocks began to flee before the poisonous serpents, towards the land southward, which was called by the Nephites Zarahemla.

---

lesson of the experience of Israel in the wilderness, and of Jaredites in the Land of Moron.

GENERAL NOTES

Scholars hold that the widespread veneration of snakes began in fear inspired by violent thunderstorms. The reptiles became the symbols of the lightning, they believed, and thereby also of the god of thunder and rain. Thus, the Tlaloc of the Aztecs held in one hand a piece of gold supposed to represent lightning. Huracan of the Quiche legend is "the strong serpent," the thunderer. Quetzalcoatl, Gucumatz, Cuculcan, Bancroft says, are all titles of the god of the air, signifying, "Bird-Serpent." This may be so. For when man, through neglect of communion with God and the indulgence in sin sets aside his knowledge of the true Ruler of Heaven and Earth, he may even believe that a golden calf is the image of Him who led Israel out of Egypt. (Exodus 32:8)

But the serpent is also the symbol of evil among some. The Apaches are said to believe that the rattlesnakes are inhabited by the souls of bad men, and that they are the emissaries of evil spirits. The Piutes believe, it is said, that the existence of a demon in the form of a serpent was in the waters of the Pyramid Lake. But whether symbols of good or bad spiritual forces, the serpents occur with many of the gods revered by the aborigines of the American continents.

Concerning some interesting antiquities discovered in California, Mr. Bancroft has this to say:

"The existence of the works of human hands buried hundreds of feet beneath the many successive layers of different rocks and earths, might not necessarily imply a greater age than one dating a few centuries before the coming of the Spaniards; although few would be willing to admit, probably, that natural convulsions so extensive have taken place at so recent an epoch. But when the work of human hands is shown to be discovered in connection with the bones of mastodons, elephants, horses, camels and other animals long since extinct, and that they have been so found, there seems to be sufficient proof, it is hardly possible with consistency to deny that these implements date from a remote antiquity." (Native Races, Vol. 4, p. 697)

AGRICULTURE IN AMERICA

According to a press dispatch dated Dec. 28, 1938, Dr. Donald D. Brand, an anthropologist of the Smithsonian Institution, has recently made the statement that civilization in America is older than that of Egypt, if agriculture is taken as evidence.

32. And it came to pass that there were many of them which did perish by the way; nevertheless, there were some which fled into the land southward.

33. And it came to pass that the Lord did cause the serpents that they should pursue them no more, but that they should hedge up the way that the people could not pass, that whoso should attempt to pass might fall by the poisonous serpents.

34. And it came to pass that the people did follow the course of the beasts, and did devour the carcasses of them which fell by the way, until they had devoured them all. Now when the people saw that they must perish they began to repent of their iniquities and cry unto the Lord.

35. And it came to pass that when they had humbled themselves sufficiently before the Lord he did send rain upon the face of the earth; and the people began to revive again, and there began to be fruit in the north countries, and in all the countries round about. And the Lord did show forth his power unto them in preserving them from famine.

He pointed out that the wide spread of plants which require cultivation for their propagation, such as maize, kidney beans, pumpkins and potatoes, indicate a long period of development. The prehistoric inhabitants of Mexico and Central America, Dr. Brand said, had more domesticated plants than any people in a similar area anywhere in the world.

ABLOM

A place on the Atlantic Seaboard of the northern continent, east of the Hill Cumorah. The Lord in a dream warned Omer, King of the Jaredites, to flee from his native land at the time his Kingdom was overthrown by Akish and his friends. This he did and after a long journey settled at Ablom. Nimrah, a son of Akish, with a number of adherents afterwards joined Omer at Ablom. After many years Omer was restored to his Kingdom and returned to his own land.

CUMOM

The Cumom was a useful animal known to the Jaredites. By some it is supposed to be the Mastodon, by others, the Alpaca or Llama.

CURELOM

The Curelom was a useful animal known to the Jaredites. By some it is supposed to be the Elephant, by others, the Llama or Alpaca. (Ether 9:19)

CHAPTER 10

1. *Riplakish, the wrong-doer.*

1. And it came to pass that Shez, who was a descendant of Heth—for Heth had perished by the famine, and all his household save it were Shez — wherefore, Shez began to build up again a broken people.

2. And it came to pass that Shez did remember the destruction of his fathers, and he did build up a righteous kingdom; for he remembered what the Lord had done in bringing Jared and his brother across the deep; and he did walk in the ways of the Lord; and be begat sons and daughters.

3. And his eldest son, whose name was Shez, did rebel against him; nevertheless, Shez was smitten by the hand of a robber, because of his exceeding riches, which brought peace again unto his father.

4. And it came to pass that his father did build up many cities upon the face of the land, and the people began again to spread over all the face of the land. And Shez did live to an exceeding old age; and he begat Riplakish. And he died, and Riplakish reigned in his stead.

5. And it came to pass that Riplakish did not do that which was right in the sight of the Lord, for he did have many wives and concubines, and did lay that upon men's shoulders which was grievous to be borne; yea, he did tax them with heavy taxes; and with

---

VERSES 1-4. *Shez.* Heth and his family having perished in the famine (Ether 9:30), Shez, a descendant of Heth, succeeded him as head of the government. The people were in a deplorable condition. Their number had been reduced by famine, pestilence, and emigration. The arable land was just beginning to emerge from a condition of desolation, and pioneer work had to be done over again. The cattle had perished. Under the circumstances, Shez remembering the destruction wrought and the mercy and power of God in bringing Jared and his Brother across the great Deep, undertook to restore the people to normal activities and prosperity. As he was in earnest to succeed, he kept near to the Lord, and led a life of righteousness both public and private. There is no other sure way to success.

And yet, he had great sorrow in seeing his firstborn, also named Shez, gathering up wealth for himself, and then heading a rebellion, in which he, the wayward son, was assassinated by a robber who turned out to be one of his partners in crime.

After this the people enjoyed a season of peace. Cities were built, and the population multiplied. Shez lived to an exceeding old age.

VERSES 5-8. The successor of Shez was a different character. He offended God and man by gathering around him a great number of seductive women. To meet

the taxes he did build many spacious buildings.

6. And he did erect him an exceedingly beautiful throne; and he did build many prisons, and whoso would not be subject unto taxes he did cast into prison; and whoso was not able to pay taxes he did cast into prison; and he did cause that they should labor continually for their support; and whoso refused to labor he did cause to be put to death.

7. Wherefore he did obtain all his fine work, yea, even his fine gold he did cause to be refined in prison, and all manner of fine workmanship he did cause to be wrought in prison. And it came to pass that he did afflict the people with his whoredoms and abominations.

8. And when he had reigned for the space of forty and two years the people did rise up in rebellion against him; and there began to be war again in the land, insomuch that Riplakish was killed, and his descendants were driven out of the land.

2. Morianton, the reformer.

9. And it came to pass after the space of many years, Morianton, (he being a descendant of Riplakish) gathered together an army of outcasts, and went forth and gave battle unto the people; and he gained power over many cities; and the war became exceeding sore, and did last for the space of many years; and he did gain power over all the land, and did establish himself king over all the land.

10. And after that he had established himself king he did ease the burden of the people, by which he did gain favor in the eyes of the people, and they did anoint him to be their king.

11. And he did do justice unto the people, but not unto himself because of his many whoredoms;

---

the expenses of a vast court, reveling in luxury, he levied oppressive taxes and built prisons which he filled with laborers who were unable to pay the dues he imposed. His numerous places of incarceration became what we would call concentration camps, where working men were forced to slave incessantly for him and his lewd women. And if they refused to work according to his will, they were put to death. This reign of terror lasted for forty-two years. Then the people rose in uncontrollable fury. Riplakish was killed and his family driven into exile.

Verses 9-12. *Morianton anointed King.* At the violent death of Riplakish, the people were not in a hurry to elect another king. There was an interregnum of *many years.* During that time the government may have been administered by a representative body elected by popular vote.

This form of government was brought to an end by an invader. Morianton, a descendant of Riplakish, entered the country at the head of an army of *outcasts,* overturned the administration and proclaimed himself King. He secured popularity by lightening the tax burdens, and causing general prosperity. The people became wealthy, in buildings, gold, silver, grain, flocks and herds. (Compare Ether 9:17-19)

wherefore he was cut off from the presence of the Lord.

12. And it came to pass that Morianton built up many cities, and the people became exceeding rich under his reign, both in buildings, and in gold and silver, and in raising grain, and in flocks, and herds, and such things which had been restored unto them.

3. Other Monarchs and their wars.

13. And Morianton did live to an exceeding great age, and then he begat Kim; and Kim did reign in the stead of his father; and he did reign eight years, and his father died. And it came to pass that Kim did not reign in righteousness, wherefore he was not favored of the Lord.

14. And his brother did rise up in rebellion against him, by which he did bring him into captivity; and he did remain in captivity all his days; and he begat sons and daughters in captivity, and in his old age he begat Levi; and he died.

15. And it came to pass that Levi did serve in captivity after the death of his father, for the space of forty and two years. And he did make war against the king of the land, by which he did obtain unto himself the kingdom.

16. And after he had obtained unto himself the kingdom he did that which was right in the sight of the Lord; and the people did prosper in the land; and he did live to a good old age, and begat sons and daughters; and he also begat Corom, whom he anointed king in his stead.

In their enthusiasm they caused him to be anointed King; that is, they conferred religious authority on him, the prerogatives of the Priesthood. But that was misplaced confidence. Morianton, as did his predecessors, surrounded himself with loose women and was "cut off from the presence of the Lord." In other words, he was deprived of the Priesthood and excommunicated. But, it seems that he continued his administration as King.

This is a remarkable example in early history of a perfect democracy and the complete separation of the church from the state, as far as their respective governments are concerned.

VERSES 13-14. *Kim.* The son and successor of Morianton. He reigned eight years before his father died. After the death of his father, the aged Morianton, Kim forfeited the favor of the Lord by unrighteousness. He was made a prisoner of war by his brother who rose up in rebellion against him, and remained in captivity until released by death. And Kim "begat sons and daughters in captivity, and in his old age he begat Levi."

VERSES 15-16. *Levi.* The son of Kim, was born in captivity and remained a prisoner for forty-two years. Then he began a successful war on the reigning monarch. As the head of the state, Levi served the Lord. The people prospered under his regime. He lived to a good age and enjoyed domestic happiness.

17. And it came to pass that Corom did that which was good in the sight of the Lord all his days; and he begat many sons and daughters; and after he had seen many days he did pass away, even like unto the rest of the earth; and Kish reigned in his stead.

18. And it came to pass that Kish passed away also, and Lib reigned in his stead.

4. The Land Southward.

19. And it came to pass that Lib also did that which was good in the sight of the Lord. And in the days of Lib the poisonous serpents were destroyed. Wherefore they did go into the land southward, to hunt food for the people of the land, for the land was covered with animals of the forest. And Lib also himself became a great hunter.

20. And they built a great city by the narrow neck of land, by the place where the sea divides the land.

5. The Land Northward, Inhabited.

21. And they did preserve the land southward for a wilderness, to get game. And the whole face of the land northward was covered with inhabitants.

22. And they were exceedingly industrious, and they did buy and sell and traffic one with another, that they might get gain.

23. And they did work in all

VERSES 17-18. *Corom.* The son and successor of Levi, had been anointed King before the death of his father. He did what was good for the people, seeking the approval of the Lord. His private life was one of all around happiness, and he passed away at a good old age, "like unto the rest of the earth."

VERSE 18. *Kish.* The son and successor of Corom. Nothing more is recorded of his reign, but from an expression in verse nineteen, we may conclude that he was a righteous King.

VERSES 19-20. *Lib.* The accession to the throne by Lib, the son of Kish, marks the beginning of an important era in the history of the Jaredites. The following events are mentioned:

(1) In his day the poisonous serpents (Ether 9:31) were destroyed and communication established with the Land Southward (Zarahemla).

(2) This land was then covered with forests which were the habitat of various kinds of animals. Hunting expeditions opened the way into this country.

(3) These hunters, of whom many remained in the Land Southward, "built a great city by the narrow neck of land, by the place where the sea divides the land."

(4) During the reign of Lib the entire land northward became densely populated, "covered with inhabitants." (v. 21)

Forests in which animals might be hunted for pelts, bones, horn, etc., if not for food, and a shipping port may have been of vital importance at this time to the flourishing industries in the Land Northward. Marquis de Nadaillac, who describes

manner of ore, and they did make gold, and silver, and iron, and brass, and all manner of metals; and they did dig it out of the earth; wherefore they did cast up mighty heaps of earth to get ore, of gold, and of silver, and of iron, and of copper. And they did work all manner of fine work.

24. And they did have silks, and fine-twined linen; and they did work all manner of cloth, that they might clothe themselves from their nakedness.

25. And they did make all manner of tools to till the earth, both to plow and to sow, to reap and to hoe, and also to thrash.

26. And they did make all manner of tools with which they did work their beasts.

27. And they did make all manner of weapons of war. And they did work all manner of work of exceedingly curious workmanship.

28. And never could be a people more blessed than were they, and more prospered by the hand of the Lord. And they were in a

---

certain mounds in North America, and artifacts found therein which evidently had crossed a large part of the continent, came to the conclusion that it is not improbable that articles from Mexico or Florida could, as far back as the time of the mound-builders, have found their way to what is now New England and Minnesota.

Gold, Silver, Iron, Brass. Nadaillac says that ornaments of shell, stone, and even wood, have been unearthed in North American mounds. The wooden trinkets were covered with copper. Some of the ornaments were made of copper, plated with gold, silver, or iron. Mica was used for mirrors. (*See, Prehistoric America*, Nadaillac, pp. 46-132)

VERSE 24. *Silks and fine twined linen.* See, Ether 9:17. Fine twined linen was the fiber twisted into strands, or threads, ready for the loom. It was, perhaps, the very material from which the silks were made.

VERSE 25. *Tools to till the earth.* The plow used in Peru at the time of the arrival of the Spaniards is described by Prescott. Probably it was not materially different from that of the Jaredites. It consisted of a strong sharp-pointed stake, traversed by a horizontal piece some inches from that point. The ploughman forced the lower part of the stake into the ground by means of a rope, to make a furrow. Women followed with rakes, breaking up the sod. (*Peru*, Prescott, Vol. I, p. 115)

To thrash. In oriental countries during historic times, thrashing was done on a thrashing floor in the open air. The floor was a hard-beaten spot. Often a flail was used. Or oxen were made to tramp the grain out of the sheaves.

Weapons of War. Including bows and arrows, lances, darts, swords, battle-axes, slings, shields, and a tunic of quilted cotton, were among their weapons of war. Spears and arrows were tipped with copper, or bone. At least, such were the contents of the arsenals of warring Indians of later ages.

All manner of Work. Stone mortars, implements for boring, daggers, arrowheads, beads of shell and bear's teeth, are a few of the curios found in North American shell heaps and mounds. Central and South American ruins have, as is well known, yielded thousands of specimens of the products of ancient American civilizations.

VERSE 28. *A people blessed by the Lord.* This verse indicates the religious character of the people. Prescott, *Peru*, Volume 1, p. 85, observes that the originals or aborigines, of America, notwithstanding many superstitions, had attained to the sublime

land that was choice above all lands, for the Lord had spoken it.

29. And it came to pass that Lib did live many years, and begat sons and daughters; and he also begat Hearthom.

30. And it came to pass that Hearthom reigned in the stead of his father. And when Hearthom had reigned twenty and four years, behold, the kingdom was taken away from him. And he served many years in captivity, yea, even all the remainder of his days.

31. And he begat Heth, and Heth lived in captivity all his days. And Heth begat Aaron, and Aaron dwelt in captivity all his days; and he begat Amnigaddah, and Amnigaddah also dwelt in captivity all his days; and he begat Coriantum, and Coriantum dwelt in captivity all his days; and he begat Com.

32. And it came to pass that Com drew away the half of the kingdom. And he reigned over the half of the kingdom forty and two years; and he went to battle

---

conception of a Great Spirit, the Creator of the Universe, Who was not to be dishonored by visible representation. Students of what is generally known as prehistoric America need the Book of Mormon to explain such facts as these.

VERSES 30-34. Hearthom, the son of Lib, after having been the head of the administration for twenty-four years, was made a prisoner of war and spent the rest of his life in captivity.

Heth II. His son, Heth, remained in servitude all his life.

Aaron. He, too, lived all his life in captivity. Aaron, it will be remembered, was the eloquent brother of Moses, who was called to be the interpreter, or mouth, of the great liberator before Pharaoh. He was born in Egypt three years before Moses. The name means *mountaineer.*

Amnigaddah, the son of Heth II, lived and died in captivity.

Coriantum, the son of Amnigaddah, also lived in captivity all his days.

Com. This son of Coriantum managed to rise above the condition of servitude, and to be elected King over one-half of the kingdom. Amgid was the King of the other half. Com reigned for forty-two years. Then he began war on Amgid, and after years of warfare, the Kingdom was united under Com as the regent.

During his reign secret organizations flourished and sought to destroy the government. Com was unable to suppress the activities of these enemies of the people.

GENERAL NOTES

Writing about the industries of the Nahuas, Dr. Bancroft says:

"The finer kinds of cloth were made of cotton, of rabbit hair, of the two mixed, or of cotton mixed with feathers. The rabbit hair fabrics were pronounced equal in finish and texture to silk." (*Native Races,* Volume 2, p. 484)

SHEZ

A Jaredite Prince, the eldest son of the King of the same name. He rose in rebellion against his father, but while thus traitorously engaged, a robber killed him in the endeavor to obtain some of his riches which the Book of Ether informs us were great.

against the king, Amgid, and they fought for the space of many years, during which time Com gained power over Amgid, and obtained power over the remainder of the kingdom.

33. And in the days of Com there began to be robbers in the land; and they adopted the old plans, and administered oaths after the manner of the ancients, and sought again to destroy the kingdom.

34. Now Com did fight against them much; nevertheless, he did not prevail against them.

AMGID

A King of the Jaredites of the dynasty that overthrew the reigning monarch in the days of Hearthom. In Amgid's days a descendant of Hearthom named Com, having first drawn away half of the Kingdom, after a lapse of forty-two years, went to war with Amgid for the other half. The war lasted many years and ended in Com obtaining power over the whole Kingdom.

CHAPTER 11

1. *The Story of Com Continued: Jaredite Prophets Predict Utter Destruction of Their People Unless They Repent*—2. *The Warning Unheeded; Shiblom, Seth, Ahah, Ethem, Moron, Coriantor, Ether.*

1. *The story of Com continued.*

1. And there came also in the days of Com many prophets, and prophesied of the destruction of that great people except they should repent, and turn unto the Lord, and forsake their murders and wickedness.

2. And it came to pass that the prophets were rejected by the people, and they fled unto Com for protection, for the people sought to destroy them.

3. And they prophesied unto Com many things; and he was blessed in all the remainder of his days.

4. And he lived to a good old age, and begat Shiblom; and

VERSES 1-3. *Com.* This ruler, although unable to suppress the activities of the secret, criminal, organizations in his country, (Ether 10:33-34) became the protector of persecuted servants of God. He took a bold stand for religious liberty, and was blessed by the Lord as long as he lived.

The Prophet Joseph Smith was a consistent defender of religious liberty. Referring to the persecution in early days of Baptists and Quakers in Boston, the burning of *witches* in Salem, and the destruction of a Catholic convent more recently, he says of the persecutors:

"Well did the Savior say concerning such, 'By their fruits ye shall know them.' And if the wicked mob who destroyed the convent, and the cool, calculating, religious lookers on, who inspired their hearts with deeds of infamy, do not arise and redress the wrong, and restore the injury fourfold, they, in turn, will receive of the measure they have meted out, till the just indignation of a righteous God is satisfied. When will man cease to war with man and wrest from him his sacred right of worshiping his God according as his conscience dictates? Holy Father, hasten the day!" (*History of the Church*, Volume 2, p. 465)

Religious liberty is one of the inalienable rights belonging to each individual child of God. It is the foundation of all true liberty. The authority to legislate in religious matters cannot be transferred to any political legislature.

Luther stressed this fact in his great speech before the Diet of Worms, April 17, 1521. The Emperor Charles V, princes of Germany, papal nuncios, dignitaries of all grades, were there. Luther, being urged to recall his teachings, replied in an eloquent, forceful and yet humble speech. He spoke for two hours. He admitted that human infirmity, no doubt, marked some of his writings. This he did not deny. But, as far as the word of God, that he could not recant. "Confute me," he said, "by proofs of Scripture, or else by plain, just, arguments; I cannot recant otherwise. For it is neither safe nor prudent to do aught against conscience. Here I stand. I cannot do otherwise. God help me." Luther, at that moment, proved himself faithful to liberty, to humanity, to God.

VERSES 4-9. *Shiblom.* Shiblom succeeded his father, Com. During his reign, prophets arose, who foretold a time of trouble and destruction—an indication of the

Shiblom reigned in his stead. And the brother of Shiblom rebelled against him, and there began to be an exceeding great war in all the land.

5. And it came to pass that the brother of Shiblom caused that all the prophets who prophesied of the destruction of the people should be put to death;

6. And there was great calamity in all the land, for they had testified that a great curse should come upon the land, and also upon the people, and that there should be a great destruction among them, such an one as never had been upon the face of the earth, and their bones should become as heaps of earth upon the face of the land, except they

should repent of their wickedness.

7. And they hearkened not unto the voice of the Lord, because of their wicked combinations; wherefore, there began to be wars and contentions in all the land, and also many famines and pestilences, insomuch that there was a great destruction, such an one as never had been known upon the face of the earth; and all this came to pass in the days of Shiblom.

8. And the people began to repent of their iniquity; and inasmuch as they did the Lord did have mercy on them.

9. And it came to pass that Shiblom was slain, and Seth was brought into captivity, and did dwell in captivity all his days.

2. The warning unheeded.

10. And it came to pass that Ahah, his son, did obtain the kingdom; and he did reign over

the people all his days. And he did do all manner of iniquity in his days, by which he did cause

---

Godless character of his administration. Disaster began when his brother rebelled and plunged the country into the throes of civil war. This conflict was at first confined to one country, probably to Moron, but it spread to "all the land," and the consequences were famine, pestilence and destruction everywhere. The bones of the dead were figuratively speaking, "as heaps of earth upon the face of the land." A striking simile, suggested, we believe, by the shell heaps and earth mounds, which have been a familiar sight to the people of some localities.

The destruction had the effect intended. The transgressors repented, and the Lord had mercy on them. Shiblom, the chief offender, was slain.[1]

VERSES 10-23. *Seth, Ahah, Ethem, Moron, Coriantor, Ether.* Seth, the son of Shiblom, was made a prisoner of war for the remainder of his life. The entire period

---

[1]The foregoing note takes it for granted that Shiblom in this chapter and Shiblon in Ether 1:12 are identical. That is the general understanding. Perhaps they are. But another supposition is at least permissible. Shiblom may have been the rebel brother of Shiblom; the brother who is said to have caused the prophets to be slain, and to have brought the calamity of civil war and destruction on the people. He must have usurped the government in order to do this. In that case it may have been Shiblon who ordered the death of Shiblom, and the degradation of his own son, Seth, to a state of servitude for life. If this understanding of the text is correct, the royal lineage, at the death of Com, diverged from Shiblon to Shiblom, both sons of Com, and continued through the latter to Ether. Shiblom, although king for a short time, had no place in the genealogical table.

the shedding of much blood; and few were his days.

11. And Ethem, being a descendant of Ahah, did obtain the kingdom; and he also did do that which was wicked in his days.

12. And it came to pass that in the days of Ethem there came many prophets, and prophesied again unto the people; yea, they did prophesy that the Lord would utterly destroy them from off the face of the earth except they repented of their iniquities.

13. And it came to pass that the people hardened their hearts, and would not hearken unto their words; and the prophets mourned and withdrew from among the people.

14. And it came to pass that Ethem did execute judgment in wickedness all his days; and he begat Moron. And it came to pass that Moron did reign in his stead; and Moron did that which was wicked before the Lord.

15. And it came to pass that there arose a rebellion among the people, because of that secret combination which was built up to get power and gain; and there arose a mighty man among them in iniquity, and gave battle unto Moron, in which he did over-

throw the half of the kingdom; and he did maintain the half of the kingdom for many years.

16. And it came to pass that Moron did overthrow him, and did obtain the kingdom again.

17. And it came to pass that there arose another mighty man; and he was a descendant of the brother of Jared.

18. And it came to pass that he did overthrow Moron and obtain the kingdom; wherefore, Moron dwelt in captivity all the remainder of his days; and he begat Coriantor.

19. And it came to pass that Coriantor dwelt in captivity all his days.

20. And in the days of Coriantor there also came many prophets, and prophesied of great and marvelous things, and cried repentance unto the people, and except they should repent the Lord God would execute judgment against them to their utter destruction;

21. And that the Lord God would send or bring forth another people to possess the land, by his power, after the manner by which he brought their fathers.

22. And they did reject all the words of the prophets, because

---

covered by these paragraphs was one of wicked governments, rebellions, war and rejection of divine messengers.

AHAH

Ahah was the son of Seth. He died in captivity.

ETHEM

Ethem, a descendant of Ahah's son in Ether 1:9. In his day prophets foretold the destruction of the people, unless they should repent. Being rejected, the prophets withdrew, and the unbelievers were left without the inspired word of God.

of their secret society and wicked abominations.

23. And it came to pass that Coriantor begat Ether, and he died, having dwelt in captivity all his days.

AHAH

Ahah is Egyptian. It was the name of a watchman at the gates of one of the many gods of Egyptian mythology.

MORON

Moron, the son of Ethem, was deprived of one-half of his Kingdom by rebels. Twice he was forced to fight for his crown. The second war was ended with the rebels victorious. Moron was made a prisoner and died in captivity.

CORIANTOR

Coriantor was born and died in captivity. Prophets were again heard in the land. They predicted the utter destruction of the Jaredite Kingdom, and the coming of another people, referring to the descendants of Lehi and Mulek, "after the manner in which He brought their fathers." That is, across the sea.

ETHER

Ether was the son of Coriantor, who died in captivity.

CHAPTER 12

1. *The Prophet Ether and Coriantumr.*

1. And it came to pass that the days of Ether were in the days of Coriantumr; and Coriantumr was king over all the land.

2. And Ether was a prophet of the Lord; wherefore Ether came forth in the days of Coriantumr, and began to prophesy unto the people, for he could not be restrained because of the Spirit of the Lord which was in him.

3. For he did cry from the morning, even until the going down of the sun, exhorting the people to believe in God unto repentance lest they should be destroyed, saying unto them that by faith all things are fulfilled—

4. Wherefore, whoso believeth in God might with surety hope for a better world, yea, even a place at the right hand of God, which hope cometh of faith, maketh an anchor to the souls of men, which would make them sure and steadfast, always abounding in good works, being led to glorify God.

VERSES 1-5. *The days of Ether were in the days of Coriantumr.* Coriantumr was the last King over the Jaredites in "all the land." That is, Moron and adjacent countries. His parentage is not given in the genealogy of Ether in Chapter 1. In the Book of Omni (vv. 20-22), it is related that a large engraved stone was brought to King Mosiah in Zarahemla. On this stone was an account concerning Coriantumr. He had wandered southward, after the Battle of Ramah, and reached Zarahemla, where he lived nine months (moons). He had, presumably, prepared the record on the stone that was brought to King Mosiah for translation.

Ether was a "descendant" of Coriantor. (Ether 1:6) Descendant here stands for *son,* for Coriantor was his father. (Ether 11:25) Coriantor was the legal king. His name, therefore, appears in the genealogy notwithstanding he was held in captivity. Coriantumr must have been an usurper, holding and wielding illegal authority.

In the days of this unrighteous ruler, the Spirit of the Lord came upon Ether and called him to the prophetic office. His special mission was to preach repentance. As Jonah was sent to Nineveh, or Jeremiah to Judah, to warn of disaster unless the people repented, so Ether was sent to the Jaredites, and so faithfully did he discharge his mission that he cried repentance "from the morning, even until the going down of the sun." It was a tremendous mission, if he was the only missionary at work to make the whole nation conscious of the fact that wickedness would end in destruction, and that repentance, alone, would bring Salvation. Ether also taught that hope and faith "make an anchor to the souls of men." In other words, that through them, men feel safe even when furious hurricanes hurl destructive waves against their frail crafts. At such times faith is the chain that connects the ship with the firm anchorage. The storms, no matter how terrifying, are only on the surface; the divine anchorage is always safe.

5. And it came to pass that Ether did prophesy great and marvelous things unto the people, which they did not believe, because they saw them not.

2. A discourse by Moroni on faith.

6. And now, I, Moroni, would speak somewhat concerning these things; I would show unto the world that faith is things which are hoped for and not seen; wherefore, dispute not because ye see not, for ye receive no witness until after the trial of your faith.

VERSES 6-22. *Things hoped for.* Moroni begins his discourse on faith with a definition of that term: "Faith is things," that is, a strong, firm, belief that things exist even though they cannot be seen. He says, "Things which are hoped for and not seen." The Apostle Paul (Hebrews 11:1) defines *faith* as the "substance of things hoped for, the evidence of things not seen." The word *substance* means that which *stands under,* or the underlying reality of things. It is that which sustains the qualities by which matter becomes perceptible to us. For instance, here is an object. We examine it. We find that it has a certain weight, and a peculiar color; that it is impervious to the action of most acids; that it amalgamates readily with mercury, and that, for practical purposes it forms valuable alloys with silver, or copper, etc., we call it gold. Another object, with a different combination of qualities, we call silver; another copper, etc. That which sustains these qualities is the *substance.*

What substance is in the material world, faith is in the spiritual world. It is the very foundation of *hope,* and also of other qualities essential to the Christian character, namely love, humility, peace, joy, benevolence, etc. Faith is one of the conditions of Salvation, and the Apostle after having quoted Habakkuk 2:4, "The just shall live by his faith," gives the foregoing explanation of just what *faith* is. The two definitions of both Moroni and St. Paul are essentially the same, that in the Book of Ether being more concise.

By faith, we may assure ourselves of the existence of that, which, to our ordinary sight, is not seen. It is the power through which unseen things are made real.

Theologians say that there is an historical faith that accepts as facts the records concerning Christ, or for that matter, any of the great men who have had outstanding characteristics portrayed in any of the annals of mankind. But there is also a saving faith which is entirely different. This is implicit *trust* and confidence in the divine work of the Redeemer, with a complete surrender to His will and obedience to His commandments. The word *trust* as we use it here is fully exemplified by reading the sixth and seventh verses of Chapter 7, Book of Alma: "I trust . . . that ye look forward . . . with an everlasting faith. . ." Trust means "confidence in the integrity or acts of another"; the assured reliance on their moral soundness; the assured anticipation of something. That is the hope, based on a perfect faith that saves from all evil. It is the faith which as Christ, our Savior and Redeemer, was made in the likeness of man, causes the man of faith to grow into the likeness of Christ. (Romans 6:5-7; Philippians 2:7-9)

Faith has also a third important meaning. The Apostle Paul writes (Galatians 3:24-26): "Before faith came we were kept in ward under the Law, shut up unto the faith which should afterwards be revealed. So that the Law hath been our schoolmaster to bring us unto Christ, that we might be justified by faith. But now that faith is come, we are no longer under a schoolmaster. For we are all sons of God, by faith in Christ Jesus." Here the Apostle contrasts law and faith. Law is the

THE BOOK OF ETHER

7. For it was by faith that Christ showed himself unto our fathers, after he had risen from the dead; and he showed not himself unto them until after they had faith in him; wherefore, it must needs be that some had faith in him, for he showed himself not unto the world.

8. But because of the faith of men he has shown himself unto the world, and glorified the name of the Father, and prepared a way that thereby others might be partakers of the heavenly gift, that they might hope for those things which they have not seen.

9. Wherefore, ye may also have hope, and be partakers of the gift, if ye will but have faith.

Law of Moses, or the Mosaic Dispensation, which was the schoolmaster with authority until faith, that is, the Dispensation of the Gospel of Jesus Christ came.

Moroni makes the same distinction in verse 11 in this Chapter, when he says: "But in the gift of His Son hath God prepared a more excellent way," than the Law of Moses.

No witnesses until after trial. Moroni adds this memorable truth, that faith must stand trial before it witnesses to the truthfulness or falsity of a thing hoped for. Or as we call it, a testimony is obtained, which brings absolute and lasting certainty. "Wherefore," he says, "dispute not because ye see not, for ye receive no witness until after the trial of your faith."

VERSES 7-9. By faith Christ showed Himself. Again, Moroni states an important truth. Christ must be seen through the eye of faith or not at all:

"He showed not Himself unto them, until after they had faith in Him."

This is illustrated in the appearances of the Lord immediately after His resurrection. The women who went to the sepulcher to perform a last service of love before the final entombment of Jesus, as they thought, were told by an angel that Jesus, for Whom they were looking, was not there. He was risen. The angel commanded them to return to Jerusalem and inform the disciples of what they had seen and heard. Faith now filled their hearts with joy, and as they were wending their way back to Jerusalem with their message, behold, Jesus met them; they saw Him, and worshiped Him. (Matthew 28:1-10)

The experience of the two men on the road to Emmaus illustrates the same principle. Jesus came and walked with them. But they knew Him not. He listened to their account of the sad tragedy of Calvary. Still they did not recognize Him. He explained the Scriptures to them. His words stirred up emotions in their breasts reminiscent of the hours they used to spend with the Master before His departure; still He was not known to them. It was first when He broke and blessed the bread that faith opened their eyes, and they saw and recognized their beloved Lord. (Luke 24:13-48)

In every instance of an appearance of Jesus, be it to individuals, as Peter, Thomas or Paul, or to multitudes as the disciples in Jerusalem, or to the five hundred in Galilee, faith prepared the way for the glorious visions. Faith is the light that enables the spiritual eye to see clearly the things that bring joy and happiness, where, without faith, all is dark.

In the case of the appearance of our Lord in the Land Bountiful, the same principle is apparent. His advent there preceded by extraordinary convulsions of nature, and the destruction of wicked populations. (III Nephi 9:1-12) A terrifying voice was heard. It was the voice of our Lord. An awe-inspiring silence followed.

10. Behold it was by faith that they of old were called after the holy order of God.

11. Wherefore, by faith was the law of Moses given. But in

the gift of his Son hath God prepared a more excellent way; and it is by faith that it hath been fulfilled.

12. For if there be no faith

Again the voice was heard. (III Nephi 10:1-8) During the time of convulsions and destruction, the righteous were saved. (III Nephi 10:12) They had faith in the prophecies. And it was to this believing remnant that our Lord appeared. They had met on the Temple grounds in expectation of the fulfilment of the divine word. (III Nephi 11:1-10)

The Apostle Paul expresses the same thought concerning faith and seeing; he writes: "So Christ was once offered to bear the sins of many; and unto them that look for Him shall He appear the second time without sin unto salvation." (Hebrews 9:28) *"Unto those who look for Him."* To those His second coming will bring deliverance.

It has been observed that the religious world from the Apostolic era to the Reformation did not look for a second advent of our Lord. Most of the orthodox speakers and writers of the darkened times explained all the prophecies on that subject as applicable to the church. The Kingdom of Christ was only a spiritual organization, and the coming of its King, the Savior of the world, would be the end of the earth and the last judgment. It is evident that with such an understanding of the prophecies, nobody was really looking for the coming of that King, and nobody made preparations to receive Him. It is equally clear that He could not, or would not, come when nobody expected Him.

After the Reformation some prominent writers began to interpret the prophecies literally and maintain that our Lord would gather Israel and have a Millennial Kingdom on this earth. They were vehemently opposed by others, and the ideas proposed by both became confused in the public mind. Common pople were at a loss to know what to believe. Very few were looking for the Lord to come. The majority were content with faith in Christ as the bearer of "the sins of many," without expecting to see Him appearing "a second time without sin" to Salvation.

Now it is different. In 1830 the Church of Jesus Christ of Latter-day Saints was organized. Revelation was restored as of yore. The literal gathering of Israel and Judah, preliminary to the actual return of our Lord in great power and glory, was proclaimed as an essential element of the everlasting Gospel. (Doctrine and Covenants 1:12; 35:15; 49:6; 133:17, and many other texts. *See* also Doctrine and Covenants on Gathering, 29:7, 8; 133:9)

The Message is summed up thus: "Verily I say unto you, the coming of the Lord draweth nigh, and it overtaketh the world as a thief in the night." (Doctrine and Covenants 106:4) Thousands of faithful Elders of the Church have proclaimed this word of the Lord in all parts of our globe with great spiritual force. Some have sealed their testimony with their blood upon the Altar of Martyrdom as heralds of the advent of the King of kings. All the world has heard the midnight cry: *"Behold the Bridegroom cometh."* Many, wise and foolish, have been aroused from their drowsy slumbers and are even now examining "their lamps" and supply of oil. The wise are ready. They are eagerly awaiting their opportunity to join the *Bridal* torch procession, and they are praying daily: "Even so, Come Lord Jesus." (Revelation 22:20)

VERSE 10. *The Holy Order of God.* (Doctrine and Covenants 76:57; 84:19-22; 107:1-4) A few commentators hold that the name *Melchizedek* means, "Zedek is my king," and that Zedek was the name of some village divinity. But that is a

among the children of men God can do no miracle among them; wherefore, he showed not himself until after their faith.

13. Behold, it was the faith of Alma and Amulek that caused the prison to tumble to the earth.

14. Behold, it was the faith of Nephi and Lehi that wrought the change upon the Lamanites, that they were baptized with fire and with the Holy Ghost.

---

misrepresentation. The author of Genesis introduces him as "the priest of the *Most High God*" (Genesis 14:18), and St. Paul, who is the infallible authority on that question says: "For this Melchizedek, King of Salem, priest of the Most High God . . . first being by interpretation King of Righteousness, and after that also King of Salem, which is, King of Peace." (Hebrews 7:1-2) (Salem—believed to be Jerusalem) Melchizedek, High Priest of God, was King of Righteousness and of Peace, as everyone who holds the Higher Priesthood is, or ought to be. For there is no real peace without righteousness, and no righteousness without peace.

Verse 11. *By Faith, the Law of Moses Given.* Moses was the most outstanding lawgiver the world ever had because his implicit faith in God, although at times wavering, enabled him to serve as the mouthpiece of the infinite Ruler of the Universe.

Verse 12. *If there be no faith.* God does not show forth His glory nor His power unto the working of mighty miracles among them, unto men who do not believe in Him, that He is. Therefore, we understand more fully the meaning of the words of Jesus Christ: "Come unto Me, O ye Gentiles, and I will show unto you the greater things, the knowledge which is hid up because of unbelief." (Ether 4:13-14) Belief and faith are sometimes used synonymously, or being alike, or nearly alike in meaning or significance. Certainly belief engenders faith. Our faith in God becomes an impelling agent unto righteousness in the same ratio as our belief in Him grows stronger.

"For behold, I am God; and I am a God of miracles; and I will show unto the world that I am the same yesterday, today, and forever; and I work not among the children of men save it be according to their faith." (II Nephi 27:23)

"For I perceive that ye desire that I should show unto you what I have done unto your brethren at Jerusalem, for I see that your faith is sufficient that I should heal you." (III Nephi 17:8)

Verse 13. *Alma and Amulek.* The incident referred to is recorded in Alma 14: 25-29. A solemn warning against the folly of defying the Almighty is therein seen. The Ammonihahites, angered because of Alma's rebuke to them for their wickedness, were seeking ways to destroy him and his missionary companion, Amulek. They were arrested and while in prison suffered almost every indignity and torment human ingenuity could suggest or evil power achieve. At length, Alma, under a sense of unjust treatment, cried: "How long shall we suffer these great afflictions, O Lord? O Lord, give us strength according to our faith which is in Christ, even unto deliverance."

The Lord heard and answered his appeal. They were immediately delivered from their bands. By faith this was brought about. The judges and priests who sought to destroy God's servants and thereby in doing so defied His power, were themselves destroyed. "Be not deceived: God is not mocked; for whatsoever a man soweth, that shall he also reap." (Galatians 6:7) "It is a fearful thing to fall into the hands of the living God." (Hebrews 10:31)

Verse 14. *Nephi and Lehi.* Helaman 5:20-52. This incident tells of a remark-

15. Behold, it was the faith of Ammon and his brethren which wrought so great a miracle among the Lamanites.

16. Yea, and even all they who wrought miracles wrought them by faith, even those who were before Christ and also those who were after.

17. And it was by faith that the three disciples obtained a promise that they should not taste of death; and they obtained not the promise until after their faith.

18. And neither at any time hath any wrought miracles until after their faith; wherefore they first believed in the Son of God.

---

able instances of the protecting care of God of His faithful servants. Such divine solicitude is not always manifested in supernatural encircling flames, as in this case; nor is it by the visible presence of a guardian angel, as in the case of Shadrach, Meshach, and Abednego in the heated furnace in Babylon. But the Lord never forgets His children. "As thy days, so shall thy strength be." (Deuteronomy 33:25) Or, as we sing, "As thy days may demand, so thy succor shall be."

VERSE 15. *Ammon and his Brethren.* With a constant faith in the providential care of the Lord, Ammon and his brethren toiled incessantly for fourteen long years to carry the Word of the Lord to the benighted Lamanites. (*See* Alma 17-26 Chapters) Their faith in His marvelous ways, and their undying conviction that He would overrule all to His honor and glory, so filled their hearts and minds that through much fasting and prayer they with divine guidance "wrought so great a miracle among the Lamanites." Their faith in His *word* was undaunted, their works to His honor and glory were untiring, together through their *faith and works* God was able to crown their efforts with a bounteous harvest of those who loved the Lord and who ever afterwards sought to do His will.

VERSE 17. *The Three Disciples.* (*See* III Nephi 28:7-9) When, on an occasion, Jesus asked His Twelve Nephite Disciples: "What is it that ye desire of me, after I am gone to the Father?" all but three gave answer. "And they sorrowed in their hearts, for they durst not speak unto Him the thing which they desired." "And He said unto them: Behold, I know your thoughts, and ye have desired the thing which John, My beloved, who was with Me in My ministry, before that I was lifted up by the Jews, desired of Me."

They were promised that they should not die, but that, at the second coming of the Lord, their bodies would be "changed in the twinkling of an eye from mortality to immortality," they were never to feel pain, nor worldly sorrow; they were to have the privilege of beholding the dealings of God with the children of men in the successive following dispensations "even until all things shall be fulfilled."

Moroni's purpose in referring to the incidents above mentioned is to impress upon the mind of the reader of his earnest warning that faith is the contributing cause of all action. Faith urges exertion of strength or faculties to bring an issue to full success, or in other words, faith makes real the things we cannot see.

All these things were consummated because of faith. They were not accidents. What sometimes seems to us as being accidental is really not so. The accidents of man are the inspirations of God, and the incidents of this life are the leadings and the guidings of Him Who made it.

Another incident of note in further examining this particular theme is found in Alma's instructions to his son, Helaman: "And now, my son, I have somewhat

19. And there were many whose faith was so exceeding strong, even before Christ came, who could not be kept from within the veil, but truly saw with their eyes the things which they had beheld with an eye of faith, and they were glad.

20. And behold, we have seen in this record that one of these was the brother of Jared; for so great was his faith in God, that when God put forth his finger he could not hide it from the sight of the brother of Jared, because of his word which he had spoken unto him, which word he had obtained by faith.

21. And after the brother of Jared had beheld the finger of the Lord, because of the promise which the brother of Jared had obtained by faith, the Lord could not withhold anything from his sight; wherefore he showed him all things, for he could no longer be kept without the veil.

22. And it is by faith that my

---

to say concerning the thing which our fathers call a ball, or director—or our fathers called it *Liahona*, which is, being interpreted, a compass; and the Lord prepared it. And behold, there cannot any man work after the manner of so curious a workmanship. And behold, it was prepared to show unto our fathers the course which they should travel in the wilderness. *And it did work for them according to their faith in God;* therefore, if they had faith to believe that God could cause that those spindles should point the way they should go, behold, it was done; therefore, they had this miracle, and also many other miracles wrought by the power of God, day by day. Nevertheless, because those miracles were worked by small means it did show unto them marvelous works. They were slothful, and forgot to exercise their faith and diligence and then those marvelous works ceased, and they did not progress in their journey. (Alma 37:38-41)

We have already quoted Paul, and he further explains that "through faith we understand that the worlds were framed by the word of God, so that things that are seen were not made of things which do appear"; for, no matter what scientists may assert, the beginning of things, origins, being outside our sphere of experience or observation can be known only through faith. Only through faith do we comprehend that the universe of which we are part is the Divine idea which received form in the material creation. Abel, Enoch, Noah, Abraham, Sarah, Isaac, Jacob, Joseph, Moses, Joshua, Samuel, and many others are mentioned as examples of what mortals can accomplish, if they have the power that comes from faith in God.

It is important to remember that *faith* means not only the conviction of the mind, but also that which is believed, the Gospel, the creed, which, in the mind of the Apostle, is a long step in advance of the Mosaic Law. (*See* Acts 6:7; 13:8; 14:22; Romans 1:5; 3:27; 10:8; Galatians 1:23; 2:16; 3:2; 3:5; Ephesians 2:8; 1 Timothy 1:2; 4:1.) When this is kept in mind, it is evident that there is no conflict between the views of Paul and James. For when it is argued that Salvation is by faith and not by works, as for instance in Galatians 3, it is not maintained that a Christian is without works of righteousness, but that it is the Gospel and not the Law of Moses that has *saved* him, and made him capable of living a righteous life.

"For behold, I am God; and I am a God of miracles; and I will show unto the world that I am the same yesterday, today, and forever; and I work not among the children of men save it be according to their faith." (II Nephi 27:23)

VERSES 19-21. *Saw with their eyes.* (*See* Ether 3:8-16; 4:4)

fathers have obtained the promise that these things should come
unto their brethren through the

Gentiles; therefore the Lord hath
commanded me, yea, even Jesus
Christ.

3. The Jaredite and Nephite languages.

23. And I said unto him: Lord,
the Gentiles will mock at these
things, because of our weakness
in writing; for Lord thou hast
made us mighty in word by faith,
but thou hast not made us mighty
in writing; for thou hast made
all this people that they could
speak much, because of the Holy
Ghost which thou hast given
them;

24. And thou hast made us
that we could write but little, because of the awkwardness of our
hands. Behold, thou hast not
made us mighty in writing like
unto the brother of Jared, for
thou madest him that the things
which he wrote were mighty even
as thou art, unto the overpowering of man to read them.

25. Thou hast also made our

words powerful and great, even
that we cannot write them;
wherefore, when we write we behold our weakness, and stumble
because of the placing of our
words; and I fear lest the Gentiles shall mock at our words.

26. And when I had said this,
the Lord spake unto me, saying:
Fools mock, but they shall mourn;
and my grace is sufficient for the
meek, that they shall take no advantage of your weakness;

27. And if men come unto me
I will show unto them their weakness. I give unto men weakness
that they may be humble; and
my grace is sufficient for all men
that humble themselves before
me; for if they humble themselves before me, and have faith
in me, then will I make weak

VERSE 22. *These things.* The Book of Mormon, and especially the Plates of
Ether.

VERSES 23-25. *Our Weakness in Writing.* Moroni humbly apologizes to the Lord
for the imperfections in the record he was making. Having complied with the divine
instruction to write, he expresses fear that the Gentiles would mock at his efforts,
because of his lack of literary ability. As a trusting child, speaking to a beloved
parent, he reminds his Heavenly Father of the fact that He had not been pleased
to make him, or his people "mighty in writing," as He had in the spoken word.
This is a notable observation, for Moroni, feeling very inadequate to the task required
of him, in his prayer to the Lord, said: "And Thou hast made us that we could
write but little, because of the awkwardness of our hands. Behold, Thou hast not
made us mighty in writing like unto the Brother of Jared, for Thou madest him that
the things which he wrote were mighty even as Thou art, unto the overpowering
of man to read them."

VERSE 27. *I will make weak things become strong.* A promise that has singularly
been fulfilled in the mission fields of the Church. Every sincere missionary of the
Latter-day Saints can testify to that. The Book of Mormon, itself, is a witness of
the irresistible power of truth. From the early days of Mormonism till the present

things become strong unto them. 28. Behold, I will show unto the Gentiles their weakness and I will show unto them that faith, hope and charity bringeth unto me—the fountain of all righteousness.

---

time, converts have been raised up by hearing the humble testimonies concerning the divine origin of that record.

Then, is it not a truth in everyone's experience that the Lord magnifies the worthy man in whatsoever position he may occupy? The weak are made strong, and the strong become stronger. This is probably true in part because the truths of Christ's Gospel need no studied or strong defense, and it should be remembered that the utmost strength of man, when compared to God's, is absolute weakness, and his wisdom but foolishness.

VERSE 28. *The Fountain of All Righteousness.* Jesus Christ is the *Fountain of All Righteousness.* Faith, Hope, and Charity, are living waters that flow therefrom. (*Fountain* is properly the source or springhead of waters. Metaphorically, God is called the Fountain of Living Waters. (Jeremiah 2:18) Springs or fountains are called *living,* when they never cease, but are always sending forth their waters. All spiritual graces and refreshments communicated by the Spirit, are also compared to a fountain. (Joel 3:18; Zechariah 13:10.)

"And when my father saw that the waters of the river emptied into the Red Sea, he spoke unto Laman, saying: O that thou mightest be like unto this river, continually running into the *Fountain of All Righteousness!*" (I Nephi 2:9)

"And it came to pass that I beheld that the Rod of Iron, which my father had seen, was the word of God, which led to the *Fountain of Living Waters,* or to the Tree of Life; which waters are a representation of the love of God; and I also beheld that the Tree of Life was a representation of the love of God." (I Nephi 11:25) Christ, the Fountain of Living Waters, Who, also, is represented by the Tree of Life, shows in God's greatest gift to mankind the satisfaction of His highest ideal for His children, Eternal Life in His Kingdom. God's love can show no more than that He gave His Only Begotten Son that whosoever believeth on Him should have Eternal Life. "He that loveth not knoweth not God; for God is love. In this was manifested the love of God toward us, because that God sent His Only Begotten Son into the world, that we might live through Him." (I John 4:8-9) "Wherefore, I, Moroni, am commanded to write these things that evil may be done away, and that the time may come that Satan may have no power upon the hearts of the children of men, but that they may be persuaded to do good continually, that they may come unto the *Fountain of All Righteousness* and be saved." (Ether 8:26)

In this verse Christ, Himself, calls Himself, *The Fountain of All Righteousness,* and that Faith, Hope, and Charity, will bring the Gentiles unto Him thereby making them strong. Faith, Hope, and Charity, are Godly graces.

Faith, by some, is called an eye, *even the eye of faith.* By it we see things which do not appear to the natural eye. In a religious sense, faith makes real that for which we hope. We perceive that which has been promised, but not yet given. It enlarges our scope, so that the horizon of our vision is far beyond worldly concept. With it, we see within the veil. (vv. 19-21)

"Do you exercise faith in the redemption of Him Who created you? Do you look forward with an *eye of faith,* and view this mortal body raised in immortality, and this corruption raised in incorruption, to stand before God to be judged according to the deeds which have been done in the mortal body?" (Alma 5:15) In this verse Alma calls *Faith,* an *eye.* So it is! The more it is used, the clearer becomes its per-

4. *Faith, Hope, and Charity.*

29. And I, Moroni, having heard these words, was comforted, and said: O Lord, thy righteous will be done, for I know that thou workest unto the children of men according to their faith;

30. For the brother of Jared said unto the mountain Zerin, Remove — and it was removed. And if he had not had faith it would not have moved; wherefore thou workest after men have faith.

ception. In it there is no impaired vision; no corrective measures need be taken. Alma asked the people of Zarahemla to whom he spoke: "Do you look forward with an *eye of faith?*" Do you, we imagine him asking, view your unworthy bodies, each with its own certain traces of death, raised to immortality and Eternal Life? The weaknesses of the flesh, and its other afflictions; those ill-omens of death and corruption, do you see them "swallowed up in everlasting and glorious victory through Christ, our Lord?" Do you see yourselves standing before God "to be judged according to the deeds which have been done in the mortal body?"

VERSE 29. *I know that Thou workest unto the children of men according to their faith.* Moroni was comforted by the words of the Lord because all righteous men seeking to discern the mind and will of God have, at times, been troubled at heart to know His purposes concerning the Gentiles, or those who are in darkness because of unbelief. "O Lord, Thy righteous will be done," was Moroni's paean in praise of Him Who reigns On High. And inasmuch as the Lord then gave him assurance that the Gentiles would be shown their weakness and thereby made strong, he shouted praises because, "I know that Thou workest unto the children of men *according to their faith.*" " Come unto Me, O ye Gentiles, and I will show unto you the greater things, the knowledge which is hid up because of unbelief." (Ether 4:13)

"And there was also written upon them a new writing, which was plain to be read, which did give us understanding concerning the ways of the Lord; and it was written and changed from time to time, according to the faith and diligence which we gave unto it. And thus we see that by small means the Lord can bring about great things." (I Nephi 16:29)

"And that He manifesteth Himself unto all those who believe in Him, by the power of the Holy Ghost; yea, unto every nation, kindred, tongue, and people, working mighty miracles, signs, and wonders, among the children of men *according to their faith.*" (II Nephi 26:13)

"For behold, I am God; and I am a God of miracles; and I will show unto the world that I am the same yesterday, today, and forever; and I work not among the children of men save it be *according to their faith.*" (II Nephi 27:23)

"Yea, and they did obey and observe to perform every word of command with exactness; yea, and even *according to their faith* it was done unto them" . . . (Alma 57:21)

See also, Jarom 1:4; Mosiah 27:14; Alma 12:30; 14:28; 37:40; 57:21; III Nephi 5:14; Mormon 9:37.

VERSE 30. *Remove, and it was removed.* Moroni refers to an incident in the history of the Jaredites, not recorded elsewhere. The Brother of Jared said to Mount Zerin, Remove! and it was removed. Where and how this happened we do not know. But it is, by no means improbable, that the Jaredites during their migrations from the coast to the interior of the Continent of Asia, encountered some mountainous obstacle which the Lord removed in answer to the prayers of faith of the great

31. For thus didst thou manifest thyself unto thy disciples; for after they had faith, and did speak in thy name, thou didst show thyself unto them in great power.

32. And I also remember that thou hast said that thou hast prepared a house for man, yea, even among the mansions of thy Father, in which man might have a more excellent hope; wherefore man must hope, or he cannot receive an inheritance in the place which thou hast prepared.

Jaredite Moses. It may have been done by some physical adjustment of the earth such as an earthquake, or by some supernatural agency unknown to us. Whatever it was, be it either case, it was a miracle, a divine reward of Faith.

VERSE 31. *For thus didst Thou manifest Thyself unto Thy Disciples.* This verse undoubtedly refers to the visit of Christ to His Disciples as recorded in III Nephi 27.

VERSE 32. *Wherefore, man must hope.* In the Plan of Salvation *Hope* is necessary as well as Faith. "Man must hope, or he cannot receive an inheritance in the place which Thou hast prepared." "In My Father's house are many mansions: if it were not so, I would have told you. I go to prepare a place for you. . ." (John 14:2) *Hope* for a place in one of these mansions is one of those fair and fragrant flowers of Christ's Gospel, and the sweet fruit of *Faith.*

It is easy to understand that *Hope* and *Faith* are inseparable; Faith reveals things the possession of which we hope. Hope is a desire to obtain what Faith reveals. Hope becomes greater as through *the eye of faith* we see the glories and the rewards of righteous living. *Hope* is the power that urges us onward along that path which is Straight and Narrow. Hope stresses *ardor,* and to us it connotes *striving.*

"And again, my beloved brethren, I would speak unto you concerning *Hope.* How is it you can attain unto faith, save ye shall have hope? And what is it that ye shall hope for? Behold I say unto you that ye shall have hope through the Atonement of Christ and the power of His resurrection, to be raised unto Life Eternal, and this because of your faith in Him according to the promise. Wherefore, if a man have faith he must needs have hope; for without faith there cannot be any hope." (Moroni 7:40-42)

"But before ye seek for riches, seek ye for the Kingdom of God. And after ye have obtained a *hope* in Christ ye shall obtain riches, if ye seek them. . ." (Jacob 2:18-19)

"For, for this intent have we written these things, that they may know that we knew of Christ, and we had a *hope* of His glory many hundred years before His coming; and not only we ourselves had a *hope* of His glory, but also all the holy prophets which were before us." (Jacob 4:4)

"And if ye have no *hope* ye must needs be in despair; and despair cometh because of iniquity." (Moroni 10:22)

Reference is hereby made to every mention of the word, HOPE as used in the Book of Mormon:

HOPE

1 Nephi	19-24	That ye may have hope as well as your
2 Nephi	31:20	Having a perfect brightness of h.
	33:9	For none of these can I h. except

Jacob	2:19	After ye have obtained a h. in Christ
	4:4	Christ, and we had a h. of his glory
	4	Not only we ourselves had a h. of his glory
	6	Having all these witnesses we obtain a h.
	11	Obtained a good h. of glory in him
	7:5	He had h. to shake me from the faith
Alma	5:10	What grounds had they to h. for salvation
	7:24	See that ye have faith, h., and charity
	13:29	Having a h. that ye shall receive eternal
	22:16	Thou shalt receive the h. which thou
	25:16	Thus they did retain a h. through faith
	27:28	For their h. and views of Christ and the
	28:12	Yet they rejoice and exalt in the h.
	30:13	Bound down under a foolish and a vain h.
	32:21	Ye h. for things which are not seen
	34:41	With a firm h. that ye shall one day rest
	38:2	I h. that you will continue in keeping
	58:11	We should h. for our deliverance in him
3 Nephi	3:10	Lachoneus, and I h. that ye will deliver
	4:4	Which time they did h. to destroy the
Mormon	6:4	Here we had h. to gain advantage over
Ether	12:4	Might with surety h. for a better world
	4	Which h. cometh of faith
	8	They might h. for those things which
	9	Wherefore ye may also have h.
	28	Show unto them that faith, h., and charity
	32	Man might have a more excellent h.
		Wherefore man must h., or he cannot
Moroni	7:1	Which he spake concerning Faith, H.,
	3	And that have obtained a sufficient h.
	40	I would speak unto you concerning H.
	40	Can attain unto faith, save ye shall have h.?
	41	And what is it that ye shall h. for?
	41	Ye shall have h. through the atonement
	42	If a man have faith he must needs have h.
	42	For without faith there cannot be any h.
	43	He cannot have faith and h. save he
	44	If so, his faith and h. is vain
	48	See him as he is, that he may have this h.
	8:14	For he hath neither faith, h., nor charity
	26	Which Comforter filleth with h.
	9:25	Long suffering, and the h. of his glory
	10:20	There must be faith, there must also be h.
	20	And if there must be h., there must also
	21	Neither can ye if ye have no h.
	22	If ye have no h. ye must needs be in despair

Let us now refer to some passages of Scripture found in the Holy Bible:

"Happy is he that hath the God of Jacob for his help, whose *hope* is in the Lord his God." (Psalm 146:5)

"O Lord, the *Hope of Israel*, all that forsake Thee shall be ashamed, and they that depart from me shall be written in the earth, because they have forsaken the Lord, the Fountain of Living Waters." (Jeremiah 17:13)

33. And again, I remember that thou hast said that thou hast loved the world, even unto the laying down of thy life for the world, that thou mightest take it again to prepare a place for the children of men.

34. And now I know that this love which thou hast had for the children of men is charity; wherefore, except men shall have charity they cannot inherit that place which thou hast prepared in the mansions of thy Father.

35. Wherefore, I know by this thing which thou hast said, that if the Gentiles have not charity, because of our weakness, that thou wilt prove them, and take away their talent, yea, even that which they have received, and give unto them who shall have more abundantly.

36. And it came to pass that I prayed unto the Lord that he would give unto the Gentiles grace, that they might have charity.

37. And it came to pass that the Lord said unto me: If they have not charity it mattereth not unto thee, thou hast been faith-

---

"And not only they, but ourselves also, which have the first-fruits of the Spirit, even we ourselves groan within ourselves waiting for the adoption, *to wit*, the redemption of our body. For we are saved by *hope*: but *hope* that is seen is not *hope*: for what a man seeth, why doth he yet *hope* for? But if we hope for that we see not, then we do with patience wait for it." (Romans 8:23-25)

"Looking for that blessed *hope*, and the glorious appearing of the great God and our Savior Jesus Christ." (Titus 2:13)

VERSES 33-37. *And now I know that this love which Thou hast had for the children of men is Charity. Charity* is expressed most often in Christian love. The word, *Charity*, is used only in the New Testament, and nowhere else in the Bible. In the Revised Version *Charity* is always translated love. It is Divine love for man. Mortals can show Charity best by, or in the act of loving all men as brothers because he sees them as sons of God.

Charity is the love of Christ which prompted Him to sacrifice Himself for the children of men. And this, Moroni says is the kind of love, or charity, which men must have to inherit a place in the mansions of the Father.

The greatest of these is Charity. "Though I speak with the tongues of men and of angels, and have not charity, I am become as sounding brass, or a tinkling cymbal.

"And though I have the gift of prophecy, and understand all mysteries, and all knowledge; and though I have all faith, so that I could remove mountains, and have not charity, I am nothing.

"And though I bestow all my goods to feed the poor, and though I give my body to be burned, and have not charity, it profiteth me nothing.

"Charity suffereth long, and is kind; charity envieth not; charity vaunteth not itself, is not puffed up,

"Doth not behave itself unseemly, seeketh not her own, is not easily provoked, thinketh no evil;

"Rejoiceth not in iniquity, but rejoiceth in the truth;

"Beareth all things, believeth all things, endureth all things.

"Charity never faileth: but whether there be prophecies, they shall fail; whether there be tongues, they shall cease; whether there be knowledge, it shall vanish away.

ful; wherefore, thy garments shall be made clean. And because thou hast seen thy weakness thou shalt be made strong, even unto the sitting down in the place which I have prepared in the mansions of my Father.

5. *A Farewell Address of Moroni.*

38. And now I, Moroni, bid farewell unto the Gentiles, yea, and also unto my brethren whom I love, until we shall meet before the judgment-seat of Christ, where all men shall know that my garments are not spotted with your blood.

39. And then shall ye know that I have seen Jesus, and that he hath talked with me face to face, and that he told me in plain humility, even as a man telleth another in mine own language, concerning these things;

40. And only a few have I written, because of my weakness in writing.

41. And now, I would commend you to seek this Jesus of whom the prophets and apostles have written, that the grace of

---

"For we know in part, and we prophesy in part.

"But when that which is perfect is come, then that which is in part shall be done away.

"When I was a child, I spake as a child, I understood as a child, I thought as a child: but when I became a man, I put away childish things.

"For now we see through a glass darkly; but then face to face: now I know in part; but then shall I know even as also I am known.

"And now abideth faith, hope, charity, these three; but the greatest of these is *charity.*" (I Corinthians 13)

"And again, behold I say unto you that he cannot have faith and hope, save he shall be meek, and lowly of heart.

"If so, his faith and hope is vain, for none is acceptable before God, save the meek and lowly in heart; and if a man be meek and lowly in heart, and confesses by the power of the Holy Ghost that Jesus is the Christ, he must needs have charity; for if he have not charity he is nothing; wherefore he must needs have charity.

"And charity suffereth long, and is kind, and envieth not, and is not puffed up, seeketh not her own, is not easily provoked, thinkest no evil, and rejoiceth not in iniquity but rejoiceth in the truth, beareth all things, believeth all things, hopeth all things, endureth all things.

"Wherefore, my beloved brethren, if ye have not charity, ye are nothing, for charity never faileth. Wherefore, cleave unto charity, which is the greatest of all, for all things must fail—

"But *charity is the pure love of Christ,* and it endureth forever; and whoso is found possessed of it at the last day, it shall be well with him." (Moroni 7:43-47)

"Wherefore, there must be faith; and if there must be faith there must also be hope; and if there must be hope there must be charity.

"And except ye have charity ye can in nowise be saved in the Kingdom of God; neither can ye be saved in the Kingdom of God if ye have not faith; neither can ye if ye have no hope." (Moroni 10:20-21)

God the Father, and also the Lord | may be and abide in you forever.
Jesus Christ, and the Holy Ghost, | Amen.
which beareth record of them,

VERSE 38. *And now I, Moroni, bid farewell unto the Gentiles.* Moroni addresses his word of farewell to Gentiles and also to his brethren of the House of Israel. He reminds them of the solemn truth that we shall all meet before the Judgment-Seat of Christ, and there, he says, "all men shall know that my garments are not spotted with your blood." He then testifies that he had seen Jesus, Who talked with him and told him "concerning these things." His closing admonition is: "And now, I would commend you to seek this Jesus of whom the prophets and apostles have written, that the grace of God the Father, and also the Lord Jesus Christ, and the Holy Ghost, which beareth record of them, may be and abide in you forever. Amen."

CORIANTUMR

Coriantumr was the last of the Jaredites of whom we have any record. We are first introduced to him as King of the whole land. In his day the Prophet Ether raised his warning voice, but all his words of exhortation and reproof were rejected by that rapidly-decaying race. They cast him out of their midst, and he spent his days in a mountain cave; while thus hidden he wrote the history of his times. Troublous and terrible times they were, for the war that commenced in the first year of Ether's concealment lasted until the nation was destroyed. This war became one of the most bloodthirsty, cruel and vindictive that ever cursed our fair planet. It was not the work of a day, it was the outgrowth of centuries of dishonor, crime and iniquity. Men's most savage passions were worked up to such an extent that every better feeling of humanity was crushed out. The women and children armed themselves for the fray with the same intense hate as the men. It was not a conflict of armies alone; it was the crushing together of a divided house that had long tottered because of internal weakness, but which now fell in upon itself.

Coriantumr, although we believe that he was a usurper of the royal position he held, still was a mighty prince, well versed in the art of war, cunning, diplomatic, and learned, but exceedingly corrupt. Like his people, he gave no heed to the prophecies of Ether. The war commenced in a powerful revolution against him, led by some of the most influential men in the Kingdom, who acted as leaders of the secret, Gadianton-like bands that overspread the nation. In the first year of the war much blood was spilled; Coriantumr's own sons were among the foremost in the defense of their father's rights. In the second year Ether again appeared and declared that if the people repented not they should every one be slain, except Coriantumr. They heeded not his voice, but sought to slay him; and he again retired to his place of concealment. In the third year, Shared, a leader of the revolutionists, defeated Coriantumr and held him a prisoner. In the fourth year, the sons of Coriantumr released their father and placed him again upon the throne. Then war extended over all the continent, every man with his band, fighting for what he desired to get. It was a reign of anarchy and crime; men's hatreds and evil passions growing more intense as the bloodshed spread. At last, the vast armies of Coriantumr and Shared met in the Valley of Gilgal and fought for three days. The King was victorious, and he followed his foe to the Plains of Heshlon. There Shared turned upon the victorious army of Coriantumr's and drove them back to the Valley of Gilgal. Another desperate battle took place in this Valley in which Shared's forces were beaten. Shared, himself, was slain and Coriantumr was so severely wounded that he did not come out to battle again for two years, during which time the people in all the land were shedding blood and there was none to restrain them.

Two years after Shared's death, his brother uprose to take his place. But he was defeated by Coriantumr, and his forces driven into the Wilderness of Akish where another exceedingly bloody battle was fought. After a time, the armies of Gilead, the brother of Shared, made a night attack on a portion of Coriantumr's hosts. They being drunken were easily overcome, and Gilead, the conqueror, marched to the Land of Moron and placed himself upon the throne where, a short time afterwards, he was slain by his high-priest.

Coriantumr continued in the wilderness for two years, during which time he gained many accessions to his forces. When strong enough, personally, having recovered from his battle-acquired wounds, he attacked the giant Lib who had assumed the kingly authority. In the first battle Coriantumr was victorious, though again wounded. He pursued Lib who had retreated to the seashore where another battle was fought, and Coriantumr's armies were forced back into the Wilderness of Akish, and yet farther, even to the Plains of Agosh. Coriantumr gathered up all the people as he retreated. Another horrible conflict ensued. Lib was killed, but his brother, Shiz, assumed command of Lib's army and utterly routed the forces of Coriantumr. The horrors of war now grew apace; the whole country was ravaged, its face was covered with the bodies of the dead, for neither women nor children were spared by the ruthless warriors. The pursuit did not stop until Coriantumr was forced back across the continent to the seashore. There they fought for three days, when Coriantumr's star was again in the ascendancy, and he drove Shiz back to the Land of Corihor. As Shiz retreated, he swept off all the inhabitants of the lands through which he passed who would not join him. Shiz and his forces halted in the Valley of Corihor, and Coriantumr established himself in the Valley of Shurr and from the neighboring Hill of Comnor challenged Shiz. The latter made two unsuccessful attacks upon Coriantumr, and after a third desperate battle he was victorious, for Coriantumr was terribly wounded and fainted from loss of blood. But the loss of men, women and children, was so great on both sides that Shiz was not strong enough to take advantage of his victory. At this time, some four or more years before the final battles around and near the Hill Ramah (otherwise Cumorah), two millions of warriors had been slain, besides their wives and children. How many millions actually fell before the last terrible struggle ended, when Coriantumr stood alone, the sole representative of his race, it is impossible to tell from the record that has been handed down to us, but we think we are justified in believing that for bloodshed and desolation no such war ever took place before, or ever occurred since in the history of the world; if the annals of any nation have a record of its equal, it is not known to us.

When Coriantumr sensed how great was the slaughter of his people, he wrote to Shiz, offering to withdraw from the conflict that the bloodshed might cease. But Shiz refused, unless Coriantumr surrendered that Shiz might have the gratification of slaying him, himself. So the war was renewed with intensified bitterness. Shiz was victorious, and the defeated army of Coriantumr fled as far as the waters of Ripliancum, supposed to be Lake Ontario. In this region another hotly contested battle was fought in which Coriantumr was once more severely wounded, but his troops were the victors and drove the enemy to the neighborhood of the Hill Ramah. Here they rested at bay for four years, both parties scouring the country for recruits, until every man, woman or child in all their domain had been enlisted on one side or the other. There, filled with the spirits of demons they confronted each other, and when the fight began it did not cease until every soul was slain except the commanders of the opposing forces, themselves. The Sacred Record says, "They had all fallen by the sword, save it were Coriantumr and Shiz, behold Shiz had fainted with the loss of blood." Coriantumr also was faint. He rested his weary frame upon the sword he still grasped, and when he had recruited enough strength to end the bloody struggle, he smote off the head of his last antagonist. This final act of combat took Coriantumr's utmost strength for it is recorded of him, "Coriantumr fell to the earth, and became as if he had no life."

Coriantumr, when he had regained consciousness, wandered forth aimlessly and alone, the last of his associates. A whole continent lay round about him, but there was nothing in any place to invite him to tarry or depart. Weakened by the trials and excesses of the last campaign, he staggered on, placing as great a distance as his limited powers would permit between himself and that battleground. He passed onward through each deserted valley, each tenantless town; in neither was there any human voice to greet or to chide him; the homes of his own people and those of his enemies were alike—a silent desolation; all the land seemed like a wilderness.

How long he thus wandered to and fro, wretched, comfortless and forelorn, we do know not, but at last he reached the southern portion of the northern continent, thousands of miles from Ramah, and there, to the astonishment of both, he found the people of Mulek, who had been led by the hand of the Lord from Jerusalem. With them he spent his few remaining days and when nine moons (months) had grown and waned, he passed away to join the hosts of his people in the unknown world of spirits.

CHAPTER 13

1. Ether and his predictions.

2. His life sought.

1. And now I, Moroni, proceed to finish my record concerning the destruction of the people of whom I have been writing.

2. For behold, they rejected all the words of Ether; for he truly told them of all things, from the beginning of man; and that after the waters had receded from off the face of this land it became a choice land above all other lands, a chosen land of the Lord; wherefore the Lord would have that all men should serve him who dwell upon the face thereof;

3. And that it was the place of the New Jerusalem, which should come down out of heaven, and the holy sanctuary of the Lord.

4. Behold, Ether saw the days of Christ, and he spake concerning a New Jerusalem upon this land.

5. And he spake also concerning the house of Israel, and the Jerusalem from whence Lehi should come—after it should be destroyed it should be built up again, a holy city unto the Lord;

Verse 2. *They rejected all the words of Ether.* In the first part of this chapter, the message of Ether is briefly recorded. It bears a marked resemblance to the prophecies of Enoch, as preserved in the Pearl of Great Price. The mission of Enoch was to warn the people who lived before the flood of their wickedness. Ether was sent to the Jaredites with a similar word of warning. The Ante-diluvians rejected Enoch. The Jaredites refused to listen to the words of Ether.

In his pleas that they abandon their iniquities and turn unto righteousness, Ether explained to them the Plan of Salvation from the beginning to the end of all things. The Gospel that Ether preached was the Gospel of Adam, of Enoch and the Patriarchs. It was also the Gospel of Noah, handed down through his sons to Eber, Peleg and his brother, Joktan, and to Jared. It was the same Gospel that was entrusted by our Lord to His Apostles for dissemination throughout the world. It was, in one word, *the Everlasting Gospel of Jesus Christ.*

From the beginning of man. Enoch says: "The Heavens He (God) made; the Earth is His footstool; and the foundation thereof is His . . . an host of men hath He brought in upon the face thereof." (Moses 6:44) Moses, in the first, or the opening statement of his great work, *The Book of Moses*, gives what is, perhaps, the most sublime sentence ever penned by man: "In the beginning God created the Heaven and the Earth." (Genesis 1:1) A philosopher who has become lost in the midst of the wonders and riddles of Nature, as in a labyrinth, without an Ariadne-thread by which to find the way out, may ask, bewildered: Where am I? Who am I? The Gospel answers: You are, O mortal! in God's Universe, in God's house. He has placed you here. Not as a stranger, but as a child in His home and your own.

wherefore, it could not be a new Jerusalem for it had been in a time of old; but it should be built up again, and become a holy city of the Lord; and it should be built unto the house of Israel.

6. And that a New Jerusalem should be built upon this land, unto the remnant of the seed of Joseph, for which things there has been a type.

7. For as Joseph brought his father down into the land of Egypt, even so he died there; wherefore, the Lord brought a remnant of the seed of Joseph out of the land of Jerusalem, that he might be merciful unto the seed of Joseph that they should perish not, even as he was merciful unto the father of Joseph that he would perish not.

8. Wherefore, the remnant of the house of Joseph shall be built upon this land; and it shall be a land of their inheritance; and they shall build up a holy city unto the Lord, like unto the Jerusalem of old; and they shall no more be confounded, until the end come when the earth shall pass away.

9. And there shall be a new heaven and a new earth; and they shall be like unto the old save the old have passed away, and all things have become new.

10. And then cometh the New Jerusalem; and blessed are they who dwell therein, for it is they whose garments are w h i t e through the blood of the Lamb; and they are they who are numbered among the remnant of the

---

As such you have His care, His protection, His Fatherly love and responsibility; all on condition of filial trust and obedience. "For a wise and glorious purpose," He "has placed us here on Earth."

The Flood. It is not necessary to discuss, here, any controversial questions relating to the deluge. Many nations and many tribes have traditions in which the story of some such catastrophe has been preserved. There are, besides the account of it in Genesis and reference to it in other parts of the Bible, Ovid's Greek story of Deucalion and Pyrrha, who were saved in an ark when Zeus destroyed all other inhabitants of Hellas by a flood; also the stories of the Hindus, and the Persians, who say that the waters washed away the evils of Ahriman, the Evil One; further, traditions or legends by Babylonians, Assyrians, Scandinavians, Mexicans, Peruvians, and others. The point that Ether makes is this, that the Lord, after the deluge, declared the American Continents to be a "choice land above all other lands," and that all who dwell thereon are under obligation to serve Him. (Compare Ether 1:42-43) And this directs the attention of Moroni to the revelation given through Ether on the New Jerusalem (vv. 3-13), an element of the Everlasting Gospel of Salvation evidently of first importance to the compiler of the works of the last Jaredite Prophet.

The place of the New Jerusalem. For a better understanding of this section, one is referred to the visions of Enoch recorded in the Pearl of Great Price, Moses 7:60-62.

Enoch, it will be remembered, ascended a high mountain, where the Lord revealed to him the future of the human family. The advent of our Lord and Savior, Jesus Christ, was shown to him. At that time, the Lord declared: "As I live, even so will I come in the last days, in the days of wickedness and vengeance, to fulfill the oath which I have made unto you concerning the children of Noah."

Enoch had asked, "When shall the Earth rest?" and the Lord answered, that

seed of Joseph, who were of the house of Israel.

11. And then also cometh the Jerusalem of old; and the inhabitants thereof, blessed are they, for they have been washed in the blood of the Lamb; and they are they who were scattered and gathered in from the four quarters of the earth, and from the north countries, and are partakers of the fulfilling of the covenant which God made with their father, Abraham.

12. And when these things come, bringeth to pass the scripture which saith, there are they who were first, who shall be last; and they are they who were last, who shall be first.

---

the day of rest would come, but it would be preceded by a period of deep night and destructive revolutions. We read:

"Before that day the heavens shall be darkened, and a veil of darkness shall cover the earth; and the heavens shall shake and also the earth; and great tribulations shall be among the children of men, but My people will I preserve; and righteousness will I send down out of Heaven; and truth out of the earth, to bear testimony of My Only Begotten; His resurrection from the dead; yea, and also the resurrection of all men; and righteousness and truth will I cause to sweep the Earth as with a flood, to gather out Mine elect from the four quarters of the Earth unto a place which I shall prepare, an holy City, that My people may gird up their loins, and be looking forth for the time of My coming; for there shall be My tabernacle, and it shall be called ZION, a New Jerusalem." (Moses 7:61-62)

Two Cities. In the account of the life of Enoch, as recorded in the "Writings of Moses," Pearl of Great Price, two cities of outstanding prominence are mentioned, viz., the City of Zion, and the New Jerusalem. Concerning these we note the following information:

The City of Zion. As a fruit of the missionary labors of Enoch among the Ante-diluvians, the righteous of all nations were gathered together. They were the people of the Lord, and He called them Zion, "because they were of one heart and one mind, and dwelt in righteousness; and there was no poor among them." (Moses 7:18) Then Enoch undertook to build a city as the chief center thereof, we may suppose, of the country of the gathering place, and that city became known as "The City of Holiness, even Zion." (v. 19)

Zion, the Abode of the Lord for ever. This done, Enoch expressed the hope that the organization of the people of Zion, and their magnificent city might remain forever. "Surely," he said, "Zion, the City shall dwell in safety forever."

The Lord answered, in substance, that it would, "Zion have I blessed, but the residue of the people have I cursed." His answer was amplified by a vision of the future of the inhabitants of the Earth. "And lo, Zion, in process of time was taken up into Heaven." There it would remain in safety forever with its perfect organization, its palaces and temples, and there the Lord would dwell: "And the Lord said unto Enoch: Behold mine abode forever." (v. 21) If it has pleased the Lord to establish His permanent home, His Royal Residence, in the City of Zion on the other side of the veil, then that City is the *Capital of the Kingdom of God* forever.

Missionary work after the removal of the City of Zion. The Patriarch now was shown that missionary work was continued among the Ante-diluvians after he and his City were taken unto Heaven. "And Enoch beheld angels" — Gospel messengers — "descending out of Heaven, bearing testimony of the Father and Son; and the Holy Ghost fell on many."

What about these on whom the Holy Ghost fell?

"And they were caught up by the powers of Heaven." So they, too, became citizens of the heavenly Zion, of which Enoch says, "And Thou hast taken Zion to Thine own bosom, from all Thy creations, from all eternity to all eternity."

Thus the righteous of the Ante-diluvians were saved from destruction. The impenitent perished in the Flood. And the work of Enoch, as seen in the results attending his city and its people on the other side of the veil, far surpassed in magnitude and importance anything that the Patriarch could ever have hoped for.

A New Jerusalem. Enoch had glorious visions of the advent of the Only Begotten in the meridian of time. Also visions of His Second Coming in the last days. A New Jerusalem is closely connected with this great event yet future.

The place revealed. In a revelation given to the Prophet Joseph Smith and six elders at Kirtland, Ohio, September 22, 1832, we read:

"Yea, the word of the Lord concerning His Church, established in the last days for the restoration of His people, as He has spoken by the mouth of His prophets, and for the gathering of His Saints to stand upon Mount Zion, which shall be the City of the New Jerusalem. Which City shall be built, beginning at the Temple Lot, which is appointed by the finger of the Lord, in the western boundaries in the State of Missouri, and dedicated by the hand of Joseph Smith, Jun., and others with whom the Lord is well pleased." (Doctrine and Covenants 84:2-3)

A wonderful reunion. The Lord told Enoch about the marvelous destiny of this City to be built in Missouri. In the first place, our Lord, Himself, and Enoch and the inhabitants of Zion, the City of our Lord before the Flood, are to meet the Saints in the New Jerusalem, in a most affectionate reunion. In the second place, the Lord will make it His abode temporarily, "It shall be Zion, which shall come forth out of all the creations which I have made"; the affairs of the Kingdom of God will be directed from there, and the Earth shall rest for a thousand years. Enoch saw that the Lord would come in the last days to dwell in the New Jerusalem on the Earth in righteousness for the space of a thousand years. That is the glorious hope and expectation of the people of God. They know that the last word in the controversy between the agents of good and evil; the final word of triumphant victory, will be spoken, not by any slave of Lucifer, but by the Son of God, the Savior and the Redeemer of mankind.

A Jerusalem from Heaven. Note that the New Jerusalem mentioned in verse 3 as coming down out of Heaven and the holy sanctuary, is the City of Zion, which had been taken up into Heaven. (Moses 7:19-20) It is the heavenly pattern of the city yet to be built upon the Earth.

Upon this Land. The New Jerusalem of this paragraph is the City that is to be reared in Jackson County, Missouri. Here the Saints of God will meet the Saints of the last days. President Brigham Young may have had this marvelous reunion in mind when he told the Saints:

"About the time that the Temples of the Lord will be built and Zion is established —pretty nigh this time, you will see, (those who are faithful enough) the first you know, there will be strangers in your midst, walking with you, talking with you; they will enter into your houses and eat and drink with you, go to meeting with you, and begin to open your minds, as the Savior did the two disciples who walked out in the country in the days of old.

"About the time the Temples are ready, the strangers will be along and will converse with you, and will inquire of you, probably, if you understand the resurrection of the dead. You might say you have heard and read a great deal about it, but you do not properly understand it; and they will then open your minds and tell you the principles of the resurrection of the dead and how to save your friends; they will point out the Scriptures in the Old and New Testaments, in the Book of Mormon and other revelations of God, saying 'Don't you recollect reading so-and-so, that saviors should come up on Mount Zion?' etc., and they will expound the Scriptures to you. You have got your temples ready; now go forth and be baptized for those good people. There are your father and mother—your ancestors for many generations back—the people that have lived upon the face of the Earth since the Priesthood was taken away, thousands and millions of them, who have lived according to the best light and knowledge in their possession.

"Many of the elders of Israel in Mount Zion will become pillars in the Temple of God, to go no more out. They will eat and drink and sleep there; and they will often have occasion to say, 'Somebody came to the Temple last night; we did not know who he was, but he was no doubt a brother, and he told us a great many things we did not before understand. He gave us the names of a great many of our forefathers that were not on record, and he gave me my true lineage and the names of my forefathers for hundreds of years back. He said to me, 'You and I are connected in one family; there are the names of your ancestors; take them and write them down, and be baptized and confirmed, and save such and such ones, and receive the blessings of the eternal Priesthood for such and such an individual, as you do for yourselves." (*Journal of Discourses*, Vol. 6, pp. 294-295. Also *See*, *Discourses of Brigham Young*, Widtsoe, pp. 627-628.)

The reason why the Saints of Enoch's Zion will visit the Saints of the Zion in the Last Days, during the Millennium, appears clearly in the remarkable sermon just quoted. The personal calls of the "strangers" are in the interest of the Temple Service, in which both the Heavens and the Earth are equally interested.

The Jerusalem of Lehi. Having spoken of the New Jerusalem, Ether turns, in his prophetic discourse, to the City from which Moroni, the abridger of the translation King Mosiah made of the twenty-four gold plates which contained Ether's record, says that Lehi should come; that is, Jerusalem in Palestine. That City is to be built up again, and become a "holy City unto the Lord, and it should be built unto the House of Israel."

The New Jerusalem. This City, as explained, will be upon the American Continent "unto the remnant of the seed of Joseph, for which things there has been a type."

There has been a type. If we understand, correctly, these paragraphs, the thought is there conveyed that the exodus of Jacob with his household from Canaan, at the instance of his son, Joseph, was a prototype of the migration of Lehi and his little company from the Land of Jerusalem, in compliance with a divine command; for, as the father of Joseph was brought to Egypt in order that he and his house might be saved from perishing in an almost universal famine, so Lehi and his family were led to the New World, in order to escape the Babylonian siege and destruction of Jerusalem. In both these instances of notable migration, the purpose of the Lord was the salvation of a "remnant of the House of Joseph" from annihilation.

They shall build a city. The reason for the miraculous preservation of a "remnant of the Seed of Joseph" is here stated. That remnant has a special mission to perform in the Kingdom of God. They are to build the New Jerusalem on this Continent. We read in verse eight: "The remnant of the House of Joseph shall be built upon this land." That is to say, "It shall be a land of their inheritance; and they shall build up a Holy City unto the Lord, like unto the Jerusalem of old." That is the mission of the remnant of Joseph's seed.

A new Heaven and a new Earth. The preceding sentence (v. 8) refers to a certain time "when the Earth shall pass away." In verse nine it is asserted that there will be a new Heaven and a new Earth, and that the new creations are to be "like unto the old," except for the fact that they are new.

This, if modern phraseology alone is considered, might be regarded as a prediction of the end, literally speaking, of the entire universe. But the context does not permit such a sweeping interpretation. The passing away of the Heaven and the Earth is not the end (finis) of either; it is the continuation of their existence, but under such entirely new conditions and circumstances as to enable the people of God to build both the New and the Old Jerusalem on this Earth.

In the ancient writings, the expression "heaven and earth" sometimes means the entire universe as in Genesis 1:1. But sometimes it is a figure of speech, referring to the existing order of things; that is for example, the organization of a kingdom, its rulers and subjects. So used, the *Sun, moon, and the stars* are the symbols of kings and governors, while the *earth* stands for the common people. Our Lord, undoubtedly, referred to the kings and governors, when He said that immediately after the tribulation preceding His coming, "The sun shall be darkened and the moon not give her light, and the stars shall fall from heaven, and the power of heaven shall be shaken." (Matthew 24:29) Compare Revelation by John, 8:10; and 9:1 for the figurative meaning of "star."

In Isaiah 51:13 and 16, we find the literal meaning, and also the figurative. Our Lord, in this prophecy, first reminded Israel of the fact that He had "stretched forth the heavens and laid the foundations of the earth," literally, in the Creation. He then said that He had put His words in the mouth of Israel, and preserved the people, in order to "plant the heavens and lay the foundations of the earth" — that is, create a new heaven and a new earth, figuratively speaking — and say unto Zion Thou art My people.

In the text under consideration (v. 9) "heaven" and "earth" are to be understood in this figurative — we may even call it political — sense. The true meaning, therefore, is this, that before the coming of the new era, with a New Jerusalem in Jackson County, Missouri, and the Old Jerusalem in Palestine rebuilt, the entire social and political organizations of mankind will be radically changed as to make the establishment of the Kingdom of God among men possible. In that sense there will be a new earth under a new heaven.

Let us now pause a moment and ask whether this change has not been going on for some time. Is the Earth today what it was, say a hundred years ago, speaking socially and politically? Look at the automobiles in streets where formerly ox teams and horses took care of the traffic. Listen to the planes in the air that have made it possible to breakfast in San Francisco and dine in New York the same day. Consider the radio, by means of which a speaker, or singer, in Salt Lake City may entertain an audience in Australia; or a politician in Washington D.C. can converse with a colleague in London, Berlin, or Rome, as if the two were face to face with each other in the same room. Consider the changes affected in the industrial world— agriculture, for instance, with its costly and intricate machinery, or in the conditions of the laboring man generally. Think of the progress made in engineering, in the medical sciences, in education, and the discoveries made by means of the microscope on one hand and the telescope on the other. Our earth is indeed *new*, if we compare it to that of our ancestors. Were some of them to arise in our midst, they would not know or recognize their old home town, or their farms. They would be in strange surroundings, where miracles would be to them an every-day occurrence. We are already now living on a "new" earth, and further changes are going on daily.

Then cometh the New Jerusalem. When this change of the earth has been completed, then the New Jerusalem will be built in Jackson County, Missouri. (*See* paragraph 4, this chapter)

Through the blood of the Lamb. The inhabitants of the New Jerusalem are they "who are numbered among the remnant of the Seed of Joseph," or, in other words, "the House of Israel." That is, the Saints of the latter days, whose "garments are white through the Blood of the Lamb." (Compare Revelation 7:13-17) The white garments were a sign of victory. Those who wore them had overcome every trial during the tribulation of the last days. But their victory was, properly considered, the triumph of the Lamb of God who offered His Atoning Blood on Calvary. In other words, the victory of the white-robed Saints in the New City was due to the conquest by the Savior of the powers of hell, or all evil, which was made manifest in the lives of His faithful followers. To Him, therefore, be all honor and glory for ever.

Jerusalem of Old. At the time when the New Jerusalem is coming into existence in Jackson County, Missouri, Jerusalem in Palestine will be restored to a magnificence and importance never before attained by that City. Even the glory of the period of David and Solomon will be far surpassed. The inhabitants thereof, we read, "Have been washed in the Blood of the Lamb." That is, they have accepted our Lord as the Messiah, who, by His Atoning Sacrifice on Calvary, became "The Lamb of God, Which taketh away the sin of the world." (John 1:29-36) And thus were they *washed,* or made clean, in the Blood of the Lamb.

Scattered and gathered. The inhabitants of the restored City of Jerusalem are, further, described as having been "scattered and gathered in from the four corners of the Earth"; that is, from the entire globe. Up to this time, the mission of Israel and Judah, as the custodians of the divine promises to Abraham, by which all nations of the Earth are to be blessed, required them to live in dispersion. Now that mission is ended. A new era, one of consolidation of the scattered descendants of Abraham into political unity and importance is about to begin. The restoration of Jerusalem is one of the signs of the new era.

From the North Countries. The best understanding of this not-quite-definite expression may be gathered from the revelations on the subject.

On April 3, 1836, Moses appeared to the Prophet Joseph Smith and Oliver Cowdery in the Kirtland Temple, and committed to them the "keys of the Gathering of Israel from the four parts of the Earth, and the leading of the Ten Tribes from the land of the north." (Doctrine and Covenants 110:11) This makes it plain that the "north countries" are the regions where the Ten Tribes found a refuge after having escaped the Assyrian captivity.

Here historic research may come to our aid. According to the Apocryphal II Esdras 13:40-50, the Ten Tribes were deported across the Euphrates by the Assyrian Shalmaneser. This was about 722 B.C. But this ruler had trouble of his own, and in the political confusion prevailing, the captives, for such they were, found an opportunity to recross the great river, and then to turn northward to reach an uninhabited country, where they were safe from pursuit. Esdras says that they traveled a year and a half to a region called Arsareth, and there, he adds, "They dwelt until the latter time, and when they came forth again, the Most High shall hold still the springs of the river again, that they may go through."

Here, then, we learn that the exiled Tribes traveled a year and a half to reach their new home, the "north countries."

Lieutenant C. A. L. Totten[1] refers to Herodotus as follows: "He tells us that in his day (450 B.C.), a warlike, virtuous, and powerful race, called Cumbri, lived around the northern coasts of the Black Sea, and centrally at the Crimea. . . . Herodotus further tells us that this people had originally come from Media, the which, he adds, however, had not been their birthplace, and he puts them there, in Media, as sojourners only. (Circa 600 B.C.) "Mr. Totten concludes from this information by the "father of history" and from numerous other references, that the

---

[1] *Our Race,* Study Number 3, p. 73. We may not agree with all the conclusions of this author, but his quotations can always be accepted.

3. *He dwells in a cave.*

13. And I was about to write more, but I am forbidden; but great and marvelous were the prophecies of Ether; but they esteemed him as naught, and cast him out; and he hid himself in the cavity of a rock by day, and by night he went forth viewing the things which should come upon the people.

Ten Tribes gradually emerged fom the region of the Caucasus and appeared in northern and western Europe as Angles, Jutes, Saxons, Danes, Normans, Goths, etc. All, he says, were kindred, all Cimri, all Scythians, all Scots, all from Crimea and the Asia Minor and Black Sea region of Herodotus.

If these statements are historically correct, we may look for the "north countries" in the regions where these nationalities are liberally represented, especially Great Britain, the German States, and the Scandinavian countries. Northern mythology, which, as preserved in the exquisite Icelandic poetry, especially the *Older Edda,* reminds one of a kinship with the early parts of the Old Testament, and seems to lend some support to this view.

The following modern revelation (Doctrine and Covenants 133:23-30) should be studied in this connection:

"He shall command the great deep, and it shall be driven back into the north countries, and the islands shall become one land; and the Land of Jerusalem and the Land of Zion shall be turned back into their own place, and the Earth shall be like it was in the days before it was divided. And the Lord, even the Savior, shall stand in the midst of His people, and shall reign over all flesh. And they who are in the North Countries shall come in remembrance before the Lord; and their prophets shall hear His voice, and shall no longer stay themselves; and they shall smite the rocks, and the sea shall flow down at their presence. And an highway shall be cast up in the midst of the great deep. Their enemies shall become a prey unto them. And in the barren deserts there shall come forth pools of living water; and the parched ground shall no longer be a thirsty land. And they shall bring forth their rich treasures unto the children of Ephraim, My servants."

This is all highly figurative language, but the general meaning seems to be clear.

Partakers of the Covenant. This Covenant was made with Abraham. See a previous paragraph headed "Scattered and Gathered." God, Himself, was He Who made the Covenant with the *Father of the Faithful:*

"I will make thy seed to multiply as the stars of heaven, and will give unto thy seed all those countries; and in thy seed shall all the nations of the Earth be blessed." (Genesis 26:4)

This Covenant was repeated to Jacob, the grandson of Abraham and the son of Isaac:

"And thy seed shall be as the dust of the Earth, and thou shalt spread abroad to the west, and to the east, and to the north, and to the south; and in thee and in thy seed shall all the families of the Earth be blessed." (Genesis 28:14)

Such is the mission of the descendants of Abraham, through Isaac and Jacob. (Genesis 15:1-6 and 18) "In Isaac shall thy seed be called." (Genesis 21:12; Hebrews 11:18)

VERSES 13-14. *In the cavity of a rock.* Moroni here explains that he was about to write more of Ether's predictions, but he was restrained from doing so. Ether prophesied many things that to Moroni were "great and marvelous," and, no doubt thought that the future readers of his account would be impressed as he was with them.

4. *Views by night the destruction falling upon his people.*

14. And as he dwelt in the cavity of a rock he made the remainder of this record, viewing the destructions which came upon the people, by night.

15. And it came to pass that in that same year in which he was cast out from among the people there began to be a great war among the people, for there were many who rose up, who were mighty men, and sought to destroy Coriantumr by their secret plans of wickedness, of which hath been spoken.

16. And now Coriantumr, having studied, himself, in all the arts of war and all the cunning of the world, wherefore he gave battle unto them who sought to destroy him.

17. But he repented not, neither his fair sons nor daughters; neither the fair sons and daughters of Cohor; neither the fair

A prophet not only foretells the future, but also he interprets the past, and explains and makes clear the Scriptures. Ether told the wicked Jaredites "of all things from the beginning of man." (v. 2) He saw "the days of Christ," and testified of His mission. (v. 4) This great land in which we now live, he told them, was a "chosen land of the Lord"; and made the solemn declaration that "the Lord would have that all men should serve Him who dwell upon the face thereof." Ether took this awe-inspiring proclamation, of which he was the herald, as a basis for his call on them to repent. Because the Jaredites had been chosen by God to dwell in this favored land, they, we may assume he argued, were under obligation to serve Him. And right here let us say that we, in living upon this same land, are, too, commanded to serve Him. Well we may say: "Thy will, O God, is my command," and we will remember God's gracious promise to Nephi of Old; it is to us as it was to him, a pledge given by the Lord: "And inasmuch as ye shall keep My commandments, ye shall prosper" in the land. This land is to us a "Land of Promise." The promise is sure! It is a land which God has prepared for us as much as for Nephi and his seed, "Yea, a land which is choice above all other lands." Then, we may argue, why should not we, who enjoy a liberty of which He is the Author and for which the Nephites fought and bled, serve Him, and make manifest our appreciation of His great love; for is He not the loving Father of all men? (*See,* I Nephi 2:20; also, Alma 53:17)

But, we have pointed out that the Jaredites rejected Ether's voice of warning, "they esteemed him as naught," and sought to take away his life. Knowing his work was not yet finished, and the account of his people that he was making was not complete, he took every precaution that presented itself to protect and preserve his life. "He hid himself in the cavity of a rock by day, and by night he went forth viewing the things which should come upon the people." It was while protecting himself thusly, he "made the remainder of" his record.

VERSES 15-31. *The great war.* The warning voice of Ether aroused bitter enmity among the people of Moron against the chosen prophet of God. He was cast out, and as we have said, found refuge in a cave. There he finished his record.

The prophet having found a place of safety, the momentous war broke out in all its fury. Coriantumr, the King, had many enemies. After three years of civil struggle he was made a prisoner of war by Shared. But in the fourth year, his sons

sons and daughters of Corihor; and in fine, there were none of the fair sons and daughters upon the face of the whole earth who repented of their sins.

18. Wherefore, it came to pass that in the first year that Ether dwelt in the cavity of a rock, there were many people who were slain by the sword of those secret combinations, fighting against Coriantumr that they might obtain the kingdom.

19. And it came to pass that the sons of Coriantumr fought much and bled much.

20. And in the second year the word of the Lord came to Ether, that he should go and prophesy unto Coriantumr that, if he would repent, and all his household, the Lord would give unto him his kingdom and spare the people—

21. Otherwise they should be destroyed, and all his household save it were himself. And he should only live to see the fulfilling of the prophecies which had been spoken concerning another people receiving the land for their inheritance; and Coriantumr should receive a burial by them; and every soul should be destroyed save it were Coriantumr.

22. And it came to pass that Coriantumr repented not, neither his household, neither the people; and the wars ceased not; and they sought to kill Ether, but

---

succeeded in liberating him. But the people sunk deeper and deeper in corruption, and the war flames continued roaring. Shared was slain in the Battle of Gilgal. Coriantumr was wounded so seriously that he was unfit for active military service for two years. However, this did not deter the people from shedding each other's blood, "and as there was none to restrain them," the whole face of the land lay festering in its own wantonness and filthiness.

THE NEW JERUSALEM, A RESUME

We have now read the principal Scripture passages relating to this subject. A brief resume of the points noted is now offered.

Enoch, before the flood, gathered a considerable number of converts in a place to which the Lord gave the name of Zion. (Pearl of Great Price, Moses 7:18) Enoch built a city in this place. It was called, "The City of Holiness," or "The City of Zion." In course of time, the inhabitants of this gathering place and this City were taken up into Heaven, whereupon the Lord declared: "Behold Mine Abode forever." We naturally infer that the Saints of the Zion of Enoch, had, beyond the veil, the same perfect social organizations that they had here; that, in other words, they had a heavenly gathering place and City of Zion, and that the Lord graciously selected the latter to be the permanent Capital of His Kingdom, on both sides of the veil. (v. 32) See, also, v. 47, where Enoch, in his vision, seeing the Lamb of God slain on Earth, took comfort in the thought that Zion still existed: "Behold Zion is with me." The absence of the King was only temporary.

In his vision concerning the second advent of our Lord, Enoch saw a new City of Zion, a New Jerusalem, on this (the American) Continent. (v. 62; also, Doctrine and Covenants 84:3) He saw that Jesus, the King, that he himself (Enoch), and many Saints from the City of Enoch beyond the veil, were to meet the Saints of the latter days in this City of New Jerusalem in America. Those Saints of the Zion

he fled from before them and hid again in the cavity of the rock.

23. And it came to pass that there arose up Shared, and he also gave battle unto Coriantumr; and he did beat him, insomuch that in the third year he did bring him into captivity.

24. And the sons of Coriantumr, in the fourth year, did beat Shared, and did obtain the kingdom again unto their father.

25. Now there began to be a war upon all the face of the land, every man with his band fighting for that which he desired.

26. And there were robbers, and in fine, all manner of wickedness upon all the face of the land.

27. And it came to pass that Coriantumr was exceedingly angry with Shared, and he went against him with his armies to battle; and they did meet in great anger, and they did meet in the valley of Gilgal; and the battle became exceeding sore.

28. And it came to pass that Shared fought against him for the space of three days. And it came to pass that Coriantumr beat him, and did pursue him until he came to the plains of Heshlon.

29. And it came to pass that

---

of Enoch and the Saints gathered from every part of the Earth are to be the inhabitants of the New Jerusalem in Jackson County, Missouri, (v. 63; Ether 13:3)

Here the Lord will dwell for a thousand years, governing His Kingdom on both sides of the veil, and completing the Plan of Salvation. (vv. 64-65; Revelation 21:1-5)

OUR RELATIONSHIP TO ABRAHAM

"Look unto Abraham your father, and unto Sarah that bare you, for I called him alone and blessed him, and increased him.

"For the Lord shall comfort Zion: He will comfort all her waste places; and He will make her wilderness like Eden, and her desert like the garden of the Lord; joy and gladness shall be found therein, thanksgiving, and the voice of melody." (Isaiah 51:2-3.)

These sacred words were spoken or written about seven hundred years before the birth of the Savior, and they point unmistakably to the latter days. Who was this man, Abraham, of whom the prophet tells? He was the father of the faithful, the friend of God, the great progenitor of the House of Israel; and the exhortation of the prophet is unto Israel in modern times. He is endeavoring to turn the hearts of the children to their father, their ancestor, the rock from which they were hewn.

How do we trace our lineage—we Latter-day Saints—back to Abraham, or from Abraham down? Briefly thus: Abraham had a son named Isaac; Isaac had a son named Jacob; Jacob had twelve sons, the head of the Twelve Tribes of Israel, and one of those sons was Joseph, who was sold into Egypt. Joseph had two sons, Manasseh and Ephraim, and we are of Ephraim, the "first-born of God in the great work of Israel's conversion and gathering in the last days." (From a sermon by Apostle Orson F. Whitney, March 9, 1924; Deseret News, March 15, 1924)

SHARED

A Jaredite military commander opposed to Coriantumr during a part of the great series of wars that ended in the destruction of that race. Nothing is said of him until he comes to the front as the leader of an army which gave battle to Coriantumr

Shared gave him battle again upon the plains; and behold, he did beat Coriantumr, and drove him back again to the valley of Gilgal.

30. And Coriantumr gave Shared battle again in the valley of Gilgal, in which he beat Shared and slew him.

31. And Shared wounded Coriantumr in his thigh, that he did not go to battle again for the space of two years, in which time all the people upon the face of the land were shedding blood, and there was none to restrain them.

---

and defeated him. This appears to have been a lengthy campaign and not one solitary fight for we are told that "in the third year he (Shared) did bring him into captivity. And the sons of Coriantumr, in the fourth year, did obtain the kingdom again unto their father." The war, at this period, would seem to have grown beyond control of the military leaders and to have degenerated into a condition of affairs in which every man's hand was against his neighbor and mobs, instead of disciplined armies, carried bloodshed and devastation far and wide, throughout the land. Bands of brigands and robbers committed all manner of outrages and the whole country was the scene of anarchy and horror from one end to the other. After a time, Coriantumr, being exceedingly angry, gathered his forces and met Shared in the Valley of Gilgal. The fight, which lasted three days, was a desperate and stubborn one. Shared was beaten and retreated as far as Heshlon where he again withstood Coriantumr, and this time he was victorious, driving his foe back to their former battleground—the Valley of Gilgal. Here another fierce battle was fought in which Shared was slain and his troops defeated. In after years, Gilead, a brother of Shared's, took his brother's place and continued the bitter conflict with Coriantumr.

GILGAL, VALLEY OF

A valley mentioned as the locality of several desperate battles in the last Jaredite war. The first of these battles was between the armies of Shared and those of Coriantumr; it lasted three days. The losses on both sides were exceedingly heavy and ended in a victory for Coriantumr who pursued his enemy as far as the Plains of Heshlon. There another hotly contested fight took place, in which the tide of battle turned and Coriantumr was driven back to the Valley of Gilgal. Here a third conflict ensued in which Shared was killed and Coriantumr wounded. Nothing more is said in the Book of Ether that gives any clue to the locality in which Gilgal was situated.

NEW JERUSALEM

The City spoken of by John in the Book of Revelation; but ages before that time, prophesied of by Ether, the last seer of the Jaredites. (Ether 13:3-10) Among the other things of which he prophesied, Ether foretells that this blessed City shall be built upon the American Continent. Jesus, in His teachings to the Nephites, confirms the truth of this prophecy. (III Nephi 20:22; 21:23-24)

CORIHOR

Corihor was a prominent Jaredite of the latest generation (between 700 and 600 years before Christ). He appears to have been an associate of Coriantumr's, and to have had many fair sons and daughters. Further than this nothing is known of him.

CHAPTER 14

1. *A curse upon the land.*

1. And now there began to be a great curse upon all the land because of the iniquity of the people, in which, if a man should lay his tool or his sword upon his shelf, or upon the place whither he would keep it, behold, upon the morrow, he could not find it, so great was the curse upon the land.

2. Wherefore every man did cleave unto that which was his own, with his hands, and would not borrow neither would he lend; and every man kept the hilt of his sword in his right hand, in the defence of his property and his own life and of his wives and children.

VERSE 1. *There began to be a great curse upon all the land because of the iniquity of the people.* Some of the demoralizing influences of war upon a nation are noted in these paragraphs. In the murderous conflict between Shared and Coriantumr, and their followers, the walls of civilization were broken down, and a tidal wave of immorality, notably dishonesty and violent savagery, destroyed all signs of decent culture. We believe that history proves every great war has been followed by just such a wave of crime, degradation, and filth, especially violence, destruction of mutual confidence among neighbors, and therefore of human happiness.

But that is not all. In a great war millions of beings are slaughtered as so many no consequence, loss, however, of which, post-mortem empty orations and useless pyrotechnics are no compensation. According to Professor L. Hersch, a Swiss statistician, 41,435,000 were slain in World War I. These were, generally speaking, the physically and intellectually strong and fit, in their best age. Their prospective careers as leaders in civilization and progress were cut short in the unspeakable mud puddles of modern battlefields. Many survivors, as has been made evident in after years, lost during the years of "military discipline," their personal will power and initiative, to such a degree that they became the blind, deaf and dumb, victims of calculating adventurers.

The cost of a great war in the loss of valuable property, pensions, bonuses, taxes, etc., can never be ascertained except approximately. It has been estimated that the United States, since 1865 until a few years after World War I, has paid no less than $14,500,000,000 in pensions alone. And that is only one item. The total cost is incalculable. But the World War of which we have spoken taught us that whatever it is, both parties are the losers. Both pay the price of blood. National hatreds are revived. Expenditures on account of armaments have been ruining both victors and vanquished, and it has been found that no restitution in cash or trade can be enforced without lessening the chances of prosperity everywhere.

War is nothing but a curse!

2. Continued Strife and Bloodshed.

3. And now, after the space of two years, and after the death of Shared, behold, there arose the brother of Shared and he gave battle unto Coriantumr, in which Coriantumr did beat him and did pursue him to the wilderness of Akish.

4. And it came to pass that the brother of Shared did give battle unto him in the wilderness of Akish; and the battle became exceeding sore, and many thousands fell by the sword.

5. And it came to pass that Coriantumr did lay siege to the wilderness; and the brother of Shared did march forth out of the wilderness by night, and slew a part of the army of Coriantumr, as they were drunken.

6. And he came forth to the land of Moron, and placed himself upon the throne of Coriantumr.

7. And it came to pass that Coriantumr dwelt with his army in the wilderness for the space of two years, in which he did receive great strength to his army.

8. Now the brother of Shared, whose name was Gilead, also received great strength to his army, because of secret combinations.

9. And it came to pass that his high priest murdered him as he sat upon his throne.

10. And it came to pass that one of the secret combinations murdered him in a secret pass, and obtained unto himself the kingdom; and his name was Lib; and Lib was a man of great stature, more than any other man among all the people.

11. And it came to pass that in the first year of Lib, Coriantumr came up unto the land of Moron, and gave battle unto Lib.

12. And it came to pass that he fought with Lib, in which Lib did smite upon his arm that he was wounded; nevertheless, the

---

VERSE 8. *Now the brother of Shared, whose name was Gilead.* The first notable engagement of the great Jaredite war, after the death of Shared in the Valley of Gilgal, was fought in the sparsely-settled Wilderness of Akish. After Gilgal there was peace for two years. But at the expiration of that time, Gilead, the brother of Shared, attacked Coriantumr unsuccessfully, and fled to the Wilderness of Akish, closely pursued by his antagonist. This notable place of conflict must have been close to the border of Moron.

Kish is a Jaredite word. It was also the name of an important city in Mesopotamia thousands of years ago. It is a Hebrew word, said to mean a "bow," or a "horn." It was the name of the father of King Saul. (I Samuel 9:1)

For an account of Akish, the son of Kimnor, and the daughter of Jared, the son of Omer, *See* Ether 8:9-18 and 9:1-12. The Wilderness may have been his homeland and so named after him.

The fortunes of war are always uncertain. In the first period of this war, Coriantumr lost a large part of his army, and also his throne. Gilead took charge of the government of Moron, and Coriantumr established himself in the Wilderness of Akish. Two years later, the brother of Shared was murdered by his chief ecclesiastical officer.

army of Coriantumr did press forward upon Lib, that he fled to the borders upon the seashore.

13. And it came to pass that Coriantumr pursued him; and Lib gave battle unto him upon the seashore.

14. And it came to pass that Lib did smite the army of Coriantumr, that they fled again to the wilderness of Akish.

15. And it came to pass that Lib did pursue him until he came to the plains of Agosh. And Coriantumr had taken all the people with him as he fled before Lib in that quarter of the land whither he fled.

3. Coriantumr not to fall by the Sword.

16. And when he had come to the plains of Agosh he gave battle unto Lib, and he smote upon him until he died; nevertheless, the brother of Lib did come against Coriantumr in the stead thereof, and the battle became exceeding sore, in the which Coriantumr fled again before the army of the brother of Lib.

17. Now the name of the brother of Lib was called Shiz. And it came to pass that Shiz pursued after Coriantumr, and he did overthrow many cities, and he did slay both women and children, and he did burn the cities.

18. And there went a fear of Shiz throughout all the land; yea, a cry went forth throughout the land—Who can stand before the army of Shiz? Behold, he sweepeth the earth before him!

19. And it came to pass that the people began to flock together in armies, throughout all the face of the land.

20. And they were divided; and a part of them fled to the army of Shiz, and a part of them fled to the army of Coriantumr.

21. And so great and lasting had been the war, and so long had been the scene of bloodshed and carnage, that the whole face of the land was covered with the bodies of the dead.

22. And so swift and speedy was the war that there was none left to bury the dead, but they did march forth from the shedding of blood to the shedding of blood, leaving the bodies of both men, women, and children strewed upon the face of the land, to become a prey to the worms of the flesh.

23. And the scent thereof went

Retaliation. The patriarchal law, given through Noah for the protection of human life, never revoked, is this: "Whoso sheddeth man's blood, by man shall his blood be shed; for in the image of God made He man." (Genesis 9:6) In the case of this blasphemous murderer retaliation came before long. He was assassinated by another aspirant to the throne, Lib.

Lib, and Coriantumr. Coriantumr attacked Lib in the Land of Moron with so much savage impetuosity that the false king, that is Lib, and his confused army fled "to the borders upon the sea shore," pursued by his antagonist. There Lib rallied and drove Coriantumr back to the Wilderness of Akish. On the Plains of Agosh the two armies again met.

forth upon the face of the land, even upon all the face of the land; wherefore the people became troubled by day and by night, because of the scent thereof.

24. Nevertheless, Shiz did not cease to pursue Coriantumr; for he had sworn to avenge himself upon Coriantumr of the blood of his brother, who had been slain, and the word of the Lord which came to Ether that Coriantumr should not fall by the sword.

25. And thus we see that the Lord did visit them in the fulness of his wrath, and their wickedness and abominations had prepared a way for their everlasting destruction.

26. And it came to pass that Shiz did pursue Coriantumr eastward, even to the borders of the seashore, and there he gave battle unto Shiz for the space of three days.

27. And so terrible was the destruction among the armies of Shiz that the people began to be frightened, and began to flee before the armies of Coriantumr; and they fled to the land of Corihor, and swept off the inhabitants before them, all them that would not join them.

28. And they pitched their tents in the valley of Corihor; and Coriantumr pitched his tents in the valley of Shurr. Now the valley of Shurr was near the hill Comnor; wherefore, Coriantumr did gather his armies together upon the hill Comnor, and did sound a trumpet unto the armies of Shiz to invite them forth to battle.

29. And it came to pass that they came forth, but were driven again; and they came the second time, and they were driven again the second time. And it came to pass that they came again the third time, and the battle became exceeding sore.

30. And it came to pass that Shiz smote upon Coriantumr that he gave him many deep wounds; and Coriantumr, having lost his blood, fainted, and was carried away as though he were dead.

31. Now the loss of men, women and children on both sides was so great that Shiz commanded his people that they should not pursue the armies of Coriantumr; wherefore, they returned to their camp.

VERSES 16-27. *Shiz, the brother of Lib, pursues Coriantumr.* At the Battle of Agosh Lib fell (v. 16), but his brother took his place as commander of Lib's army, and the slaughter was continued until Coriantumr fled. The war now became a general massacre of men, women and children. The entire country was drenched in blood. A terrible battle was fought at the "borders of the sea shore."

VERSES 28-31. *Two Camps.* After three days of carnage on the sea shore Shiz established his camp in the Valley of Corihor, while Coriantumr gathered his forces on the Hill Comnor, in the Valley of Shurr. Shiz attacked Coriantumr three times in vain. The loss of lives on both sides was terrific. Coriantumr was wounded and carried away as dead. But Shiz commanded his army not to risk further bloodshed at that particular time, then they also went into camp.

GILEAD

A Jaredite military commander who contended with Coriantumr for the throne. He succeeded his brother Shared in the command of the armies opposed to Coriantumr. Their first battle occurred in the wilderness of Akish, when many thousands were slain. Gilead remained for a time in the wilderness, watched by Coriantumr; but eventually he made a night attack on the enemy, and the latter, being drunken, suffered great loss. Gilead, then placed himself on the throne of Coriantumr, and both commanders busied themselves in gathering men to strengthen their respective armies. Gilead, who had the sympathy of some of the secret combinations, received great strength during the two years they were thus engaged but he was slain by his own high priest as he sat on the throne; an evidence of the intensely corrupt state of society among the Jaredites of that time (towards the close of the seventh century B.C.).

SHIZ

Shiz was the last of the great military commanders opposed to King Coriantumr in the final war between the Jaredite factions. Shiz was the brother of Lib, another mighty warrior who did battle with Coriantumr. In one of the many engagements fought duing this series of wars, Lib was slain and Shiz took command of his brother's forces and routed Coriantumr following him in quick pursuit from the Plains of Agosh where the battle took place, to the seashore. Shiz's march was one of horror and terror to the people along his way. As he swiftly pressed forward he destroyed everything within his reach, burning the cities and slaying their inhabitants, sparing neither man, woman or child as he swept along, and the cry of despair went up through all the land. "Who can stand before the army of Shiz?" So rapid were the movements of the contending armies that the slain remained unburied, and the stench from their rotting bodies filled the air with a devastating omen of coming pestilence. Those yet alive hastened to join one or the other of the contending hosts, either from predilection or because they were forced into its ranks. Shiz was filled with the spirit of murderous revenge. He swore that he would avenge the blood of his brother whom Coriantumr had slain. When he caught up with the latter's armies he threw himself upon them with all the energy that hatred inspires. The battle lasted for three days and ended in the repulse of Shiz, whose warriors fled to the Land of Corihor, sweeping off the inhabitants of the lands they passed through who would not join them.

In the Valley of Corihor, Coriantumr again sought battle. He challenged Shiz, from the Hill Comnor, by the sound of the trumpet, and Shiz was in no temper to disregard the summons. Twice Shiz attacked his over-confident foe with the hordes that followed him and twice he was repulsed. On the third occasion he bore so heavily upon Coriantumr that the latter was wounded and fainted from loss of blood. Their leader stricken, his motley following of old and young fell back, but Shiz was in no condition to take advantage of his victory. Both had lost so heavily that they were unable to renew the contest. Two millions of men, with their wives and children, had already fallen in this inhuman, relentless war.

At this point the heart of Coriantumr was touched with the miseries of his people, so he wrote to Shiz stating that he would surrender the Kingdom if the lives of his followers would be spared. Shiz's brutal soul was yet untouched, he replied that if Coriantumr would give himself up so that he (Shiz) might slay him with his own sword, he would spare the lives of the people. To this proposal, Coriantumr would not accede. With rekindled anger and hatred both armies prepared for renewed hostilities. Shiz was victorious in the battle and Coriantumr with his army retired to the neighborhood of the Great Lakes. Another furious battle followed and Coriantumr triumphed, while Shiz retreated southward to a place called Ogath, near the Hill Ramah. Here the two commanders gathered their hosts for the final struggle. All, babe and grandsire, men and women, had to join one side or the other. The spirit of bloody vengeance filled every heart. Into the trembling hands of the aged and the feeble grasp of children alike were thust the sword and spear, while shield and breastplate defended the body strong enough to bear their weights. When once begun, the dwindling fight kept on from day to day, while night was made hideous by the yells and lamentations, the curses and oaths of the survivors, who were frenzied with anger, even as a man is drunken with wine. Thus they fought, struggled and fell with utter exhaustion until one night there remained of all the soldiers of Coriantumr but fifty-two, and sixty-nine of the followers of Shiz. But they did not rest. The next morning or during the following day, thirty-two of the adherents of Shiz confronted twenty-seven of Coriantumr's. Next day the battle was continued until the remnants of the two great armies grew faint from exertion and loss of blood. After three hours' desperate fighting the men of Coriantumr attempted to flee, but Shiz and his warriors prevented them from doing so. And so they continued until the two commanders remained alone on the battlefield, all their followers having been slain, and Shiz, himself, had fainted. Then Coriantumr, having rested to gain sufficient strength, smote off the head of Shiz who in his dying throes raised himself on his hands and knees as if to renew the contest, fell over, struggled for breath and died.

LIB

A commander of the opposing forces to Coriantumr in the great series of wars that ended in the destruction of the Jaredite Race. In size, he was a giant, being the largest man in the nation. He was also high in authority among the members of the secret associations that at that time had almost unbounded power among the people. He came to the throne through the murder of his predecessor, having himself committed the vile deed. In the first year of his reign Coriantumr came up against him and drove his forces to the borders of the sea. In this battle, however, Lib and Coriantumr met in single combat, and the latter was severely wounded by his adversary. A second battle took place on the seashore in which Lib was victorious and his enemies retreated to the Wilderness of Akish and thence to the Plains of Agosh. Here Coriantumr made another stand and in the battle Lib was killed. His brother, Shiz, took command, continued the fight and obtained a decisive victory.

COMNOR

A hill near the Valley of Shurr, location unknown, but apparently nearer the Atlantic than the Pacific Seaboard of North America. In one of the last great wars that took place among the Jaredites, Coriantumr massed his soldiers upon this Hill, and there challenged them to battle, the armies of Shiz by the sound of trumpets. A series of battles then ensued which, in the end, resulted disastrously for Coriantumr.

AGOSH, PLAINS OF

A place, locality unknown, in North America, where a great battle was fought in the last Jaredite war. The commanders of the contending armies were Coriantumr and Lib. After a victory by the latter in the Wilderness of Akish, he pursued Coriantumr as far as the Plains of Agosh when another battle was joined in which Coriantumr was victorious and Lib was slain. Shiz, the brother of Lib, assumed command of the place his brother had held and attacked and defeated Coriantumr. Probably about B.C. 600.

CORIHOR

LAND AND VALLEY

The Land and Valley of Corihor was the scene of some of the most hotly-contested battles between Shiz and Coriantumr in the last great Jaredite war. Its locality is not known, but evidently on the northern continent. Shiz having failed to conquer Coriantumr and in turn was defeated by him, retreated to this valley, sweeping before him the inhabitants who would not join him. There his army pitched tents, and when the armies of Coriantumr were sufficiently rested, challenged Shiz. Three battles ensued. Shiz was, in the end victorious, but so weakened were his followers that they could not follow up their victory, and from sheer exhaustion ceased for a time.

AKISH, WILDERNESS OF

A place in North America, apparently not far from the Atlantic Coast. Here a severe battle was fought in the last great war which ended in the extinction of the Jaredite Nation. The conflict was between the armies of Gilead and Coriantumr, in which many thousands were slain. It appears to have been indecisive as Gilead remained in the wilderness and Coriantumr lay siege thereto. But one night Gilead unexpectedly sallied forth and slew a part of the army of his enemy, they being drunken. This, for the time being gave him the advantage. In a later campaign, after Gilead had been assassinated, a battle was fought between Coriantumr and Lib in which the latter was victorious, and the former fled to the Wilderness of Akish, but being pursued by Lib, Coriantumr continued his retreat to the Plains of Agosh where another desperate conflict occurred.

CHAPTER 15

1. *Coriantumr repents.*

1. And it came to pass when Coriantumr had recovered of his wounds, he began to remember the words which Ether had spoken unto him.

2. He saw that there had been slain by the sword already nearly two million of his people, and he began to sorrow in his heart; yea, there had been slain two millions of mighty men, and also their wives and their children.

3. He began to repent of the evil which he had done; he began to remember the words which had been spoken by the mouth of all the prophets, and he saw them that they were fulfilled thus far, every whit; and his soul mourned and refused to be comforted.

4. And it came to pass that he wrote an epistle unto Shiz, desiring him that he would spare the people, and he would give up the kingdom for the sake of the lives of the people.

5. And it came to pass that when Shiz had received his epistle he wrote an epistle unto Coriantumr, that if he would give himself up, that he might slay him with his own sword, that he would spare the lives of the people.

Verses 1-5. *Coriantumr began to remember the words of Ether.* The miserable monarch, slowly recovering from the ugly wounds of primitive weapons, found time to reflect upon the situation into which his country had been placed. The words of the prophets had been fulfilled. Two million mighty men, many with their wives and children, had perished during the insane conflict. The government had, of course, been neglected. No doubt, anarchy prevailed, and neither life nor property was safe. Sorrow filled the heart of the suffering king, and he refused to listen to false comforters. (v. 3) In this frame of mind he offered his rival, Shiz, the kingdom as the price of peace.

A generous proposition from his point of view, but had King Coriantumr abrogated his throne in favor of Shiz would it have righted any wrong already done? It appears that the legally-elected king was Coriantor, the father of Ether, and that he had been held as a prisoner all his life, presumably by Coriantumr. (Ether 1:7; 11:23) In that case Coriantumr ought to have set the prisoner free and placed him on the throne, a position Coriantor justly was entitled to. The kings of the Jaredites were elected by the people. They could not be made or unmade by politicians, nor by commanders of insurgent armies. (6:24-30)

Coriantumr began to remember. The words of the prophets, although rejected, were not lost on Coriantumr. His awakening conscience repeated them, and caused him to fear and tremble. Shiz, however, rejected the proposition. He demanded the life of Coriantumr.

2. The Battle of Ripliancum.

6. And it came to pass that the people repented not of their iniquity; and the people of Coriantumr were stirred up to anger against the people of Shiz; and the people of Shiz were stirred up to anger against the people of Coriantumr; wherefore, the people of Shiz did give battle unto the people of Coriantumr.

7. And when Coriantumr saw that he was about to fall he fled again before the people of Shiz.

8. And it came to pass that he came to the waters of Ripliancum, which, by interpretation, is large, or to exceed all; wherefore, when they came to these waters they pitched their tents; and Shiz also pitched his tents near unto them; and therefore on the morrow they did come to battle.

9. And it came to pass that they fought an exceedingly sore battle, in which Coriantumr was wounded again, and he fainted with the loss of blood.

3. Ogath and Ramah.

10. And it came to pass that the armies of Coriantumr did press upon the armies of Shiz that they beat them, that they caused them to flee before them; and they did flee southward, and did pitch their tents in a place which was called Ogath.

11. And it came to pass that the army of Coriantumr did pitch their tents by the hill Ramah; and it was that same hill where my father Mormon did hide up the records unto the Lord, which were sacred.

12. And it came to pass that they did gather together all the people upon all the face of the land, who had not been slain, save it was Ether.

VERSES 6-9. *The Waters of Ripliancum.* The first onslaught of Shiz after the peace offer was rejected was so viciously violent that Coriantumr fled for his life. He halted at the Waters of Ripliancum, and prepared for defense. The name *Ripliancum* means large or to exceed all. Orson Pratt in early editions of the Book of Mormon remarks in a footnote: "Supposed to be Lake Ontario," but he does not indicate his authority for this. That some large inland lake is referred to is, however, probable. The unfortunate fugitive was closely pursued by his irreconcilable enemy, and in the conflict which ensued, he was again severely wounded.

VERSES 10-12. *Shiz defeated.* The success of Shiz was of short duration. The forces of Coriantumr, determined to revenge the apparent loss of their leader, redoubled their efforts and drove Shiz and his supporters from the field. These fled to a place called Ogath, southward from the battlefield at the lake shore. (v. 10) This, Orson Pratt says: "Brought them into the region, near the Hill, called by the Nephites, Cumorah."

Coriantumr selected the country close by this Hill, which the Jaredites called *Ramah,* as his military headquarters. "It was there," Moroni says, "where my father, Mormon, did hide up the records unto the Lord, which were sacred." (v. 11)

4. *The Battle of Ramah.*

13. And it came to pass that Ether did behold all the doings of the people; and he beheld that the people who were for Coriantumr were gathered together to the army of Coriantumr; and the people who were for Shiz were gathered together to the army of Shiz.

14. Wherefore, they were for the space of four years gathering together the people, that they might get all who were upon the face of the land, and that they might receive all the strength which it was possible that they could receive.

15. And it came to pass that when they were all gathered together, every one to the army which he would, with their wives and their children — both men, women and children being armed with weapons of war, having shields, and breastplates, and head-plates, and being clothed after the manner of war — they did march forth one against another to battle; and they fought all that day, and conquered not.

16. And it came to pass that when it was night they were weary, and retired to their camps; and after they had retired to their camps they took up a howling and a lamentation for the loss of the slain of their people; and so great were their cries, their howlings and lamentations, that they did rend the air exceedingly.

17. And it came to pass that on the morrow they did go again to battle, and great and terrible was that day; nevertheless, they conquered not, and when the night came again they did rend the air with their cries, and their howlings, and their mournings, for the loss of the slain of their people.

There are now two great military camps, or headquarters, one at Ogath and one at Ramah. There the preparations were made for what was the last historic struggle.

VERSES 13-32. *Elaborate Preparations.* It took the two military leaders four years to prepare for the final duel. And then the end came.

The Battle of Ramah lasted for eight days.

First Day. The two forces engaged all day in their sanguinary butchery. At evening both were exhausted and retired. But before they closed their eyes in sleep, "they took up a howling and a lamentation for the loss of the slain of their people; and so great were their cries, their howlings and lamentations, that they did rend the air exceedingly." (vv. 15-16) The lines quoted should be noted, for they are important as evidence of the authenticity of the record.

Mourning, anciently, was an important and elaborate ceremony. When a person died, his relatives rent their garments and gave vent to their feelings in loud lamentations. Hired mourners often added to the noisy expressions of grief their own vocal efforts. (Jeremiah 9:17-19) It is absolutely certain that just such a scene as here described ended the day of death.

Second Day. The terrible slaughter continued, and the evening was again made hideous by noisy mourning.

18. And it came to pass that Coriantumr wrote again an epistle unto Shiz, desiring that he would not come again to battle, but that he would take the kingdom, and spare the lives of the people.

19. But behold, the Spirit of the Lord had ceased striving with them, and Satan had full power over the hearts of the people; for they were given up unto the hardness of their hearts, and the blindness of their minds that they might be destroyed; wherefore they went again to battle.

20. And it came to pass that they fought all that day, and when the night came they slept upon their swords.

21. And on the morrow they fought even until the night came.

22. And when the night came they were drunken with anger, even as a man who is drunken with wine; and they slept again upon their swords.

23. And on the morrow they fought again; and when the night came they had all fallen by the sword save it were fifty and two of the people of Coriantumr, and sixty and nine of the people of Shiz.

24. And it came to pass that they slept upon their swords that night, and on the morrow they fought again, and they contended in their might with their swords and with their shields, all that day.

25. And when the night came there were thirty and two of the people of Shiz, and twenty and seven of the people of Coriantumr.

26. And it came to pass that they ate and slept, and prepared for death on the morrow. And they were large and mighty men as to the strength of men.

27. And it came to pass that they fought for the space of three hours, and they fainted with the loss of blood.

28. And it came to pass that when the men of Coriantumr had received sufficient strength that

---

Coriantumr again offered Shiz the Kingdom for peace, but the offer was rejected. "Satan had full power over the people." (vv. 17-19)

Third Day. The armies fought all day and retired without disarming themselves.

Fourth Day. By this time the armies fought as if they were drunken, or insane, in their anger. They did not disarm at night. (vv. 21-22)

Fifth Day. The battle was resumed, and at evening it was found that only fifty-two of the supporters of Coriantumr and sixty-nine of the people of Shiz survived. They slept on their arms. (vv. 23-24)

Sixth Day. In the evening of this day, Shiz had only thirty-two and Coriantumr but twenty-seven survivors. They prepared for death on the morrow. (vv. 24-26)

Seventh Day. After three hours of combat they were all exhausted. Coriantumr's men, although weak, endeavored to save themselves by flight, but Shiz prevented them doing so and swore that he would have the life of his enemy. (vv. 27-28)

Eighth Day. This day began with another grim struggle between the survivors. All died except the two principal actors of the drama. Shiz was lying in a stupor on the ground. Coriantumr was leaning for a moment's rest on his sword. After this

they could walk, they were about to flee for their lives; but behold, Shiz arose, and also his men, and he swore in his wrath that he would slay Coriantumr or he would perish by the sword.

29. Wherefore, he did pursue them, and on the morrow he did overtake them; and they fought again with the sword. And it came to pass that when they had all fallen by the sword, save it were Coriantumr and Shiz, behold Shiz had fainted with the loss of blood.

30. And it came to pass that when Coriantumr had leaned upon his sword, that he rested a little, he smote off the head of Shiz.

31. And it came to pass that after he had smitten off the head of Shiz, that Shiz raised upon his hands and fell; and after that he had struggled for breath, he died.

32. And it came to pass that Coriantumr fell to the earth, and became as if he had no life.

5. *The Last Words of Ether*

33. And the Lord spake unto Ether, and said to him: Go forth. And he went forth, and beheld that the words of the Lord had all been fulfilled; and he finished his record; (and the hundredth part I have not written) and he hid them in a manner that the people of Limhi did find them.

34. Now the last words which are written by Ether are these: Whether the Lord will that I be

---

short period of rest "he smote off the head of Shiz. And it came to pass that after he had smitten off the head of Shiz, that Shiz raised upon his hands and fell; and after he had struggled for breath, he died. And it came to pass that Coriantumr fell to the earth, and became as if he had no life." (vv. 29-32)

Unfriendly critics of the Book of Mormon have objected to this account of the death of Shiz as incredible. A decapitated human body cannot, in their opinion, have acted as here represented. The obvious reply is that the case may be exceptional, even unique, but that is not a reason why we should doubt the veracity, or accuracy, of the chronicler. Exceptions to well-known rules are of daily occurrence.

But the question may be raised legitimately whether the fatal wound of Shiz consisted in the complete severance of the head from the body. Is that the fact that Moroni conveys? Coriantumr was almost exhausted when he perceived his victim on the ground. His primitive sword, which certainly was not keen Damascus blade, but must have become blunted during the preceding combat. Did Coriantumr, in his weak condition have physical strength enough to perform so great an operation with a blunt instrument? May we not rather suppose that the fatal wound which he inflicted on his enemy was a ghastly gash in the head, or the neck, causing Shiz to struggle for breath, as stated? Moroni could properly say: "He smote his head off," borrowing that expression from popular, colloquial language and using it in a figurative rather than strictly literal sense.

Verses 33-34. *His work finished.* Ether finished his record. That was part of his life's work, or mission. Then he left this "Last word,"

"Whether the Lord will that I be translated, or that I suffer the will of the Lord in the flesh, it mattereth not, if it so be that I am saved in the Kingdom of God. Amen."

translated, or that I suffer the will of the Lord in the flesh, it mattereth not, if it so be that I am saved in the kingdom of God. Amen.

OGATH

A place in North America not far from the Hill Ramah, and consequently in the modern State of New York (Ether 15:10-11). Here Shiz, for four years, gathered those of the Jaredites, men, women, and children, who sympathized with his cause, and there prepared for the final struggle which ended in the utter destruction of the Jaredite Nation.

HILL RAMAH

The Jaredite name for the Hill Cumorah. In its immediate vicinity both the Jaredite and Nephite people were destroyed. *Ramah* is Rahath, Hebrew meaning hill. Samson, after his battle with the Philistines, threw away his unique weapon, the jaw-bone of an ass, and called the place of combat *Ramath-Lehi,* "the Hill of Lehi."

THE JAREDITES

For some time after the deluge, how long neither revelation nor history informs us, the people of the whole earth were of the same language and had the same speech. And it so happened in the course of the years, that many journeyed from the east, and in their journey they found a plain in the Land of Shinar,[1] and there they rested.

Then, we are told of them, they said one to another, Come, let us make brick and burn them thoroughly; for they had brick for stone and slime for mortar. They further decided to build a city, and in it a tower whose top would be high, nigh unto heaven.

Their reason for attempting to build this tower was, we are informed, they desired to make them a name lest they be scattered abroad upon the face of the earth. But the Lord came down, and beholding the tower which the children of men were building, He said, Behold the people are the same, and they all have the same language; and this tower they begin to build, and now, nothing will be restrained from them which they have imagined, except I, the Lord, confound their language, that they may not understand one another's speech. So I, the Lord, will scatter them abroad from thence, upon all the face of the land, and unto every quarter of the earth.

And they were confounded, and left off building the city. But they hearkened not to the Lord, therefore the name of it was called Babel, because the Lord was displeased with their works, and did there confound the language of all the earth, and from thence did He scatter them abroad upon its face.

There are widespread traditions which connect Nimrod, the grandson of Ham, with this tower. By some it is asserted he was the leader or king of the people who essayed to build it. Certainly it was not earlier than his day, for when Jared and his people first began their journey they passed northward into a valley named after this same Nimrod.

But the date that Nimrod dwelt on the earth is quite uncertain. Tradition has it that he was born to his father, Cush, in the latter's old age, and some Rabbinical and Mahometan traditions make him a contemporary of the Patriarch Abraham. As men in those early days lived to be several hundred years old, this is not impossible, though it would bring the confusion of tongues to a much later date than is given in the generally accepted chronologies.

Too much trust must not, however, be placed upon chronologies dealing with those times. Two varying ones, now before us, give the

---

[1] Almost universally understood to be a portion of Lower Mesopotamia.

building of Babel at 2247 and 2207 B.C. respectively, and the birth of Abraham at B.C. 2056 and B.C. 1996.[2] We incline to the opinion that the first named event occurred at a greater distance from the universal flood than is generally asserted.

Having no fixed date upon which we can depend for the confusion of tongues, we cannot with any exactness compute the length of time that the Jaredites occupied this continent. It also prevents us forming any trustworthy estimate of who among these people were the contemporaries of the Hebrew patriarchs and prophets and the Israelitish kings. When we reach the latter ages of their history we can form some slight idea by tracing backward from Coriantumr and Ether, who evidently lived at the same time as Lehi and Nephi, Zedekiah and Mulek. On the other hand, while Abraham and Jared may possibly have lived simultaneously on the earth, the probabilities, almost amounting to a certainty, are that Orihah, the son of Jared and the first king of the Jaredites, was either in his early or later years, a contemporary of the father of the faithful.

At first sight there appears to be a ready way by which a rough estimate can be formed of the dates when each and every one of the Jaredite kings lived. It is by comparing the genealogies given by Ether and Matthew. Matthew, in his genealogical list of the ancestors of the Savior gives twenty-eight generations from Abraham to the days of the Babylonish captivity; Ether gives twenty-nine generations from Orihah to himself, and he dwelt among mankind at the time that the king of Babylon carried the people of Judah captive. But the genealogy given by Matthew, as it has reached us, is open to so many questions, and disagrees so widely with other genealogies in which the same names are introduced, that it cannot be altogether trusted. The genealogy given by Mark names many more generations during that period, and consequently does not help us in making a comparison.

JARED AND HIS BROTHER

Among the builders of the Tower of Babel were two brothers, named respectively Jared and Mahonri Moriancumer.[3] How they came to be associated with this impious work does not appear of record, and to make guesses is very unsatisfactory and also somewhat

---

[2]The latest calculations place the call of Abraham as far back as about 2280 B.C., or earlier than the generally accepted date of the building of Babel.

[3]While residing in Kirtland Elder Reynolds Cahoon had a son born to him. One day when President Joseph Smith was passing his door he called the Prophet in and asked him to bless and name the baby. Joseph did so and gave the boy the name of Mahonri Moriancumer. When he had finished the blessing he laid the child on the bed, and turning to Elder Cahoon he said, the name I have given your son is the name of the brother of Jared; the Lord has just shown [or revealed] it to me. Elder William F. Cahoon, who was standing near heard the Prophet make this statement to his father; and this was the first time the name of the brother of Jared was known in the Church in this dispensation.

perplexing, as they were righteous men and furthermore held the Holy Priesthood, which authority was vested in the descendants of Shem, while the builders of the tower appear to have been the posterity of Ham, who were cursed in this regard.[4] Abraham's family, however, dwelt in Ur[5] of the Chaldees, which was not far distant. It is therefore not stretching the probabilities to suggest that they were of the same branch of Shem's posterity as was that Patriarch.

We judge from the record of Ether that the confusion of speech among the builders of the tower did not come upon them in an instant, suddenly, but developed somewhat gradually. As the disorder increased from the mutually unintelligible jargon, Jared and his brother held a consultation in which they decided to beg the Lord that He would not confound their words so that they could not understand each other. At Jared's request, his brother, who was highly favored of the Lord, was mouth in offering this petition. Their prayers were heard, their request was granted; the language of Jared and his brother and a few of their friends was not confused, and the original tongue which Noah spoke remained with them on the earth.

Again, at the instance of Jared, his brother pled before the Lord. This time he begged that if they were driven out of the land, as others were evidently scattering in anger and dismay, that the Lord would show them whither they should go. Because of their faith, a most gracious answer was given to their prayers. The Lord told them to gather their flocks, herds and substance, and with their families and friends start on a journey to a land to which He would lead them. Regarding this land He said, "I will go before thee into a land which is choice above all the land of the earth; and there will I bless thee and thy seed, and raise up unto me of thy seed, and of the seed of thy brother, and they who shall go with thee, a great nation. And there shall be none greater than the nation which I will raise up unto me of thy seed, upon all the face of the earth."

In obedience to this call the company started on their journey. Mahonri Moriancumer was appointed by the Lord to be their leader. At their head he guided them northward into a valley, known by the name of Nimrod. Here they made the final preparations for the toilsome and lengthy pilgrimage before them. Already they had gathered their flocks, male and female of every kind; and now they secured the fowls of the air, and made a vessel in which to carry fish. Swarms of honey bees, (known to them as deseret), also formed part of their outfit, while seeds of plants and trees of every kind were collected.

---

[4]"Noah, his father, who blessed him [Ham] with the blessings of the earth, and with the blessings of wisdom, but cursed him as pertaining to the Priesthood." (Book of Abraham)

[5]Two widely distant places in Mesopotamia are named as the Ur where Abraham dwelt. We incline to the opinion that the one in the far south of that land is the correct locality, as from the Book of Abraham we discover it was intimately associated with Egypt and its rulers.

The fact was they were going, under divine guidance, to a new land; or what amounted to the same to a land whose surface had been swept bare by the waters of the flood; it had been bereft of its animal life, and the seeds of grains and fruits no longer germinated in the soil, and they took with them everything they deemed desirable to restock it with animals and vegetables. Before the flood the American continents had been the home of humanity. When Noah's ark rested it was on a new continent. From that ark went forth the creatures who replenished the earth with animal life. Many of these, especially those useful to man, were brought back to this land by Jared's colony. They also brought with them fruits and grains good for food for man and beast.

When in the Valley of Nimrod, the Lord came down and talked with the brother of Jared. But the brother of Jared saw him not, for the Lord remained concealed in a cloud. And God directed that the company should go forth into the wilderness, into that quarter where man had never yet been. As they journeyed the Heavenly Presence went before them in the cloud, instructed them and gave directions which way they should travel. In the course of their journey they had many waters—seas, rivers and lakes, to cross, on which occasions they built barges, as directed by the Lord.[6] It must have been an arduous labor, requiring much time and great patience to transport their flocks and herds, with all the rest of their cumbrous freight, across these many waters. As they advanced to a great distance from the center of population in western Asia, it is possible they traveled beyond the limits to which the larger animals had by that time scattered; and if so, they were entirely without the aid of the food obtained by the chase; on the other hand, it is probable that the fish in the lakes and rivers formed a valuable source of food supply; yet it must also be remembered they carried fish in a vessel with them.

Led by the Lord personally, instructed by His own mouth, protected by His presence, the colony at last reached the borders of the great sea which divides the continents. To the place where they tarried they gave the name Moriancumer.[7] Here they remained for a period of four years, at the end of which time the Lord again visited the brother of Jared in a cloud, talked with him for the space of three hours, and chastened him and his brethren, because of their neglect

---

[6]We have never been able to find any revelation or other authoritative statements in print with regard to the course taken by the Jaredites in their journey from the valley of Nimrod to the land of Moriancumer. It is evident that they first traveled northward, but whether they turned east or west is not so apparent. The general idea is that they turned eastward and crossed Central Asia. Elder Orson Pratt calls these waters "the inland seas of Asia."

[7]Evidently named after the brother of Jared. We have no direct information in regard to the locality of Moriancumer, but those who believe that the Jaredites traveled eastward through Central Asia, are of the opinion that it was near the mouth of one of the great rivers that flow through the Chinese empire into the Pacific Ocean.

to call upon His name. Repentance followed this reproof, and because of their repentance their sins were forgiven them.

The brother of Jared was then commanded by the Lord to build eight barges, after the same pattern as those he had previously constructed. This command he obeyed with the assistance of the company. The vessels were small, light in construction and water-tight.

These barges were so constructed that they were not only water-tight but almost air-tight and dark. They were thus compactly built that they might be able to withstand the force of the waves, when storms arose, and for the same reason the Lord permitted no windows to be cut in their sides. But He gave permission that the builders might make one hole in the top and another in the bottom of each barge, so that when the passengers began to suffer for air, the hole in the top could be opened and a fresh supply obtained. If it so happened that any water came pouring through this upper hole with the air, they could then unstop the lower hole and let it run out. The absence of windows or port holes would leave the people inside the boats in intense darkness, and as the Lord would not permit them, for some reason not given, to use artificial light, the brother of Jared felt deeply concerned to know what they should do to get over this difficulty. For it was evident that the discomforts of a long and stormy voyage would be almost unbearable in vessels filled with men, women and children, birds, beasts, insects and fishes, if they were compelled to make it in utter darkness. It is almost impossible to conceive the miseries and in all probability consequent disease, to say nothing of accidents that would doubtless happen, if they had to make the voyage without light. So Mahonri Moriancumer went up to a high mountain called Shelem, and did moulten out of the rock sixteen small, transparent stones, which had the appearance of glass. These he spread out before the Lord with an earnest and pathetic prayer that He would touch them. Said he, in part:

"Behold, O Lord, thou hast smitten us because of our iniquity, and hath driven us forth, and for this many years we have been in the wilderness; nevertheless, thou hast been merciful unto us. O Lord, look upon me in pity, and turn away thine anger from this thy people, and suffer not that they shall go forth across this raging deep in darkness, but behold these things which I have moulten out of the rock. And I know, O Lord, that thou hast all power, and can do whatsoever thou wilt for the benefit of man; therefore touch these stones, O Lord, with thy finger, and prepare them that they may shine forth in darkness; and they shall shine forth unto us in the vessels which we have prepared, that we may have light while we shall cross the sea."

This prayer, so simple, so fervent and so full of faith, was immediately answered. The Lord stretched forth his finger and touched the stones one by one, and as he touched them they shone with such exceeding brilliancy that the light they shed forth was afterwards sufficient to lighten all the barges, when one was placed at the fore and another in the aft of each vessel.

When the Lord put forth His finger the faith of the brother of Jared was so great, that his eyes were opened, the veil was removed from before them, and to his surprise he beheld the finger of God and that it was like unto that of a man. For before this he had not understood that man was made in the image of God. Then summoning courage, when he found that the hand of the Lord did not smite him, but instead thereof he heard words of encouragement and commendation, he begged the Lord to show Himself unto him. And because of his faith the Lord did so, and told him that He it was who was prepared from the foundation of the world to redeem His people; that He was Jesus Christ, in whom all mankind should have light, and that eternally. Further He said:

"Behold, this body which ye now behold, is the body of my spirit; and man have I created after the body of my spirit; and even as I appear unto thee to be in the spirit, will I appear to my people in the flesh."

And then, as Moroni informs us, Jesus administered unto the brother of Jared, "even as he ministered unto the Nephites."

All things being prepared, Jared and his people, with their animals, fishes, bees, seeds and multitudinous other things, went on board; a strong, yet favorable wind wafted them from shore, and they gradually crossed to the American coast. At the end of a somewhat stormy voyage of three hundred and forty-four days the colony reached this continent. It is generally understood that the place where they landed was south of the Gulf of California and north of the land called Desolation by the Nephites, which was north of the Isthmus of Panama.*

No sooner had the people of Jared landed than they humbled themselves before the Lord, many of them shedding tears of joy because of the multitude of His tender mercies in bringing them so safely to this new land of promise. Their next duty was to prepare for the future. They commenced to till the soil and perform the other labors incidental to founding a new home. In these efforts they prospered greatly. They began to grow and increase in numbers and in wealth; and even better than this, they were a righteous people, being taught directly from on high.

RULERS OF THE JAREDITES

In the course of time Jared and his brother grew old, and perceiving that their mortal lives were nearly finished, the latter proposed

---

*To this land the Jaredites gave the name of Moron. It was a portion of the region known to us as Central America. It appears to have been for a lengthy period, if not during the whole of their existence, the seat of government, and residence of the reigning monarch, and the center of Jaredite civilization. In the numerous fratricidal wars that disgraced the annals of the race, Moron was, more than any other land, the chief seat of war; for here the revolutionists attacked the king, and when successful drove them thence.

that they gather the people, number them, give them necessary teachings, and learn their wishes. This was done; but to the grief of the brother of Jared, the people desired that a king be anointed to rule over them. He saw, by the spirit of prophecy, that this action would lead to many evils, and he was inclined to refuse their request, but Jared pled that the wishes of the people be granted, and his brother finally consented. It was the first step in the wrong direction, and led to much sin, misery, contention and captivity. The people having the privilege granted them, chose Pagag,[8] the eldest son of their prophet. But he resolutely refused the honor, sensing, perhaps, the evils which would follow the adoption of this form of government. The people desired that his father should compel him, but he would not do so, and commanded that they should constrain no man to be their king. The result was that all of Pagag's brothers and three of the four sons of Jared followed his example, and when chosen refused to accept the proffered dignity; at last, Orihah, the fourth son of Jared, accepted.

Soon after this assembling of the people the brother of Jared died, full of years and honor. Like Enoch, he had been privileged to enter the presence of the Lord, and to have revealed to him the history of the world in all its generations. He was also a seer, having received the priceless gift of a Urim and Thummim. His faith was never exceeded by the sons of men; he laid hold of the promises of the Almighty with unshaken confidence. By that faith he performed miracles; Moroni tells us that by its power he "said unto the mountain Zerin,[9] remove, and it was removed," (Ether 12:30) but of the circumstances that attended this manifestation of divine power, we have not the slightest details. The brother of Jared is also said to have been "mighty in writing"; the uncorrupted language which he used being unquestionably most favorable for expressing niceties of thought in written characters. He was a "large and mighty man" in personal appearance, and undoubtedly as strong in his integrity to God, and in his moral courage, as he was in physical characteristics. Altogether, we deem him one of the greatest prophets and leaders of God's people that ever graced this earth. He left behind him twenty-two sons and daughters.

About this time Jared died also, and was buried in the Land Moron. Of Jared's private character we are told but little, but he appears to have been more conservative, more pliable and less energetic than his brother. The race was named after him, we presume, because one of his sons became its first king, and Jared's thus became the royal

---

[8]Nothing more is said of Pagag in the Book of Mormon, but from his action in this matter we judge him to have been a wise and God-fearing man. (Ether 6:25)

[9]No information is given in the sacred record of the locality or country in which Mount Zerin was situated.

family. Jared had four sons and eight daughters: the names of his sons were Jacom, Gilgah, Mahah and Orihah. The names of his daughters are not given.

Orihah,[10] the first king of the Jaredites, reigned in righteousness, executing judgment in justice, walking humbly before heaven and instructing his subjects in the ways of the Lord. He lived to a very great age, was the father of thirty-one children, twenty-three of whom were sons, and when he died he was succeeded on the throne by his son Kib. The Jaredites prospered and multiplied greatly under his wise and beneficent reign.

Kib was born in his father's old age, and therefore would, in all probability, be quite young when he became king. The early years of his reign appear to have been peaceful and prosperous. But he had an ambitious son, named Corihor, who became the first to fulfill the gloomy forebodings of the brother of Jared that the establishment of a monarchy would lead to trouble, bloodshed and captivity. When Corihor was thirty-two years old he rebelled against his father, and went from Moron and established himself in the Land of Nehor. There he drew many to him; when strong enough he invaded the Land of Moron, took the king, his father, captive and reigned in his stead. Kib remained in captivity many years, but during that time he had born to him a son, who he named Shule. When Shule grew to manhood he became mighty in judgment and bodily strength, and being angry with his brother, Corihor, for rebelling against their father, he raised an army, armed them with swords made by himself, gave battle to his brother at a city named Nehor, defeated the latter's forces and restored their father to the throne. Kib, being very aged, placed the sovereign power in the hands of Shule who reigned in righteousness and extended the borders of his growing people in all directions. Corihor, repentant of his former treason, received many favors from Shule and was placed in high power in the nation, the trusts whereof he faithfully performed. But as he had rebelled against his father in his early days, so in like manner one of his sons, named Noah, rebelled against him and against the king, and in this rebellion drew away all his brothers. At first, Noah was successful. He obtained possession of the Land of Moron, and reigned king in that region of Central America. Again he attacked Shule, and this time took him prisoner, carrying him captive to Moron, with the intention of putting him to death. But before he had carried out his bloodthirsty design, his cousins, the sons of Shule, broke into his house and killed the

---

[10]The fact that Orihah was the youngest son of his father appears to have been taken as a precedent, for among the Jaredites there seems to have prevailed a custom entirely opposite to that of most other nations—that of having one of the younger, generally the very youngest son instead of the eldest, succeed his father on the throne. We do not read of any queens reigning over this race.

usurper. They then went to the prison, where their father was held, released him from his confinement and replaced him on the throne of that part of the country now retained by Cohor, the son of Noah.

There were now two kingdoms, both of which were growing, while that one under the government of Shule "did prosper exceedingly and waxed great." After a time Cohor commenced war with Shule, in which he was deservedly unsuccessful, and in the conflict which ensued, he was slain. Cohor was succeeded by his son Nimrod, who, apparently deeming Shule the rightful monarch of the whole country, gave up his kingdom to him; thus once again uniting the entire Jaredite people in one nation, under one king. For this act and for his faithful allegiance, Nimrod found favor in the eyes of Shule, and he had authority given him to do "according to his desires" in the latter's kingdom.

Though the Jaredites were highly prospered at this time, they gave way to idolatry and grew hard in their hearts. This condition was no doubt intensified by the bad example of the reigning family and the miseries and cruelties of the wars which their quarrels brought about. During Shule's days the Lord sent many prophets to this people, who warned them of His impending judgments. For a time these prophets were rejected and reviled. But the king made a law that the prophets should have free access wherever they wished to go, and further decreed a punishment for all those who persecuted and reviled them. The preaching of these holy men eventually brought the Jaredites to repentance, and because of their penitance the Lord spared them and turned away His judgments, and the people prospered again. In his old age Shule begat Omer, who succeeded him on the throne. Shule's days were full of trouble and sorrow, but he reigned in righteousness, was faithful to the Lord, and executed judgment in justice towards his subjects.

KINGS OF THE JAREDITES

Shule was succeeded by his son Omer, one of the best and, in some respects, one of the most unfortunate monarchs who reigned over the Jaredites. Amongst his children was a son named Jared. This prince rebelled against his father, and by his flatteries led away the people of half the kingdom. He then gave battle to his father and took him prisoner, holding him in servitude half his days. While thus in bondage Omer begat several children, among whom were two sons named Esrom and Coriantumr. When these young men grew to manhood they espoused the cause of their father, raised an army, attacked the forces of Jared by night and utterly routed them. Jared retained his life by renouncing his rights to the throne, and Omer was reinstated in the kingly authority. But Jared's ambition would not remain dormant. He sighed and wearied for the kingly authority, until his unrest became marked by all. He had a daughter who shared her father's feelings, and at her instigation he sent for a friend of Omer's named Akish, through whom he hoped to regain the throne. An entertainment of some kind, by which Jared's daughter could be introduced, was given. By pre-arrangement with her father, she danced before Akish, and so exhibited the beauties of her person and the graces of her movements that he became desperately enamored of her. As she anticipated, Akish asked Jared to give her to him as a wife. The latter consented, but on most revolting conditions. The father and daughter had planned that the price of her hand was to be the head of her grandfather, the king.

Akish accepted this terrible responsibility. He gathered his associates at the house of Jared and there made them all swear by the God of heaven, and by the heavens, by the earth and by their heads, that whoso should vary from what he desired should lose his head, and whoso should divulge whatever he made known should lose his life. He then submitted his plans to them, which they accepted. The plot was so far successful that they overthrew the kingdom of Omer, but did not succeed in obtaining his head. For the Lord was merciful to Omer and warned him to depart out of the land. So taking those of his family who were faithful to him, he traveled for a great distance to a land called Ablom, on the shores of the Atlantic Ocean. There he and his companions tarried until the course of events permitted him to return.

Jared was again proclaimed king and Akish became his son-in-law. Soon the latter coveted the royal dignity; possibly the woman who plotted the death of her grandfather was willing to sacrifice her father also that she might be queen; such a supposition is not improbable. At any rate, Jared was slain on his throne while giving audience to his people, by some of the members of the secret society of assassins that he had been the means of calling into existence; and Akish reigned in his stead.

Under the cruel rule of Akish wickedness became almost universal; the secret societies by which he obtained power had corrupted the hearts of all the people. As may be well supposed, with such a condition of society his throne was not a stable one. He became jealous of one of his sons. What cause, if any, he had therefor, we are not told; but he shut him up in prison and slowly starved him to death. This cruel act greatly incensed another of Jared's sons, named Nimrah, and he, gathering a small number of men, fled to the exiled king, Omer, in the Land Ablom.

Now, Akish had other sons, and though they had sworn to support him in all his doings, they were not true to their oaths. They found that the hearts of the Jaredites were consumed with the love of gain, and they bribed the greater portion of the people to join them in a revolt against their father. So corrupt had the people now become that their extinction appears to have been the only remedy; they were past repentance.

A war of the most horrible character broke out, which lasted several years, and only ended when nearly every soul was slain. Of the kingdom of Akish, for which he had sinned so much, there remained but thirty souls, all the rest—men, women and children— had been swept by bloody hands into untimely graves. The people of Akish having been thus destroyed, Omer, with his friends, returned from his captivity and reigned over the feeble remnant of a wasted people. He lived to be exceedingly old, and two years before his death he anointed his son Emer to reign in his stead. His days were many and full of sorrow.

Thus has gross iniquity brought the almost entire destruction of the Jaredite race. The words of God through their forefathers had been fulfilled, that whatsoever people dwelt on this land should serve the true and living God. The few who were left had to commence the peopling of the western world anew. What a sorrowful, gloomy existence theirs must have been. Their cities tenantless, the open country deserted, and they for mutual comfort huddling together in one neighborhood, all the rest of the land but one vast sepulchre— desolation and a howling wilderness everywhere.

KINGS OF THE JAREDITES, CONTINUED

Emer, the son of Omer, was one of the best kings of his race, he executed judgment in righteousness all his days. In his reign the people greatly increased in numbers and in wealth, becoming the owners of large herds of useful animals, and rich in agricultural and mineral products, in gems and fine manufactured goods. The curse, also, which had come upon the land during the days of Akish, because of the iniquity of the people, began to be removed as they were now living more righteously. Emer's was a lengthy reign; sixty-two years are mentioned; but it is not evident whether this period covers the whole of his reign or not. When he died, full of years and honor, he was succeeded by one of his numerous sons, named Coriantum, whom he had anointed king four years before his death. It is recorded of Emer that he saw the Son of Righteousness, and did rejoice in His day.

Coriantum was a righteous, just and vigorous ruler, and in his days the Jaredites were greatly prospered and many large cities were built. But he had no children until he was exceedingly old; his wife died when she was one hundred and two years of age, after which he married a young maid, who bore him sons and daughters. He lived until he was one hundred and forty-two years old, when he died, and was succeeded on the throne by his son Com.

Com was evidently born when his father was very aged. He ascended the throne with the prospects of a bright future; but the leaven of iniquity was again beginning to work. Great prosperity, with attendant riches, was alienating the hearts of the Jaredites from God. During the peaceful and lengthy reign of Emer and Coriantum they had increased marvelously in numbers and during Com's reign this increase continued and they spread far and wide over the continent.

Com had not been long on the throne before the old murderous associations, that had well nigh destroyed the race in the days of his great-grandfather, Omer, were revived. In the forty-ninth year of his reign he had a son born whom he named Heth. This son when he grew to manhood became a leader in these unholy societies. He rose in rebellion against his father, slew him with his own sword, and became king in his stead. The Lord then sent many prophets, who called upon the people to repent, declaring that if they did not, a desolating famine should oversweep the land. The people, led and inspired by the parricide, Heth, rejected the warning of the servants of God, and cruelly abused them, some they cast out, some they threw into pits and left them to perish. Before long the rains from heaven ceased, and there was a great drouth over all the land; and poisonous serpents made their appearance and killed many people. These serpents also attacked the flocks of the Jaredites and drove them in vast bodies towards the southern continent. Many perished by the way, but some reached the land known to the Nephites as Zarahemla. Restrained by the power of God, the serpents stopped at the Isthmus of Panama, where they formed a cordon, preventing the Jaredites from further following their scattered flocks. The carcasses of the beasts which fell by the way were ravenously eaten by the famished people, until they had devoured them all. We can scarcely imagine the horrors that must have attended this famine, when the people consumed the poisoned flesh of the creatures thus killed. Disease in its most terrible forms must have followed famine. Before long even this loathsome food was all consumed and the people rapidly perished. Thus a second time was the race almost utterly destroyed. God's word was again vindicated—the people of this land must serve Him or they would be consumed by His judgments. In Omer's day it was fratricidal war that accomplished the purpose; in Heth's, famine and pestilence were the weapons of God's wrath.

When thus brought to the brink of the grave, the few that re-

mained turned in their utter misery to heaven. When they had sufficiently humbled themselves the Lord sent the long-needed rain, and
the remnants began to revive. Soon there began to be fruit in the
north country and the regions round about. All the royal family had
perished except Shez, a son or descendant[11] of Heth, who, when the
crops again began to grow, commenced to build up his desolate race.
He was a virtuous man, and taught his people righteousness, and the
sun of prosperity shone upon them. His peace, however, was marred
by the treason of his son Shez, who rebelled against him. This son,
however, was slain by a robber, and peace was restored. In the later
years of his lengthy reign, Shez built many cities, and the rapidly
increasing people spread out in various directions. This monarch
lived to an exceeding old age, was blessed with numerous children,
and when he died was succeeded on the throne by his son Riplakish,
who was apparently the youngest of his family.

Riplakish was unfortunately an unrighteous man. He greatly
afflicted his people by imposing upon them grievously heavy taxes,
and when they could not, or would not pay these exactions he cast
them into prison, where he compelled them to labor continually to
sustain him in his whoredoms and abominations, and in the erection
of costly and magnificent edifices that conduced to his luxury; if any
prisoner refused to labor he was put to death. In this way he greatly
adorned his kingdom, but he also filled it with prisons. For forty-two
years the people groaned under his oppressions, when they rose in
their anger, slew Riplakish and drove his descendants out of the land.
What form of government immediately followed is uncertain, we have
no information on this point, but we are told that after many years
one of his descendants, named Morianton, gathered an army of outcasts and invaded the Jaredite country.

The war that followed was an exceedingly severe one, and lasted
a number of years. One by one the cities of the Jaredites fell into the
hands of Morianton, until he had made himself master of the entire
country. When established in power, he conciliated the people by
lightening their burdens, so that they anointed him king. During his
mild though energetic reign the people were greatly prospered, many
new cities were built, and the nation grew exceedingly rich. He lived
to a very great age, and when too old to hold the reigns of government,
he abdicated in favor of his son Kim, Morianton surviving this action
for eight years. His character is thus summarized in the Book of
Ether: "He did do justice unto the people, but not unto himself, be-

---

[11]In the first chapter of Ether, Shez is called the son of Heth; in the tenth chapter he is
called a descendant; but these two words are used in the Book of Ether, as in the Bible and other
ancient records, interchangeably, or one for the other; and son, or daughter may mean a direct
descendant of any remoteness.

cause of his many whoredoms; wherefore he was cut off from the presence of the Lord."

KINGS OF THE JAREDITES, CONTINUED

As stated previously, Kim reigned for eight years before his father's death. He, however, did not reign in righteousness, and by his wickedness he displeased the Lord, so that He permitted the brother of the monarch to rebel against him, dethrone him and hold him in captivity all the remainder of his life. During his captivity Kim begat sons and daughters, the only one of whom whose name is mentioned is Levi, who was born to him in his old age.

Levi remained in captivity until forty-two years after the death of his father, when he rose in rebellion against his uncle, who occupied the throne, deposed him, and reigned in his stead. During his reign he did right in the sight of the Lord, and his people were greatly prospered. He lived to a good old age, was blessed with a large family, and when he died his son Corum succeeded him as king.

Corum was one of the most righteous of the Jaredite kings. It is said of him that he did good all his days, and they were many upon the earth. Nothing is told us of the events of this reign in the sacred records, so it is consistent to believe that no very important social convulsions marred the kingdom's peace. When crowned with the glory of many well-spent years Corum passed away to his reward, leaving numerous sons and daughters to emulate his example. One of these sons, named Kish, then came to the throne. Of the events of his reign and of his character, not a word is said. All that is recorded is that he reigned and died.

Lib was the son and successor of Kish. In his beneficent reign the nation prospered and multiplied greatly. As will be recollected in the reign of a former monarch, named Heth, the Lord had deeply afflicted the people because of their sins; and among other things He had caused numbers of poisonous serpents to occupy the regions adjacent to the Isthmus of Panama, and thus prevented the people from gaining access to the southern continent. In Lib's reign these venomous creatures were destroyed and the land southward was found to abound with beasts of the forest. That region was preserved as one enormous hunting ground for the nation, Lib himself becoming a mighty hunter. He also built a large city near the narrowest portion of the isthmus, apparently for the purpose of preventing an exodus into the regions south, so that it might be the source of their meat supply, for the country northward was covered with inhabitants.

In this reign the people greatly developed in the arts of civilization, they prosecuted mining with much vigor, improved in the manufacture of textile fabrics, agriculture made marked advance through the invention and application of improved machinery in the cultivation of the earth and the harvesting of their crops. They also made all manner of weapons of war, though, as this was a time of profound peace, this can only be regarded as a precautionary measure. In fact, to use the words of the sacred historian: "never could be a people more blessed than were they, and more prospered by the hand of the Lord. And they were in a land that was choice above all lands, for the Lord had spoken it." Lib lived many years, was blessed with a numerous posterity, and when he died he was succeeded by his son Hearthom.

When Hearthom had reigned twenty-four years the kingdom was wrested from him, and he was held in captivity by the triumphant party all the remainder of his days. In his captivity he begat a son named Heth. Heth was held in captivity all his days by the usurping dynasty; and so was his son Aaron, his grandson Amnigaddah, and his great-grandson Coriantum.

Of the history of the Jaredites under the new dynasty we have not a glimmer of light. They were not of the ancestry of Ether, the historian, and he treats them with silent disregard. We are not told if the monarchs of this family were righteous or wicked, if the people prospered or diminished. The record simply confines itself to the genealogy of Hearthom until it reaches Com, the son of Coriantum, when a few meager statements are given.

In Com's days the reigning monarch was named Amgid. Com, like his predecessors, was born in captivity. How he managed to obtain his liberty and inaugurate a successful rebellion is not told. But when he attained manhood "he drew away half the kingdom." When he had thus reigned forty-two years he made war with Amgid, and after a desolating conflict of many years he gained power over the whole realm. While he was king, robber bands, like the Gadiantons among the Nephites, began to appear, who administered secret and damnable oaths, after the manner of the ancients, and sought again to destroy the kingdom. Com fought these robbers with vigor, but without success, for they had the sympathy of the masses of the people, who were rapidly ripening for destruction. Many prophets came in these days, who foretold the impending destruction of the race, if the people did not repent and turn unto the Lord. But the voice of mercy and warning was rejected, and sin-sunken Jaredites sought the lives of the heaven-inspired messengers. The prophets fled to Com for preservation, and he appears to have valiantly protected them. While with him they prophesied many things for his comfort and edification, and he was blessed of the Lord all the remainder of his days. He lived to a great age, and begat Shiblom, who at his death reigned in his stead.[12]

In Shiblom's[13] day, because of the iniquity of the people many prophets appeared and foretold the woes that would attend the extinction of the race. Wars and grievous calamities also marked the reign of Shiblom. First, his brother inaugurated a bloody civil war, which extended throughout all the land. The wicked combinations, akin to the Gadianton robbers, did their part to render anarchy more complete. Famine and pestilence followed rapine, until "there was a great destruction, such an one as never had been known upon the face of the earth." In the extreme of their misery and degradation, the people began to repent and then the Lord had mercy upon them. Finally Shiblom was slain and Seth, his son, was brought into captivity. Of Shiblom's private character we have no record; but his rebellious brother issued the infamous mandate that all the prophets who prophesied of the destruction of the people should be put to death.

Seth was held in captivity all his life, but his son, Ahah, regained the kingdom and reigned over the people until his death. He did all manner of iniquity, by which he caused the shedding of much blood, but providentially his reign was but a short one. His son, Ethem, succeeded him.

In Ethem's days many prophets came and prophesied that unless the Jaredites repented the Lord would utterly destroy them from the earth. But the people hardened their hearts and repented not; and the prophets mourned over their depravity and withdrew from among them. Ethem was as his people, and did wickedly all his days; and when he died he was succeeded by his son Moron, who was like unto his father.

During Moron's reign the Gadianton-like bands which at that time flourished among the Jaredites, led a rebellion against the king and succeeded in wresting from him half the kingdom; but after many years Moron succeeded in recovering his lost provinces. Soon after, a descendant of the brother of Jared, who is described as "a mighty man," headed another revolution against Moron, and was so successful that he took possession of the whole of the kingdom, and held Moron in captivity all the rest of his days. In captivity Moron begat Coriantor.

Coriantor, son of Moron, was held a prisoner all his days. This period of Jaredite history is a particularly sad one; it is an epoch of sin and war. Many prophets appeared, who proclaimed that the Lord would execute judgment against the Jaredites to their utter destruction,

---

[12]It is somewhat strange coincidence that both kings of the Jaredites who were named Com were sons of kings named Coriantum, though they appear to have lived nearly a thousand years apart.

[13]Also spelled Shiblon.

and that He would bring forth another people to possess the land, as he had their fathers; but the people rejected all the words of these servants of God, "because of their secret societies and wicked abominations"; nevertheless, in that and the succeeding generation these prophecies were all fulfilled—the Jaredites were destroyed and the land was given to a branch of the house of Israel.

Coriantor was the father of the Prophet Ether.

THE FINAL WAR OF EXTINCTION

We now come to Coriantumr, the last of the Jaredites. We are introduced to him as king of all the land, but we are not told how long he had been so. At any rate, he must have then been of middle age, for he had sons old enough to fight in his defense. He was a mighty man of war, cunning and bold, diplomatic and learned, but withal, like the great majority of his people, exceedingly corrupt. He was as fit an instrument to execute the wrath of God as ever led a debased and decaying race to slaughter and destruction. But before the great crisis came, God in His mercy, sent another messenger to warn the Jaredites for the last time, of their impending doom, their utter desolation. This messenger was Ether, the son of Coriantor. Few greater prophets than he have graced our earth, few have had so sad, so terrible a tale to tell of human depravity, of divine mercies despised, of the overwhelming retribution that followed.

Great and marvelous were the prophecies of Ether. He saw the days of Christ, and the great work of the last dispensation, even to the coming of the New Jerusalem. Indeed, he appears to have had revealed to him a complete history of the dealings of the Lord with the inhabitants of this earth, from his own day to the end of time. He also proclaimed the near destruction of the entire Jaredite race (a prophecy which many of his predecessors uttered) with this exception, that Coriantumr should outlive all his subjects and meet another race whom God had brought to occupy the land. But the people heeded not his words, and ultimately grew weary of his threatenings and drove him from their midst. He hid himself in a cavity of a rock, coming forth in the night time to view the course of events, and occasionally appearing and repeating his warnings.

In the first year of Ether's concealment a war commenced which grew to be one of the most bloodthirsty, savage and vindictive that ever cursed this fair planet. It began in a powerful revolution against Coriantumr led by some of the most influential men in the kingdom, who were leaders of the secret, Gadianton-like bands that overspread the nation. In that year much blood was spilt, Coriantumr's own sons being among the foremost in the defense of their father's rights. There was then a lull in the tempest for a short time, the combatants rested to gain strength, and Ether again came forth to plead the cause of heaven in their deadened ears. It was then that he announced the strange message regarding Coriantumr's preservation. But the people heeded not his warnings but sought to slay him, and he again retired to his place of concealment.

The next year, a leader of the revolutionists named Shared of whom no previous mention is made, defeated Coriantumr, and held him a prisoner. In the fourth year, the sons of Coriantumr released their father and placed him again on the throne. Then bloodshed extended over all the continent, every man with his band, fighting for that which he desired. The war at this period would seem to have grown beyond the control of the great leaders, and to have degenerated into a condition of affairs in which every man's hand was against his neighbor, and mobs instead of disciplined armies, carried bloodshed and devastation far and wide, throughout the land. Bands of brigands and robbers committed all manner of outrages, and the country was a scene of anarchy and horror from one end to the other. After a time Coriantumr, being exceedingly angry, gathered his forces and met Shared in the Valley of Gilgal.[14] The fight which lasted three days, was a desperate and stubborn one. Shared was beaten and retreated as far as the Plains of Heshlon, where he again withstood Coriantumr, and this time was victorious, driving his foe back to their former battleground—the Valley of Gilgal. Here another fierce battle was fought, in which Shared was slain and his troops defeated.

In his last battle with Shared, Coriantumr was so severely wounded that he did not go to battle again for two years, during which time the people in all the land were shedding blood, and there was none to restrain them. Two years after Shared's death his brother Gilead rose up to take his place. But he was defeated by Coriantumr and his forces driven into the Wilderness of Akish, where another exceedingly bloody battle was fought, and many thousands were slain. Gilead remained for a time in the wilderness, watched by Coriantumr; but eventually he made a night attack on the enemy, and the latter, being drunken, suffered great loss. Gilead then placed himself on the throne of Coriantumr, and both commanders busied themselves in gathering men to strengthen their respective armies. Gilead who had the sympathy of some of the secret combinations, received great strength during the two years they were thus engaged, but he was slain by his own high priest as he sat on the throne; an evidence of how intensely corrupt society among the Jaredites had, at that time grown.

If we understand the record aright, this murderous high priest assumed the kingly authority. But he held it only a few short weeks

---

[14]Nothing is said in the Book of Ether that gives any clue to the locality in which Gilgal was situated.

or months for the same fate befell him that he had brought upon his predecessor. He was assassinated in a lonely pass, by a member of one of the dominant secret societies who desired to be king. This murderer was named Lib. He was a giant in size, being the largest man in the kingdom.

In the first year of his reign, Coriantumr came up against him, and drove his forces to the borders of the sea. In this battle, however, Lib and Coriantumr met in single combat, and the latter was severely wounded by his adversary. A second battle took place on the seashore in which Lib was victorious, and the enemy retreated to the wilderness of Akish,[15] and thence to the Plains of Agosh.[16] Here Coriantumr made another stand, and in the battle that ensued Lib was killed.

Lib slain, his brother Shiz, assumed command of his forces. He completely routed Coriantumr, following him in quick pursuit from the Plains of Agosh, where the battle took place, to the seashore. His march was one of horror and terror to the people. As he swiftly pressed forward, he destroyed everything within his reach, burning the cities and slaying their inhabitants, sparing neither man, woman nor child as he swept along, and a cry of despair went up through all the land, "Who can stand before the army of Shiz? Behold, he sweepeth the earth before him!" So rapid were the movements of the contending armies, that the slain remained unburied, and the stench from their bodies filled the air with pestilence. Those yet alive hastened to join one or the other of the contending hosts, either from predilection or because they were crowded into the ranks. The pursuit did not stop until Coriantumr was forced back across the continent to the seashore. Here they fought for three days, when Coriantumr's star was again in the ascendant, and he drove Shiz back to the Land of Corihor.[17]

In the Valley of Corihor, Coriantumr again sought battle. He challenged Shiz from the Hill Comnor[18] by the sound of the trumpet, and Shiz was in no temper to disregard the challenge. Twice he attacked his over-confident foe, with the horde of men, women and children who followed his banner, and twice he was repulsed. On the third occasion he bore so heavily upon Coriantumr that the latter was wounded and fainted from the loss of blood. Their leader stricken, his motley following of old and young fell back; but Shiz was in no condition to take advantage of his victory. At this time some four or more years before the final battles around and near the Hill Ramah,

---

[15]A place in North America, apparently not far from the Atlantic coast.
[16]These plains were somewhere on the northern continent, but no clue is given to their situation.
[17]A place in North America; its location is unknown.
[18]A hill near the valley of Shurr, location unknown, but apparently nearer the Atlantic than the Pacific seaboard of North America.

two millions of warriors had been slain besides their wives and children. How many millions actually fell before the last terrible struggle ended, when Coriantumr stood alone, the sole representative of his race, it is impossible to tell from the record that has been handed down to us, but we think we are justified in believing that for bloodshed and desolation no such war ever took place before, or ever occurred since in the history of this world; if the annals of any nation have the record of its equal, it is not known to us.

When Coriantumr sensed how great was the slaughter of the people, he wrote to Shiz, offering to withdraw from the conflict that bloodshed might cease. But Shiz refused, unless Coriantumr surrendered, that Shiz might have the gratification of slaying him himself. So the war was renewed with intensified bitterness. Shiz was victorious and the defeated army fled as far as the Waters of Ripliancum.[19] In this region another hotly contested battle was fought, in which Coriantumr was once again severely wounded, but his troops were the victors. Shiz retreated southward to a place called Ogath, near the Hill Ramah. There the two commanders rested for four years while they gathered their hosts for the final struggle. All, babe and grandsire, man and woman, had to join one side or the other. The spirit of bloody vengeance filled every heart. Into the trembling hands of age and the feeble grasp of infancy alike were thrust the sword and spear, while shield and breastplate defended the body strong enough to bear their weight. There, filled with the spirit of demons, they confronted each other, and when once the dwindling fight began it continued from day to day, while night was made hideous by the yells and lamentations, the curses and oaths of the survivors, who were frenzied with anger, even as men are drunken with wine. Thus they fought, struggled and fell, until one night there remained of all the race but fifty-two of the people of Coriantumr and sixty-nine of the followers of Shiz. But they rested not. The next evening, thirty-two of the adherents of Shiz confronted twenty-seven of Coriantumr's. Next day the battle was continued, until the remnants grew faint from exertion and loss of blood. After three hours' desperate fighting the men of Coriantumr attempted to flee, but Shiz and his warriors prevented them. And so they continued until the two commanders remained alone in the field, all their followers having been slain, and Shiz himself, had fainted. Then Coriantumr having rested to gain sufficient strength, smote off the head of Shiz, who in his dying throes raised himself on his hands and knees as if to renew the contest, fell over, struggled for breath and died.[20]

---

[19]Supposed to be Lake Ontario.

[20]Recorded instances are numerous of men suddenly decapitated, showing signs of vitality and will power as did Shiz, for several seconds after their heads have been cut off. This is more especially the case when they are intensely wrought up in the hatreds and excitements of

THE PEOPLE OF MULEK

Shiz slain, Coriantumr stood alone, the last of the hosts of the Jaredites. Probably the horrors of his solitary condition then took possession of his mind and overcame him, for we are told that he "fell to the earth and became as if he had no life." It is difficult to conceive the agonies of his soul as he reviewed the scenes of turmoil, carnage and woe which had ended in the destruction of his race; and combined with these mental throes was the fact that he was weak from excessive exertion and excitement, and from the loss of blood by reason of wounds received. By and by he came to himself again, and then he wandered forth the sole remnant of a continent. Companions he had none; they all had moistened earth's soil with their life's blood. The savage beasts alone remained to terrify him with their hideous cries as they held high carnival over the bodies of the unnumbered slain. Whither should he go? It mattered little, there were none to bid him tarry or depart. Aimlessly he staggered on, passing through each deserted valley, each tenantless town; in neither was there a human voice to greet or curse him; the homes of his own people and those of his enemies were alike—a silent desolation; all the land was a wilderness.

How long Coriantumr wandered to and fro, wretched, comfortless and 'forlorn, we know not; but at last he reached the southern portions of the northern continent, and there to his great surprise, and doubtless to theirs also, he found the people of Mulek.[21] With them he spent his few remaining days, and when nine moons had waxed and waned, he passed away to join the hosts of his people in the spirit world.

Coriantumr's solitary pilgrimage of so many hundred miles has appeared to some almost an impossibility.[22] But he had no enemies to impede his journey whichever way he traveled. The only seeming difficulty is the manner in which he obtained the food necessary to

---

actual combat. One of the latest instances which we have noticed is referred to in the *Popular Science Monthly* (p. 116) for June 1892. The writer (Geo. L. Kilmer) says:

"On the 17th of June [1864?] in the charge of the Ninth Corps on the Confederate works east of Petersburg, a sergeant of the Fifty-seventh Massachusetts leaped upon the parapet, and with his cap in his left hand and his musket in his right, stood cheering and gesturing with his arms to incite his comrades to come on. Suddenly a shell took his head off as completely as a knife could have done, but the tall form continued erect for some seconds, the arms still waving frantically but with ever-lessening sweep and power, until the forces of the body collapsed, when the headless trunk toppled over to the ground."

[21] A colony of Israelites who were led by divine power out of Jerusalem and brought to this continent in the same year (B.C. 589) that that city was captured by the King of Babylonia. Among their number was Mulek, the infant son of Zedekiah, the last King of Judah, in whose honor the people were named.

[22] As his wanderings lay in the direction of the flow of the great rivers, it is quite supposable that when he reached some deserted city on the banks of the Mississippi, or of one of its tributaries, he would find boats there, and appropriating one of them could hasten his journey by floating hundreds of miles down stream.

sustain his life; but being a soldier this would be only a slight trouble, the game he could slay and the wild fruit he could gather would be ample for his sustenance. There are a number of recorded instances of men who have made, without companions, journeys as lengthy and certainly more perilous than Coriantumr's, because they were exposed to the danger of falling into the hands of murderous savages. We will cite one of the best authenticated cases. In October, 1568, Sir John Hawkins, one of Queen Elizabeth's slave-trading admirals, by reason of the scarcity of food, felt compelled to land about one hundred men on the Mexican coast, near the Rio de Minas, and there leave them to their fate. Most of these men, in all probability, perished in the wilderness. Some who took south-westerly trails found their way to the city of Mexico, where, as "vile, Lutheran dogges," they received but little kindness at the hands of the dominant Spanish Catholics. Others took north-easterly trails, and one of them, David Ingram, made his way from Texas to Maine, and beyond to the St. Johns River, where he was picked up by a friendly French ship and carried to France; thence he made his way to England. The overland journey took him about eleven months; but one of his comrades, Job Hortop, was more than twenty years in getting back to England. Ingram told so many marvelous yarns that he was subjected to a searching investigation before Sir Francis Walsingham,[23] in 1582, the record of which is to be found in the British Museum, while a Ms. copy is in the library of Harvard University. The journey from the Hill Ramah to Central America is much of the way parallel to that from the Rio de Minas to the St. John's River, and we should judge not longer, making the comparison between the two the more consistent.

Thus were fulfilled the prophecies of Ether. Neither Coriantumr nor his people had repented, and speedy destruction had befallen them. He simply lived to witness the complete fulfillment of the words of the prophet and to receive a burial at the hands of the new people whom God had called to occupy the land.

JAREDITES AND THEIR CONTEMPORARIES

It is a somewhat peculiar though now generally acknowledged fact that geographical knowledge has not advanced among men with steady, orderly and ever-increasing strides; but to the contrary there have been periods of activity in geographical discovery followed by ages of inertia. Lands have been discovered, occupied, abandoned, forgotten and then, centuries after, rediscovered. The Egyptians and

---

[23]A famous statesman of Queen Elizabeth's days. He was one of her principal secretaries of state, and at different times ambassador to several foreign powers. He was also one of the commissioners for the trial of Queen Mary Stuart, of Scotland.

Phœnicians were the great navigators of early civilization. When their power waned and Rome became mistress of the world, many of their discoveries were lost sight of, the policy of the latter people being consolidation and a strong central government. Their realm formed one solid mass, reached, as a rule, by overland roads, not of remote and isolated colonies located far and wide over Europe, Asia and Africa, as did those of the Phœnicians. Thus it came that geographical knowledge was much further advanced six hundred years before Christ than at the time of the Redeemer's birth. Between the years B.C. 611-605 Africa was circumnavigated; all recollection of such a feat had passed away in His time.

It is worthy of note that this decrease in maritime activity is coincident with the era of the departure of the colonies of Lehi and Mulek for America, and of the promise which the Lord gave to the first named that as long as his seed were faithful in keeping the laws of heaven the land that had been given to them "should be kept as yet from the knowledge of other nations."[24]

If Diodorus Siculus and other ancient writers are to be believed, the Carthagenian Senate, in the year B.C. 460, to stop emigration, passed a decree condemning to death any man, woman or child who should embark for "The Lands of the West." We do not understand why so extreme a penalty should be attached to the attempt to emigrate to the Lands of the West; but the decree certainly would have the effect, so far as Carthage was concerned, of preventing any of its citizens landing in America, and in this way aiding in a most remarkable manner in the fulfillment of the Lord's promise of isolation to the seed of Lehi. And that promise was fulfilled in its completeness, for if the ancients had any knowledge of this continent it became to them a vague tradition and most certainly the people of no other nation reached its shores until long after the descendants of Lehi had turned from the Lord and had fallen nigh into the lowest depths of savagery and idolatry.[25] The existence of this era of geographical ignorance is a very interesting, though incidental, evidence of the truth of the Book of Mormon.

But were the ancient Phœnicians, Carthagenians and Egyptians acquainted with America? did they know anything of the Jaredites? We believe they did. In the first place there is nothing inconsistent in having this belief, in the second place there is direct testimony in its favor.

Surely so far as probabilities are concerned there is nothing startling in believing that the people who circumnavigated Africa,

---

[24]II Nephi 1:5-11.
[25]The Nephites were destroyed at Cumorah 385 A.D. It was not until the tenth century, at the earliest, that the Northmen landed on this continent, or more than 600 years later.

traded with China, and penetrated north, at least, as far as the Hebrides, and apparently into the Baltic, crossed the South Atlantic and landed in Brazil. To do so with their vessels and with the favorable winds usually blowing would have been no extraordinary feat. In fact we have the account of such a thing being done. A few years ago some slaves, working on a farm in the parish of Parabyba (Brazil) discovered a stone covered with Phœnician characters. These characters were translated by Senor Ladesloa Netto, director of the museum at Rio Janeiro, and gave an account, in substance, as follows:

The stone was a commemorative one, erected by some Sidonian, or as they call themselves Canaanite exiles or refugees, between the ninth and tenth years of the reign of a king named Hiram. They left the port of Eziongeber or Akaba, on the upper waters of the Red Sea and for twelve lunar months sailed along the coast of Africa. The number of the vessels and the members of the party, both male and female, is given; these details being placed between the invocations to their protecting gods and goddesses. The inscription is in eight lines of beautiful Phœnician characters, but there is no separation of the words, neither vowel points, nor quiescent letters.

There were two Phœnician kings named Hiram; one, the friend of Solomon, reigned from about 980 to 947 B.C., the other occupied the throne from 558 to 552 B.C.; the inscription does not say which of these Hirams is referred to. From this silence we conclude it was the earlier one; as if it had been the second it would have probably so stated, as long as there was only one there was no necessity to particularize. Again it could not have been in the time of the second Hiram as that was after the date of the promise made by God to Lehi that this land should be kept from the knowledge of other nations.

Diodorus Siculus[26] makes the following statement, as a fact of authentic history:

"Over against Africa lies a very great island, in the vast ocean, many days sail from Lybia westward. The soil there is very fruitful, a great part whereof is mountainous, but much likewise flat, open country, which is the sweetest and pleasantest part, for it is watered by several navigable streams and beautified with many pleasure gardens, planted with divers sorts of trees and an abundance of orchards. The towns are adorned with stately buildings and banqueting houses, pleasantly situated in their gardens and orchards. * * * The Phœnicians, having found out the coasts beyond the Pillars of Hercules,[27] sailed along the coast of Africa. One of their ships, on a sudden, was driven by a furious storm far off into the main ocean. After they had lain under this violent tempest many days, they at length arrived at this island."[28]

We ask here how could the Phœnicians have given such an exact

---

[26]A Roman historian who lived in the days of Julius Caesar.
[27]The Straits of Gibraltar.
[28]Elder George M. Ottinger, in his articles on "Old America," published some few years ago in *The Juvenile Instructor*, suggests, from the description given, that it was Central America that these Phoenicians sighted.

description of the geographical position and appearance of this continent if they had never seen it? Does it not take a much greater stretch of credulity to believe they guessed so well than that they actually told the truth; besides how well their description agrees with the high state of civilization existing among the Jaredites, according to the Book of Ether, eleven hundred years before the advent of the Savior, which is the time this voyage is said to have taken place. On the other hand how admirably this account bears testimony to the genuineness of Ether's record!

"Greek writers inform us that the Phœnicians and Carthagenians knew the way to a country beyond the Atlantic." The Egyptians knew of an island, far to the west, known as Atlantis, which sustained a great population. These people finally became desperately wicked, and the island was swept away by a deluge. Plato mentions it in his Timæus.[29] On old Venetian maps, Atlantis is put to the west of the Azores and Canaries.

Here appears to be a precise knowledge of the destruction of the Jaredites and the causes therefor; while the deluge which swept the island away would be a very convenient explanation why they could not find it after the Lord had placed His inhibition on further intercourse between the peoples of the two continents.

Dr. Hyde Clark[30] says:

"It is very questionable whether at any time there was regular intercourse over the Atlantic. * * * In what we know of the historical period, under the Greeks and the Romans, a lively knowledge of America was lost; the Greeks could not reach it from the west, and the Romans, when they settled on the shores of the Atlantic, had other cares than to risk the wide sea. A dead knowledge lingered, not only of the geography of the Americas, but of Australasia. * * * There must at one time have been men in the olden world, men who could bring back this knowledge of the Americas from their Nineveh to its Nineveh and Babel, where the empire of the four worlds got centered, and where one language was spoken and written for the government of the earth. How truly was it then said of Babel, 'And the whole earth was of one language and of one speech.' (Genesis XI:1) The fall of that power was indeed confusion of nations and of tongues. * * * The intercourse in times of yore between the new world and the old, now again brought to light, rests upon no slight evidence."

Another gentleman[31] remarks:

"There are proofs that there must have been repeated intercommunication between the new and the old worlds prior to the days of Columbus. So evident is this conclusion that some writers have tried to establish that the origin of the religions and the civilization of the old world must be sought in America."

On April 23rd, 1843, some citizens of Kinderbrook, Pike County, Illinois, while digging in a mound found about six feet from the surface of the earth the skeleton of a very tall man. On his breast were

---

[29]A Greek philosopher, born B.C. 429, died B.C. 348.
[30]Lecture given before the Anthropological Institute, 1874.
[31]M. R. G. Haliburton.

six bell-shaped brass plates, covered with engravings. These plates were taken to the Prophet Joseph Smith and he translated a portion of the characters. He states they contained the history of the persons with whom they were found, who was a descendant of Ham, through the loins of Pharaoh, king of Egypt, and that he received his kingdom from the ruler of heaven and earth.[32]

Here then we have the statement of the Prophet of God that, at any rate, one royal Egyptian came to America; but it is scarcely to be supposed that he, being of the royal blood, would come alone.

From the very meager details given us by the Prophet we may perhaps be justified in drawing the following deductions:

That as he could not have come to this land during the time of the divine inhibition, when the faithful Nephites occupied it, it is altogether more probable that as a Hametic Pharaoh, he came in the days of the Jaredites.

Evidence is accumulating that the reigning dynasty of Pharaohs in the days of the oppression and exodus of Israel were of Chaldean origin, who apparently had driven the previous dynasty, descended from Ham and Egyptus, from the throne. In this way the scriptural statement that there arose another Pharaoh, who knew not Joseph is accounted for. That the Egyptian ruler whose skeleton was found in the Illinois mound did not quietly succeed his father in the kingly authority may be surmised from the statement that he received his kingdom from God. We therefore think it not improbable that he belonged to the family of Pharaohs dethroned by their Chaldean successors, that he fled from his native country, with a certain following came to this country, and by the grace of heaven built up a kingdom here. The time of his coming would be somewhere between the days of Ephraim and Moses, and also that as he would very naturally be buried near the seat of his government we may reasonably conclude that his kingdom was situated in the great valley of the Mississippi.

From the testimony presented above we think we are justified in believing that the Jaredites were known to their contemporaries on the eastern continent.

ANCIENT RUINS FOUND IN AMERICA

We now come to the consideration of the question, Are any of the ruins found upon this continent the remains of Jaredite cities and buildings? Individually, we think that few, if any, of the ruined cities of ancient America are of Jaredite origin; indeed, we will go

---

[32]"Millennial Star," Vol. 21, pp. 40-44.

farther and say we believe but few of them date as far back as the days of the Nephites. This conclusion will doubtless surprise many of our readers, it is therefore due to them that we give our reasons.

The writers and explorers to whom English speaking people are indebted for their information regarding the ruins of this continent, the largest, best preserved and most important of which are to be found in Central America and contiguous regions, drew their conclusions from conditions which do not exist in the regions where these ruins most largely exist. The vast overgrowth of vegetation conveyed to their minds an idea of antiquity which the facts did not warrant, an error to which they were predisposed from the prevailing tendency among modern students to dabble in eons instead of centuries, and to give every thing and every event whose date was not determined a remote and indistinct antiquity. When in this frame of mind an explorer from the temperate zone discovered in Yucatan a tree which had five hundred rings, growing on a house-top, he argued that that tree must be at least five hundred years old, as in his native land the trees only added one ring a year to their growth, and if the tree was five hundred years old the house underneath must be much older. But the mistake made was this, that in that heated climate, some trees added ten or twelve rings, instead of one, a year, and consequently were only one-tenth or one-twelfth as old as he imagined.

Professor John Fiske, of Harvard College, cites the following example:

"The notion of their antiquity was perhaps suggested by the belief that certain colossal mahogany trees growing between and over the ruins of Palenque must be nearly two thousand years old. But when M. de Carnay visited Palenque in 1859, he had the eastern side of the 'palace' cleared of its dense vegetation in order to get a good photograph; and when he re-visited the spot, in 1881, he found a sturdy growth of young mahogany the age of which he knew did not exceed twenty-two years. Instead of making a ring once a year as in our sluggish and temperate zone, these trees had made rings at the rate of about one a month; the trunks were already more than two feet in diameter; judging from this rate of growth the biggest giant on that place need not have been more than two hundred years old, if as much."

M. Charnay himself speaking on this subject says:

"I may here remark that [the] virgin forests have no very old trees, being destroyed by insects, moisture, lianas,[33] etc., and old monteros[34] tell me that mahogany and cedar trees, which are most durable, do not live above two hundred years."

Another reason is that cities of the same class and description, having the same characteristics and style of architecture as the neighboring ruins, were inhabited at the time of the Spanish invasion by the people who built them. Some indeed were decaying, others were growing cities. This fact is attested by the Spanish Chroniclers. But

---

[33]Liana—a woody, high-climbing plant, having rope-like stems.
[34]Woodmen.

more than this, some of the now ruined cities, generally supposed to be very ancient, have lately been proven to have also been inhabited at this period. A native chief of Yucatan, named Nakuk Pech, wrote about the year 1562, a brief history of the Spanish conquest of that country. This chronicle, which has been translated into English, refers directly to Chichen-Itza and Izamal as inhabited towns during the time of the Spanish invasion, from 1519 to 1542. Mr. Fiske is inclined to consider the highest probable antiquity for most of the ruins of Yucatan and Central America as the twelfth or thirteenth century of our era;[35] while M. Charnay says, "Copan and Palenque may be two or three centuries older, and had probably fallen into ruins before the arrival of the Spaniards."[36]

A third reason is that ruins found in Central America, etc., in no wise agree with what we should naturally expect would be built by a people such as the Jaredites or the Nephites are represented to have been in the sacred writings of their prophets, but they are not inconsistent with a barbarous, idolatrous race of builders such as the Lamanites, after the destruction of the Nephites undoubtedly were. The Nephites were of the house of Israel and Christians. As Israelites they were forbidden by God Himself to make to themselves the likeness of any thing in the heavens above, on the earth beneath, or in the waters under the earth.[37] These ruins are full of images and representations of human beings and other animate things. As Christians, the Nephites would not indulge in the class of grotesque statuary and reliefs that so largely abound in many of these cities, especially in those that clearly point to idolatry and idolatrous customs. The occasional appearance of an ornament that somewhat resembles a cross carries no weight in our mind. The cross was used as an ornament, and with no reference to Christianity long before Jesus was crucified, and today is more the symbol of the apostate churches of Christendom than the original Church established by God Himself. The appearance of such a symbol would appeal more readily and have greater weight with Roman Catholics than with members of the true Church. The heathen has adorned his edifices

---

[35]The city of Mexico was built 1325 A.D.

[36]It is not improbable, however, that these cities were built on the foundations of older ones; and some of the masonry, sculptured stones, etc., of the more ancient city may have been incorporated in the buildings of the newer one. To do this would be very consistent with the character of the barbarous and indolent Lamanites, who would take advantage of every opportunity of this kind to lessen their labors, without any reference to the uses of sculpture, walls or foundations had been originally put to.

[37]"Thou shalt not make unto thee any graven image or any likeness of anything that is in the heaven above, or that is in the earth beneath, or that is in the water under the earth." (Exodus 20:4)

"Lest ye corrupt yourselves and make you a graven image the similitude of any figure, the likeness of male or female, the likeness of any beast that is on the earth, the likeness of any winged fowl that flieth in the air, the likeness of any thing that creepeth on the ground, the likeness of any fish that is in the waters beneath the earth. (Deuteronomy 4:16-18)

with crosses for the reason that it was a natural, easy and becoming style of ornament.

The civilization of the Jaredites very much resembled that of the Nephites and to our mind was greatly in advance of that of the builders of Copan, Palenque and their sister cities. It should here be observed that the greater portion of the cities built by the Nephites before the crucifixion of Christ were destroyed by the convulsions that attended that most momentous event, others so badly shattered that it would not pay to repair them. The Nephite remains, therefore, that we would expect to find would be those that were erected during the universal reign of peace that followed the ministry of the risen Redeemer. Is it not also consistent to believe that if any Jaredite ruins remained at the time of the Savior's death they also were destroyed by the universal convulsions? It must likewise be remembered that in the last great war the Lamanites took great delight in destroying everything Nephite.

The question now arises, Were the Jaredites the mound builders? Again we answer, We think not. The remains found in the mounds that have been opened betoken a race of builders far inferior in civilization to what Ether represents the Jaredites to have been. True, it is possible, as some have suggested, that an inferior race of later ages, may have opened these mounds and made them sepulchres for their dead, and placed therein, with the dead, the flint and quartzite arrowheads, the beads, pipes, shells, and inferior pottery and ornaments that have been there found. It is also quite supposable that the mounds scattered far and wide about this northern continent,[38] were not all built by the same race. It is affirmed with some show of evidence that some of these mounds are known to have been built by the Shawnees and Cherokees,[39] while others are ascribed to the Chickasaws and Winnebagos. It is also suggested that the Mandans and Minnitarees were at one time mound-building people.[40]

Major J. W. Powell, director of the U. S. Bureau of Ethnology, in the *Forum*, says: "No fragment of evidence remains to support the figment of theory that there was an ancient race of moundbuilders superior in culture to the North American Indians."

A lady writer (Mary Morrison) writing on this question in

---

[38]It is estimated that not less than 10,000 monuments of the mound-builders exist in Ohio, and they are scarcely less numerous in Indiana and Kentucky.

[39]Fiske's "Discovery of America," Vol. I, pp. 144-145.

[40]"There is good reason to believe that in the Natchez and Mandans, and perhaps some other tribes still existing, but in small numbers, at the advent of the whites, we have their lineal descendants." "We may infer from their bony structure that they belonged to the American family of men, and were not unlike, in structure, physical aspect, and color, the red Indian of today."—Prof. S. Newberry. Mr. John C. Southall, an able English writer, brings strong evidence to prove that the mound-builders lived not more than 1,500 years ago. Elder George M. Ottinger takes the ground that "the Toltecs and the mound-builders were the same people."

"Hearth and Hall,"[41] sums up the opinions of a number of intelligent investigators in the following statement:

"The mound-builders were formerly regarded as a race so remote from the present Indian tribes that there could be nothing between them, yet all recent theories deny this. Many Indian tribes have built burial mounds for their dead.

"Some of the mounds in Ohio have yielded from their deepest recesses articles of European manufacture, showing an origin not farther back than the historic period. Spanish swords and blue grass beads have been found in the mounds of Georgia and Florida. . . .

"The annals of the Columbian epoch have been carefully studied, and it is found that some of the mounds have been constructed in historical times, while early explorers and settlers found many actually used by tribes of North American Indians; so we know that many of the Indians were builders of mounds. The contents of these mounds have been compared with the works of art of the Indian tribes before they were influenced by Europeans and both were substantially identical."

But, on the other hand, we have the fact before us, that the skeleton of the Pharaoh, found in Kinderhook, Illinois, referred to previously, was dug out of a large mound. After penetrating about eleven feet the workers came to a bed of limestone that had been subjected to the action of fire. They removed the stones, which were small and easy to handle, to the depth of two feet more, when they found the skeleton. This was evidently a burial chamber, as with the bones, which appeared to have been burned, was found plenty of charcoal and ashes.[42] From this fact it is evident that some of the mounds are of very ancient date, as it is not supposable that this man would be the only one of his race and nation to be buried in this manner. We also suggest that this colony of Egyptians may have originated the style of architecture in this country in which so many find resemblances to the Egyptian, and which is specially characterized by the erection of vast truncated pyramids.

There is also another consideration; it is that the Jaredites built largely of wood. Undoubtedly their temples and palaces would be constructed of more lasting materials; to believe otherwise would be to believe that the habits of the Jaredites were different from those of all other civilized races; but the homes of the people appear to have been built from the product of the forest, and throwing all other considerations aside we cannot expect to now find remains of wooden dwellings built from four thousand to twenty-five hundred years ago. The proof of our assertion is that when the Nephites began to colonize the northern continent they found it admirably adapted for that purpose with the exception that it was without timber, and the reason given why it was without timber was "because of the many inhabitants who had before inhabited the land" who had consumed it.[43] To get

---

[41]Reprinted in the "Woman's Exponent," July 15th; August 1st, and August 15th, 1892.
[42]"Quincy Whig," and "Times and Seasons," reprinted in the "Millennial Star," Vol. 21, p. 44.
[43]Helaman 3:3-11.

over this difficulty the Nephites built their houses out of cement, and also imported considerable lumber from the lands of Zarahemla and Bountiful, and further they preserved "whatever tree should spring up upon the face of the land," until it was large enough for building purposes.

ANIMAL LIFE OF THE JAREDITE PERIOD

When Jared and his colony reached the Valley of Nimrod they tarried there for a season and made it their outfitting point. They gathered their flocks, male and female, of every kind, they laid snares and caught the fowls of the air, they prepared a vessel in which they carried fish, and they also took along with them swarms of honey bees.[44] Silk worms must have also formed a portion of their lading, for we read of their descendants manufacturing silks and fine twined linen,[45] as likewise did the Nephites, their successors in the occupation of this continent. But during the long era of savagery and barbarism that succeeded the destruction of the latter race the silk worm appears to have become extinct in America, as no trace was found of it by the Spaniards when they overran Mexico and Peru. The fact that no silk worms or remains of silk fabrics were found by the followers of Cortez, Pizzaro and others has been used as an argument against the divine authenticity of the Book of Mormon.[46] But it must be remembered that "in 1522 A.D. Cortez appointed officials to introduce sericulture into New Spain (Mexico), and mulberry trees were then planted and eggs were brought from Spain. The Mexican adventure is mentioned by Acosta,[47] but all trace of the culture had died out before the end of the century."[48] If then in about three-quarters of a century all trace of the culture had disappeared, where is the consistency of attacking the Book of Mormon because the Spaniards found no silk worms in Mexico, when between the destruction of the Nephites and the venture of Cortez more than twelve hundred years had passed away?

Among the creatures brought by Jared to America were, in all probability, the domestic animals afterwards mentioned in the record of Ether. These were all manner of cattle, sheep, swine, goats, horses, asses, elephants, cureloms, and cumoms, and many kinds of animals that were useful for the food of man.[49] The elephants, cureloms, and cumoms are especially noted as being "useful unto man," from which

[44]Ether 2:1-3.
[45]Ether 9:17; 10:24.
[46]See "The Discovery of America," by John Fiske, Vol. I, pp. 3, 179.
[47]Jose de Acosta, a Spanish writer, born about 1539, died 1600. In 1571 he was sent as a missionary to America, of which, after his return to Spain, he published a history.
[48]Encyclopedia Britannica.
[49]Ether 9:18, 19.

it is reasonable to conclude that the elephant was domesticated by the Jaredites and used as a beast of burden.[50]

It is not evident from Ether's narrative what the cureloms and cumoms were. Some suppose them to have been creatures akin to the elephant or mastadon; others think they were the alpaca or llama.

As we have already learned, when Jared's colony reached the great waters they, by divine command, built eight barges. Into these barges they all—men, women and children, went. We are told that they had prepared all manner of food, that thereby they might subsist upon the water, and also food for their flocks and herds, and whatsoever beast, or animal, or fowl that they should carry with them.[51] From the wording of the above passage—"whatsoever beast, etc., they should carry with them"—we do not think that the ancestors of all the various kinds of wild beasts and reptiles that were found on this continent when it was discovered by Columbus were brought in Jared's barges. It is also very improbable that room could be found therein for so many various creatures and the food necessary for their sustenance during a voyage of 344 days. In our opinion it is altogether more probable that they migrated to this continent before the days of Peleg,[52] when we are told the earth was divided.[53] It may be asked, where did that division occur? Asia and America were not then joined, or there would not have been the necessity of Jared making a voyage of nearly a year across the Pacific Ocean. It is therefore reasonable to look at the other side of the continent, and the existence of two elevated plateaus, now submerged, one running between Africa and South America, the other between Europe and North America, gives us reason to think that these, before the days of Peleg, were a portion of the dry land; that across them the wild animals wandered,[54] and when they sank beneath the level of the sea the earth was divided.[55]

---

[50]The fact that the Mexicans retained traditions of the elephant (Humboldt's "Vue des Cordilleras," pl. 15) is evidence that these animals were known to the Nephites; and if the Indians were the "mound builders" then that creature had not become extinct when the Nephites were destroyed, for one of the mounds is in the form of a huge elephant, and several objects found within the mounds have been adorned with its likeness or fashioned in its shape. The fact that the bones of the elephant, now in the Deseret Museum, were found on the top of an adobe house near Payson, confirms us in the view that elephants existed on this continent to a much later date than is the general opinion.

[51]Ether 6:4.

[52]A son of Eber, of the family of Shem.

[53]Genesis 10:25.

[54]The northwestern part of Europe has been solid continent for more than a hundred miles to the west of the French and Irish coasts; the Thames and Humber have been tributaries to the Rhine, which emptied into the Arctic Ocean, and across the Atlantic ridge one might have walked to the New World dryshod.—Fiske.

[55]Some have thought that this division of the earth in the days of Peleg was not a physical division of the continents by the great waters, but a patriarchal or political division, made by Noah, in which he divided Europe, Asia and Africa among his three sons, Shem, Ham and Japeth. Even admitting this to be true, and that the physical division did not take place in the days of Peleg, yet the presumption is strong, almost amounting to a certainty, that certain portions of the American continent were at one time joined to Europe and Africa, and over these connecting plateaus the wild animals could have migrated.

The next enquiry that naturally arises is, what caused this submergence? We answer that the most probable cause was volcanic action. We will take as our example the northern plateau;[56] and condense the statements of scientific writers in relation thereto. We are informed that in ages long since past the North Atlantic ridge was one of the principal seats of volcanic activity upon the globe; the line of volcanoes extended all the way from Greenland down into Central France. In the Hebrides, Great Britain and France they have long since become extinct but in the far north volcanic action has died out much more slowly. In the fifteenth century there was still an active volcano near the Icelandic settlement in the south of Greenland. Iceland has yet twenty active volcanoes, and unnumbered boiling springs. Among the submerged peaks in the North Atlantic explosions occasionally occur. A small volcanic island appears to have remained midway between Iceland and Greenland until 1456, when it was entirely destroyed by an eruption.[57] These examples show that the work of the volcanoes is not yet finished, and islands, etc., are still sinking; giving a reasonable basis for believing that, as the lands were once joined, this plateau was one of the bands that united them. It would indeed form one of most direct and shortest routes from the old world to the new; and furthermore is the road that some zoologists, (who do not believe the Bible statement regarding Peleg) claim that many of the animals, common to both Europe and North America, first reached the latter continent.

In reading the account of the conversations between the Lord and the brother of Jared with regard to the construction of the barges, we are struck with the solicitude manifested by the Savior concerning their ability to withstand the storms and other dangers to which they would be exposed. In one place He says:

"For behold, ye shall be as a whale in the midst of the sea; for the mountain waves shall dash upon you. Nevertheless, I will bring you up again out of the depths of the sea; for the winds have gone forth out of my mouth, and also the rains and the floods have I sent forth. And behold, I prepare you against these things; for howbeit, ye cannot cross this great deep, save I prepare you against the waves of the sea, and the winds which have gone forth, and the floods which shall come."[58]

Later we are told: "Thus they were driven forth; and no monster of the sea could break them, neither whale that could mar them."[59] Here apparently is an additional danger to that of the floods which threatened the barges. Here are whales spoken of that could mar

[56]Sometimes called the Telegraph Plateau, because the electric cables between Europe and North America are laid upon it.
[57]"Where volcanic action is declining geysers and boiling springs are apt to abound, as in Iceland; where it has become extinct at a period geologically recent, as in Auvergne and the Rhine Country, its latest vestiges are left in the hundreds of thermal and mineral springs whither fashionable invalids congregate to drink or to bathe."—Fiske.
[58]Ether 2:24-25.
[59]Ether 6:10.

them. But there were other creatures who could do more than this, they were monsters of the sea who could break them. What fish is there or animal of the great waters that now exists that could break a barge, built as these were, and of "the length of a tree"? No shark could do it, nor do we know of any other marine animal. But evidently from these monsters being mentioned before the whales, and the destructive word break being used in contradistinction to mar, they had greater strength and power than the whales had. Shall we be inconsistent in believing that some of the great amphibious or marine reptiles (Enaliosauria) of which geologists and paleontologists speak, such as the Plesiosauria[60] and Ichthyosauria[61] still existed in the Pacific Ocean; and that they had sufficient strength to break and destroy any vessel formed after the ordinary methods of ship building. To avoid a disaster of this kind befalling the Jaredites the Lord commanded them to build the peculiar barges, without windows or portholes, masts or sails, which have been the source of so much amusement to some unthinking folk.

References are now and again made in the Book of Mormon to the cattle, sheep and horses owned by the Jaredites and their successors, the Nephites and Lamanites. This has been used, like the silk-worm idea, as an argument against the genuineness of that holy record. Because the Spaniards found no horses in Mexico, Central America and Peru, and a certain tribe of Algonquins on the New England Coast were terrified by the bellowing of a bull belonging to a party of Norsemen,[62] it is arrogantly claimed that the Book of Mormon must be a fraud, because it states that the ancient inhabitants of this continent possessed these animals. When we remember the extent of this continent it would be just as reasonable to say there could not possibly have been elephants anywhere on the eastern hemisphere in the days of Cyrus, because the British soldiery under Caswollon were frightened at the appearance of these huge creatures in the ranks of the invading Romans, as to affirm that there were no cattle in any part of America a thousand years before because these Indians knew nothing about the roaring of a bull. So far as the non-existence of the horse in ancient America is concerned, the question has forever been set at rest by the discovery of the remains of this animal all over the land; and though Cortez and his followers saw

---

[60]Plesiosaurus—An extinct marine reptile, having a very long neck, a small head and paddles for swimming.

[61]Ichthyosaurus—An extinct marine reptile; its name means a fish lizard. The remains of these creatures that have been found in the rocks show them to have varied from ten to thirty feet long.

[62]It is stated that when Thorfinn Karlsefni, made an unsuccessful attempt, 1007 to 1010 A.D., to establish a colony in Vinland, the Indians were as terribly afraid of his cattle as the Aztecs were in later years of the Spanish horses. The chance bellowing of a bull sent them yelling to the woods, and they did not show themselves again for three weeks.

none alive, yet Admiral Sir Francis Drake did see large bands of wild horses on the Oregon Coast in 1579, far too early for any to have escaped from the Spaniards, grown wild, and traveled so vast a distance.[63]

THE JAREDITES AS METAL-WORKERS

One of the most marked characteristics of Jaredite civilization was the perfection reached by that people in working the metals. They were skillful in the manufacture of machinery and tools and in the fabrication of weapons of war. Gold, silver, iron, copper, brass were all wrought into things of usefulness and beauty by the hand of the cunning workman. It is somewhat strange that the fact of the use of iron by the Jaredites has been advanced as an argument against the divine authenticity of the Book of Mormon. Its opponents have declared that no remains of ancient iron implements have been found on this continent, apparently forgetting that as iron rusts and crumbles to dust far sooner than any other of the useful metals, it would be more remarkable if many finds of iron remains were made than the contrary. But notwithstanding the denunciations of objectors, sufficient ancient worked iron has been found to show that it was used by the former inhabitants of this continent and to prove that the statements in the Book of Mormon are correct. We will cite a few instances.

In digging a well at Cincinnati, Ohio, in 1820, at the depth of eighty feet, the workmen came upon the stump of a tree, three feet in diameter, rooted in its native soil, which had been cut with an ax or other sharp instrument. *Iron rust* was found on the top of the stump, as if the ax had been decomposed during the time the mass of earth rested upon it. Again the six bell-shaped brass plates found on the breast of the skeleton exhumed at Kinderhook, Illinois, already referred to, were fastened together, according to a writer in the *Times and Seasons*, by rings through each and clasped with two clasps. "The rings and clasps appeared to be of iron very much ozidated." The *Quincy Whig* says they were "secured and fastened together by two *iron* wires, but which were so decayed that they readily crumbled to dust on being handled."

Mr. Atwater, in the Report of the American Antiquarian Society for 1820, says that in the mounds, besides the various stone instruments, "there have been found very well manufactured swords and knives of iron and possibly steel." At Marietta, in 1819, in a burial mound, by the side of the skeleton, the remains of a sword were unearthed; the blade itself was not discovered but a streak of rust ex-

---

[63]For details see President George Q. Cannon's "Life of Nephi," pp. 70-73.

tended its whole length. Two or three broken pieces of a copper tube were also found filled with iron rust, and near the feet a piece of ore, which was nearly pure iron. (Report of the American Antiquarian Society, 1820, pp. 168-172.) At Circleville, lying on a mirror of isinglass, a plate of iron was found, of course oxidized. Before being broken it resembled a plate of cast iron. The Natchez, as well as the Aztecs, had a tradition that the country had been once inhabited by white people, who had the use of iron tools. (*Ibid.*, p. 273)

It will be remembered that when Limhi, king of the Nephites in the Land of Lehi-Nephi, (B.C. 122) desired to open up communication with their friends in Zarahemla, he sent out an exploring expedition which, after a lengthy absence, returned without discovering the objects of its search. The explorers had been lost in the wilderness, where they had wandered many days; they also traveled in a strange land among abundant waters, and though they did not find their fellow-countrymen of Zarahemla, they discovered a desolate land which was covered with the bones of men and of beasts, and which was full of the ruins of buildings of every kind: a land which evidently had once been the home of a mighty people. As a testimony of the truth of their statements they brought back to Lehi-Nephi twenty-four gold plates which were covered with undecipherable engravings. They also brought samples of large copper and brass breastplates, and of swords. Now, while the breast-plates were perfectly sound, the swords were in a state of decay. The hilts had perished and the blades were cankered with rust.[64] These were the remains of the once-favored Jaredites, who some four or five hundred years before had perished in fraticidal strife. That to which we wish to draw attention is that even at that time the steel and iron of their swords had rusted, while the brass and copper armor had entirely resisted the ravages of time. This being the case in less than five hundred years, how can we expect to find many traces of articles manufactured of iron, when twenty-five hundred years have passed away.

Of the language of the Jaredites we know next to nothing, except that it was at first the uncorrupted tongue spoken by the descendants of Noah until the confusion of languages at Babel. By divine condescension Jared and his companions were permitted to retain the old form of speech. The only word that we have that we are certain belonged to that language is Deseret, the honey bee. Curelom and Cumom may have belonged to the ancient tongue, most probably they did if the animals to whom these names were applied were known to Jared before his colony left Asia, otherwise they were probably first used when the animals were discovered on this continent.

---

[64]Mosiah 8:8-11.

There are several proper names used by the antediluvians and Hebrews which also appear in Jaredite history. This makes it probable that they all, in their original forms, belonged to the uncorrupted universal language. Among these names are: Aaron, Ether, Gilead, Heth, Jared, Levi, Nimrod, Noah, Omer.

INDEX

slays Lib, 192
battles with Shiz, 192
flees before Shiz, 192
not to fall by sword, 193
meets Shiz at Comnor, 193
wounded by Shiz, 193
repentance of, 197
writes to Shiz, 197
flees before Shiz, 198
goes to Ripliancum, 198
defeats Shiz, 198
camps at Hill Ramah, 198
watched by Ether, 199
final battle with Shiz, 199
slays Shiz, 201
falls wounded, 201
biographical notes, 175
Corihor, Land of, 42
Corihor, son of Kib, 121
  rebels against Kib, 121
  makes his father a captive, 122
  loses his kingdom to Shule, 122
  repents and gains favor with Shule, 122-123
Corihor, an associate of Coriantumr, 186-187
Corom, son of Levi, 48, 512
Cow, among Jaredites, 140
Cries at destruction of the Jaredites, 199
Cumoms, animals known to Jaredites, 140
Cumorah, known as Ramah to Jaredites, 198
Cureloms, animals known to Jaredites, 140
Cursed, is he who contends against the Word
  of the Lord, 99

— D —

Dance, of daughter of Jared, the dethroned
  king, 130
Day, Ether hid in cavity of rock, by, 185
Dearth, famine in days of Heth, 148
Descendants, of Riplakish, 151
Deseret, honey bee, 65
Desolation, Land of, near Moron, 121
Destruction, of Jaredites, 124, 157, 178
  caused by secret combinations, 131
Discovery, The, of the Jaredite Records, 12

— E —

Elephants, 140
Emer, son of Omer, 49
  anointed King of Jaredites, 139
  his prosperous reign, 139
End of Jaredite Record, 201
Ephraim, Hill, 40
Epistle, Coriantumr to Shiz, 197
  Shiz to Coriantumr, 197-198
Esrom, a Jaredite, son of Omer, 129
  battles with Jared, 129

Ethem, Jaredite King, son of Ahah, 46
Ether, Book of, taken from record on the 24
  plates, 44
Ether, son of Coriantor, 46, 160
  prophecies of, 162
  words of, rejected, 178
  sees days of Christ, 178
  and King Coriantumr, 187
  dwells in cavity of rock, 187
  word of the Lord, to, 193
  words of, remembered, 197
  hides records, 201
  last words of, 201
  genealogy of, 46ff
  biographical notes, 52ff

— F —

Faith, hope and charity, Chapter 12
Famine among Jaredites, 148, 158
Father, and Son, 78
Final, War of extinction, 219
Finger, of the Lord, seen by Brother of
  Jared, 76-77
Fish, carried by Jaredites, 64
Flocks, of Brother of Jared, 53
  Jaredites, rich in, 151-152
Flood, Jared and his people not to perish in,
  71
Food, animals used as, by Jaredites, 140
  hunted for, people's, 153
Fools, mocking, shall mourn, 168
Foreword, A, 7
Freedom, secret combinations, threaten to
  overthrow, 132

— G —

Gain, through traffic, 153
Game, wilderness preserved for, by Jaredites,
  153
Genealogy, of Jaredite Kings, Chapter 1
Gentiles, prayer for, by Moroni, 173
  to mock, 168
  modern, warned, 168
Gift, the heavenly, 163
Gilead, brother of Shared, 191
  fights Coriantumr, 191
  ascends throne, 191
  murdered by his High Priest, 191
Gilgah, son of Jared, 116
Gilgal, Valley of, 41
  Coriantumr defeats Shared in, 188
  Shared slain in, 189
Glass, as clear as, molten stones prepared
  by the Brother of Jared, 75
Good, whatsoever persuades men to do, is
  from the Lord, 99
Grace, prayed for unto Gentiles, 173